ORGANIC GROWTH

ORGANIC
GROWTH

Cost-Effective Business Expansion From Within

JEAN-FRÉDÉRIC MOGNETTI

JOHN WILEY & SONS, LTD

Other Wiley Editorial Offices

John Wiley & Sons, Inc., 605 Third Avenue,
New York, NY 10158-0012, USA

WILEY-VCH Verlag GmbH, Pappelallee 3,
D-69469 Weinheim, Germany

John Wiley & Sons Australia Ltd, 33 Park Road, Milton,
Queensland 4064, Australia

John Wiley & Sons (Asia) Pte Ltd, 2 Clementi Loop #02-01,
Jin Xing Distripark, Singapore 129809

John Wiley & Sons (Canada) Ltd, 22 Worcester Road,
Rexdale, Ontario M9W 1L1, Canada

British Library Cataloguing in Publication Data

A catalogue record for this book is available from the British Library

ISBN 0-470-84484-1

Typeset in 11.5/14pt Bembo by Footnote Graphics, Warminster, Wiltshire
Printed and bound in Great Britain by Biddles Ltd, Guildford and King's Lynn.
This book is printed on acid-free paper responsibly manufactured from sustainable forestry, in which at least two trees are planted for each one used for paper production.

For my quartet.

CONTENTS

10   The 3Cs

PART III: RECOGNIZE, UNCOVER, PRIORITIZE

11   Cross-Fertilization

FOREWORD

by Albert George, President, Sodexho Alliance

Sodexho Alliance, the world leader in food and management services, is rooted in the original vision of its current chairman and founder, Pierre Bellon. In the mid-1960s, after graduating from leading French business school HEC School of Management, he joined the family's Marseille-based ship handling company. Drawing on the lessons of the dissolution of the French colonial empire, he announced to his father, 'Our business, *c'est foutu*, it is over.' He decided to leave with a clear goal, that one experience of the nightmare of a futureless industry sector is enough. In 1966 with the equivalent of €15 000 he founded Sodexho, which today is listed on the Paris stock exchange with a market capitalization of €6.8 billion (before 11 September 2001). In July 2001 the company achieved its first listing in the Fortune 500, the magazine noting that it was 27th in terms of the size of its worldwide workforce.

Since he was starting from scratch and had a real ambition to achieve something, there was only one option for Pierre Bellon:

growth. Consequently, he institutionalized growth as a founding value for his new company. We still consider that growth is the most appropriate means to reconcile, over the long term, the sometimes mutually exclusive interests of our clients, staff and shareholders.

Pierre Bellon saw catering as the most attractive area for him to express his entrepreneurial talents. The French Council for Atomic Energy in Pierrelatte, 100 miles north of his home city of Marseille, was his first customer.

He intuitively adopted organic growth as the best way of expanding his business. Organic growth operated in a very straightforward way. It consisted of setting as a priority successively becoming first in one's home city, Marseille, then the region, Provence, then the country, France, and then surrounding countries, in order finally one day to gain access to the global arena.

The company motto is 'Sticking to our knitting' – we are expert in services to public and private communities and nothing else. These skills have been developed to a simple financial recipe, strictly enforced and monitored by our current chairman and the chairman's committee: growth must be financed by negative working capital while maintaining a minimum level of investment. We have been implementing these principles on a daily basis for more than 30 years.

With this pattern of growth, by year end 31 August 1994 Sodexho had reached a consolidated sales turnover of €1.74 billion. In our opinion, the conditions were in place to involve the company more specifically in external growth operations. The objective was twofold:

- *To acquire a visible position in markets that we had not yet addressed through organic growth operations.* In this context, we acquired Gardner Merchant in the UK and the Netherlands and, as early as 1995, Partena to give us a foothold in Scandinavia.
- *To consolidate our existing operations in order to reinforce our market visibility and access to area leadership.* This was achieved in 1998 with the merger of the catering division of Marriott, called Marriott Management Services, and Sodexho USA, to become Sodexho Marriott Services.

Through this second means of growth, we aimed to anticipate globalization in order to:

- *Stick more carefully to the evolution of our customers' needs.* Among these customers were blue-chip names such as IBM, Hewlett-Packard, Nortel and Chevron, but also some other effective but more surprising global players, such as the religious schools of the Lassalien brothers congregation (1500 schools in 82 countries).
- *Negotiate world supply contracts with global suppliers.* The objective is to guarantee both economic performance and permanent tracking of product quality.

By promoting organic growth as one of its founding values, Sodexho gives legitimacy to its ambitions of external growth. More precisely, what specific benefits has Sodexho gained over more than 30 years from its addiction to organic growth?

Organic growth generates a *threefold virtuous circle.*

Regarding customers:

- It expresses the positive vote of a satisfied portfolio of customers in favour of your performance. If not there is no growth…
- It justifies continual contact with the portfolio of customers, which leads to a unique relationship based on mutual respect where we claim to have developed outstanding skills in observing, listening and implementing.
- It allows the company to stick closely to the way customers' expectations are evolving and to keep innovating continually.

Regarding staff:

- It has educational value through the systematic repetition of best practice.
- It represents the most effective means of developing employment, career development and people empowerment by rejuvenating the opportunities that are inherently associated with growth.

■ It prepares our staff to become managerially speaking more nimble in terms of speed of reaction, a mandatory quality not only for organic growth but also if one starts dealing with outside opportunities.

Regarding shareholders:

■ It is one of the key criteria for assessing the value of a company.
■ It offers a faster and safer short-term return on investment than external growth.
■ It creates the conditions for gaining the effective support of shareholders for ambitious external growth projects.

Organic growth is a permanent opportunity, which is just a stone's throw from where a company is currently positioned. It simply demands sticking to a basic rule, not only to keep staying close to customers but also to develop the skills to capture the business relevance of their weak signals.

For Sodexho the fiscal year 2000–2001 illustrated once again this winning combination: 14 per cent growth including a 5 per cent positive exchange rate:

■ Solid organic growth of 7 per cent.
■ External growth of 2 per cent through two substantial acquisitions, in France (Sogérès) and the US (Wood Dining Services).

For many years I have known Jean-Frédéric Mognetti, both as a professor at HEC School of Management in Paris and as an international sales and marketing consultant. In the area of managing growth, we were both convinced that Sodexho was facing a serious challenge in terms of knowledge management. The purpose was to reach a so far unknown level of formalization to give our teams the means to keep playing a leading role in the upper league, which is easier said than done!

Through this book, I am happy to see Sodexho sharing a substantial part of its organic growth experience, associated with some brilliant global companies whose international exposure is unquestionably as relevant as ours. Together we have provided Professor Mognetti with the consulting project-based raw materials for proposing a rejuvenated integrated management tools package to systematically address organic growth and to avoid sub-optimization in this field. However, beyond the suggested techniques, I hope that this book will help readers avoid misleading business fads and provide them with the business attitudes and behaviour that will allow the word *growth* to be a fundamental topic in their organization's approach to thriving.

INTRODUCTION

O ver the last ten years, as a professor at the HEC School of Management in Paris, I have focused my academic and consulting interest on the sales and marketing consequences of strategic decisions. In this respect, I would venture to claim that I have contributed to bridging the too often observed gap between what is said and decided in boardrooms or executive committees and what is achieved in the field in front of customers. The concept of managing organic growth in business-to-business situations encapsulates my research and consulting experiences with a large variety of leading companies operating worldwide. One of them, Sodexho Alliance – the world leader in food and management services with €11 billion sales turnover, and more particularly its service vouchers and card division, with €4 billion issued annually in 24 countries – has provided me with the best arena for crafting and fine-tuning the organic growth concept. This results from fruitful teamwork and the uninterrupted leading support of Albert George, President of Sodexho Alliance, was critical for the development of this managerial technique.

ORGANIC GROWTH: YOUR IN-HOUSE RECIPE FOR BOOSTING COMPANY GROWTH

In this book I do not intend to demonstrate how I have discovered an unparalleled basic managerial technique. In my view there are already enough of these, if not too many. In my opinion the true priority is playing with what we already have, but in a more appropriate and effective manner. This is what organic growth is doing: assembling, in a reengineered and very often non-conventional way, strategic marketing and sales concepts, most of which are individually very familiar to any manager.

One of Sodexho's core businesses, catering, offers us the most accurate analogy for describing the perspective of this book, a *tour de main* as we say in French or an 'in-house' recipe for growth. Sticking to this context, this book is mainly a 'kitchen' story, bringing us to the heart of the back office in order to succeed with growth. However, before thinking about growth performance, I consider that the key question is whether the conditions for growth are in place. Then the growth rally, with its rare but permanently sought-after ingredient, the weak market signal, can fruitfully start, led by well-judged top management involvement. Sharing this experience of an in-house recipe, I intend to provide you with some insights and practical responses for designing your own growth menu, *à la carte*.

PART I

THE CHALLENGE

*I*f you don't turn off your mobile while travelling on another continent, your working day never ends. Falling into this trap, I was called in the middle of the night in Kuala Lumpur by one of my former MBA students.

'Hi, Jean-Frédéric, it's Olivier. I am in a meeting with Peter and Doug at GCC. Am I right in thinking you know a business game that would improve sales forecasts for the 29 directors of the Mediterranean region?'

'Do you want it on PlayStation or Nintendo?' I answered, waking up as quickly as I could.

More seriously, this question expressed real concern for the senior management of this company, in particular for its executive committee. In its role of assuring the present and creating the future, the executive committee of this express shipment company was facing a critical problem, how to take proper advantage of growth opportunities.

The situation was as follows: the company had planned for 25 per cent growth and had achieved 39 per cent. It was not the first year that performance had exceeded the forecast. This was apparently very good news, but two months before the end of the year the company was unable to fulfil the orders with its own resources. In fact, every morning it needed the equivalent tonnage of four additional 747s. This is not the kind of item you can find two blocks down on a shelf. Therefore, the company had to contract with outside suppliers, with the net result of lowering both the margin and the quality of service to all customers.

Olivier and Doug were reacting to an immediate problem facing them, but the real issue ran much deeper. In fact, this inaccuracy in forecasting has vicious organizational consequences, reaching into all spheres of the business. As in the vast majority of companies, tensions between headquarters and country subsidiaries reach a peak during budget preparation periods, when sales targets are established.

The archetypal scenario is the following: after achieving a 39 per cent increase the previous year, head office was confronted with an unbelievable proposal for the next year's sales target of 19 per cent. 'Are you kidding?' shouted headquarters. 'It seems like you are playing with the incentive scheme.' Eventually the subsidiary director corralled his troops into accepting a goal of 23 per cent, but this was still not enough for headquarters. Although head office had initially agreed to the 23 per cent target, during the final discussions it thrust a 27 per cent goal on the country manager. He left for home realizing that his troops – and he – would have to fulfil top management's belief, based on the previous year's numbers, that the stretch goal was achievable again. He could hope for a happy accident that meant he made his numbers and fulfilled his original 23 per cent goal, but he couldn't see a way to make this happen. He knew that no tree has ever reached the sky.

I don't need to describe more precisely the mood of this experienced manager flying home in his business-class seat trying to find hope in his Excel spreadsheet. How to help this talented manager is the starting point for our growth safari, which I propose to begin with this observation by Pablo Picasso in the back of our mind: 'Talent without technique is merely a bad habit.'

CHAPTER 1

THREE PROPOSITIONS

PROPOSITION 1

*T*he *account level* represents the arena in which managerial tools must be effectively deployed through the process of accurately establishing sales forecasts based on validated, objective information.

PROPOSITION 2

Organic growth offers a systematic approach to uncovering growth opportunities of three types:

1   Maintenance.
2   Sales development.
3   Business development.

Each of these carries a different level of exposure, risk and reward. The organic growth approach hinges not only on customer satisfaction, but also on continually reinforcing both customer intimacy and customer enthusiasm for the supplier's ability to create value. *Process-based marketing, permanent relationship marketing* and *dialogue-based marketing* form the integrated toolkit for systematically setting expectations, fulfilling promises to customers and reducing the threat of seeing key clients considering competitive offerings.

PROPOSITION 3

The dynamic of the process of organic growth demands the active commitment of the *executive committee*. This is a generic term describing the small team that effectively manages a company, a subsidiary or sometimes a business unit. The effectiveness of the executive committee can be *de facto*, it does not have to be clearly formalized through the company's organigram.

Active involvement is part of the executive committee's mission:

- To assure the company's ability to safeguard its present.
- To create the company's future.

Effectively achieving both parts of this mission will avoid the trap of making cosmetic instead of substantive changes and enable the company to respond consistently to growth opportunities with a *stealthy marketing approach* – by the time the competition notices, it will be too late for it to react.

CHAPTER 2

THE BATTLEFIELD

*I*n late 2000 the executive committee of a division of one of the four global players in bottling process equipment was running a strategic workshop. The conveyor line engineering division of this Strasbourg-based company included both hardware and process regulation. Its current strategic situation was fine, but not as brilliant as a couple of years ago and consequently not up to shareholders' expectations.

WE HAVE BECOME UNABLE TO ANTICIPATE

Each of the eight members of the executive committee delivered his or her own analysis following a predefined set of questions, structured to assess the closeness between the customer and the company. For ten years a close relationship with the customer had been justified by:

- Superior technical performance.
- Ability to innovate.

These two characteristics made the company globally appreciated by its customers and respected by its competition. However as usual a combination of competitive progress and internal comfort, associated with a dominant position in an industry sector, led to a situation of perceived performance parity, a business context where no strategic advantage can be expected. One of the main causes identified for the current lack of performance was: 'We have become unable to anticipate.'

The explanation was crystal clear. The company was mobilizing its resources for projects, without first having a global overview of the customer situation. The signal to mobilize resources was the project itself, so the company waited for a project. However, when the signal occurred it was already too late and everything became urgent, sometimes even reaching panic stations. An easy justification was, 'Unfortunately we were forced to adapt to changing customer behaviour. Management waits and waits and waits – and then they tell us they want it yesterday.'

ACCUMULATING CUSTOMER PROJECTS INSTEAD OF HAVING A CUSTOMER ACCOUNT PERSPECTIVE

'This type of large brewery investment does not happen by accident, it has to be planned.' So one of the new executive committee members (who used to be the head of production for one of the largest breweries in Europe) reminded his colleagues.

He added: 'The life span of such a line in a brewery is about 80 000 hours. So everything is planned accordingly. For return on investment reasons, instead of taking place in year 1 the investment will take place in year 2, even year 3, but it is in the pipeline and this is the information that needs to be managed in a proactive way.'

This kind of overall view of the whole portfolio of customers did not exist in this company. Consequently, one of the main decisions of this workshop was to:

> **Reengineer the company's business information approach around the idea of customer account management instead of too narrow project management.**

This designates the true battlefield.

To many readers the decisions taken in this example may seem obvious. This might have been true if the company had been performing badly, which was not the case. My purpose is to share with the reader some instances of the traps to be avoided in order to benefit from the full potential of this apparently obvious concept.

The point seems to be that there needs to be a system that regularly allows the rationale for the company's business success to be revisited, in order to confront reality with a cool head. In my experience, the individual customer account level is the place to do this. The account level becomes the arbiter of the whole approach, because the technique of sales forecasting is based on facts rather than perception. Eighty thousand hours for the life span of a bottling line is a fact, so obvious when read, but so volatile when one is caught up in day-to-day operations without the relevant information.

When actively promoting this idea of the importance of the customer account I get feedback from management. At some head offices their politically correct observation is: 'It's not our affair.'

This approach seems to be at odds with the importance they give to their existing sales orientation, which usually includes programmes focusing on customer loyalty and key account management. When they say 'It's not our affair', they mean in fact 'It's too basic, we're far more advanced.' Going beyond what I analyse in many cases as an alibi, people quickly understand what it is all about. Consequently, they are reluctant to follow this approach for two reasons:

- First, it might be perceived as a withdrawal from management development.
- Secondly, this new orientation represents a threat to functional managers at headquarters. They immediately notice that it reinforces the position of the people in the field, who will be able to deal with hard facts and not perception. Tom Peters used to illustrate this in his enthusiastic style in one of his videos, *Beyond Customer Satisfaction*:

An idiot with both hands tight behind his back but possessing the correct information could take the right decision ... while a room full of Chicago University laureates without the information can't.

THE ORGANIC GROWTH APPROACH

I collaborated with a leading express shipment company, DHL, on improving sales forecasting. When I made the suggestion of redesigning the system and the skills from the customer account perspective, it was intellectually accepted but not implemented. While this company pushed it into a corner, another large service organization – Sodexho Pass International (SPI), the meal vouchers division of Sodexho Alliance – did embrace this approach, because it quickly perceived it as a means to accelerate and reach another area of benefits from its existing customer loyalty and key account management programmes.

Very early on with SPI, we expressed a common opinion regarding these types of programmes. Even though they are necessary they can quickly become:

- *Tactically paralyzing*, because they led to a 'zero-sum game' that ends in a standoff situation.
- *Strategically misleading*, because they do not recognize the hidden strategic value of medium-sized and small accounts.

Consequently, over a period of 24 months I worked on transforming the constraints that held back DHL into a broad system encompassing the existing customer loyalty and key account management programmes while enabling SPI systematically to embrace other growth opportunities. This is the approach that I call *organic growth*.

CHAPTER 3

SIMPLE CONCEPT, DEEP MANAGERIAL CONSEQUENCES

O rganic growth is not a fad or a sophisticated, advanced, research-based academic concept. It draws its legitimacy from the day-to-day experiences – successes and failures – of managers confronted with real business challenges and with verifiable business results.

BACK TO BASICS

Last spring I had lunch with a colleague, Professor Saint Etienne from University Paris Dauphine. We were discussing the structure of a seminar to be run over the summer: 'Anticipating Tomorrow by Managing with Insight Today'.

Just before our meeting my colleague had had an interview with a financial analyst for research concerning his next book, *Scenes of Life in 2024*. He made the following comments about his meeting:

Among the analysts, I can clearly observe the appearance of a complementary view. These mega-mergers are in the vast majority of situations conceptually well founded, but now these new managing teams *are under the spotlight to demonstrate their ability to grow in their current perimeter...* which demands skills that are different from the financial engineering ones. Consequently, analysts and shareholders have become more demanding in terms of results in this area of corporate performance.

Mergers and acquisitions (M&A) and organic growth are two complementary perspectives of growth with a specific sequence, as Albert George, President of Sodexho Alliance, reminded us in his Foreword. Nevertheless, when my colleague mentioned growth he was not thinking of the whole scope of growth, which begins by stopping losses. Organic growth is not the positive result of plus and minus. Among its characteristics:

> **An organic growth-conscious organization starts by not losing customer accounts (this doesn't mean sales turnover).**

In an executive seminar, a former Xerox star salesman told me that 15 years ago, when he was in his early years with the company, one of the direct salesforce who lost a renewal sale of Xerox equipment was penalized in his next bonus. He added, 'Now we have even forgotten these relevant business practices. I don't know why, we are less straightforward, even in my own small company.'[1]

In the same vein, we can add this comment by the marketing director of the Brazilian subsidiary of SPI during a world convention in 1999 in Nice:

> After our large acquisitions, we have been obliged to focus on organic growth, because we had to find additional sources of return to face with the appropriate revenues the past investments.

KEEP SHARPENING YOUR COMPETITIVE ADVANTAGE

Some companies, such as Carrefour, were constrained in their growth by their native country's legislation regarding the opening of new hypermarkets. They were therefore forced very early on to reinvent growth opportunities from what was available. When this group extended its development policy internationally, it benefited from substantial competitive advantages that even the world leader, Wal-Mart, recognizes as distinctive. In support of this observation, a *Business Week* article[2] commented:

> Carrefour is a nimble competitor. Today a Carrefour shopper who stops to buy groceries or a pair of tennis shoes can also get a watch repaired, order a mobile-telephone service, rent a car or book plane tickets ... Wal-Mart offers few such services ... Carrefour has also been an innovator in store design.

From the description of Carrefour's characteristics the article moved to the key point. As a retail executive from Wal-Mart in South America explained, 'They are *relentless*, the toughest competitors I've ever seen anywhere.'

> **Organic growth means not losing, but it also represents an ultimate sense of speed of reaction.**

The article went on:

> When a planned Wal-Mart store opening in one Argentine city was delayed by construction problems for four months, Carrefour seized the opportunity to renovate its closest store.

PERCEPTIVELY CONFRONTING BUSINESS REALITY

Confronting business reality at Heytens

Heytens, a Belgium-based home decoration products distribution chain (wallpaper, fabrics, paint, carpets) has 100 shops in four European countries. The arrival of new shareholders revitalized the brand and was followed by the opening of 19 new shops over 1999 and 2000. Growth rocketed to nearly 20 per cent and pretax earnings exceeded 15 per cent in 2000.

CONTINUED . . . Confronting business reality at Heytens

Everything seemed globally positive. Nevertheless, if we focus our attention on organic growth and the contribution to total growth only of the shops opened before 1997, growth falls to a one-digit percentage. The shops opened from 1998 to 2000 were considered to be at an incubation stage. This information was like a cold shower for the executive committee. The company was mainly subscribing to the first of three key principles for success in multiple-outlet distribution:

1 Race to open new shops.
2 Organic growth.
3 Permanent testing of new ways to deal with customers.

but showing less concern for the rest.

The executive committee and the key executives returned to the front line, becoming involved in workshops that radically changed the basis for assessing the company's results. From now on they will stick to this renewed way to judge if they are both financially *and* strategically healthy.

Organic growth operates as an acid test for a strategy whose goal is to avoid uncontrolled growth.

Notes

1 This former student of mine and ex Xerox sales and then marketing manager was offered by Xerox to start an exclusive Xerox dealership with a colleague, which turned out to be a real success – $1 million turnover in 1994, up to $15 million in 2000.
2 'En garde Wal-Mart', *Business Week*, September 13 1999.

CHAPTER 4

PROCESS PERSPECTIVE

Organic growth is a double-barrelled system for spurring growth. It is based on *excellence in process* and also, under specific circumstances, on *getting priority dividends in the form of more information from customers because of their confidence in the company*. Organic growth requires the systematic extraction of relevant information to uncover growth opportunities from the existing business, so that the company can resegment the client–product side of its current business while maintaining a reliable and responsive process.

Meal voucher lookalikes

For many years in Europe and South America, meal vouchers have been recognized as a means of offering a fringe benefit. For instance in Europe, if a company gives its employees a meal voucher with a face value of 100 cents for each day worked, the employee pays between 20 and 50 cents and the company sponsors the voucher with between 50 and 80 cents. This amount is not included in the employee's taxable revenue and the company does not pay social taxes on the tickets or

CONTINUED . . . Meal voucher lookalikes

cheques given to staff. These practices are strictly regulated. The employer pays cash in exchange for the vouchers and gives them to its employees who use them in a network of affiliates. These outlets were initially restaurants but these were quickly followed by other types of shop dealing with food. They in turn present the cheque to the supplier to gain reimbursement some time later.

The voucher supplier has developed new applications in collaboration with its customers, for instance a special voucher for Christmas. Nevertheless, for each new specific organic growth opportunity the process is carried out in the same way or with minor adjustments, which does not reshuffle the organization's portfolio of skills.

One of the advantages of the voucher process is that it is a way to secure a flow of funds that can be traced. This information can be critical to some organizations. For instance the Belgian government, following a European Commission recommendation, launched a policy to combat the underground economy and to help people who are unemployed for more than two years join the workforce through ancillary jobs.

The goal was to avoid under-the-counter cash payments for small jobs, instead giving the worker a voucher. This new system represented an incentive for all the parties involved. In this specific case, the employer is the person who needs to be assisted. The unemployed person is paid with a cheque and gets cash when returning the cheque to the affiliate: the town hall. The supplier, Sodexho Pass International (SPI), is applying its well-used business model for meal vouchers, but in a different context. It is simple, which does not mean that it is easy to achieve!

The Belgian government represents a new profile of customer for SPI, which is used to dealing with private companies. Nevertheless, the process for this application is virtually the same, so the risk associated with this new business

CONTINUED ... Meal voucher lookalikes

opportunity is minimized. Consequently, SPI can carefully extend its portfolio of services to a new business group, governments. Under the name of 'Social Benefits', it provides them with solutions for handling welfare-related issues. Moreover, the first success opened up a new avenue of business. SPl invented the 'refugee cheque' together with the government of the Berlin region, and this contributed to a successful bid to the British government concerning a voucher system for asylum seekers in early 2000.

Organic growth finds new business opportunities in the subtle application of processes to a target group that had previously had no idea that SPI could provide them with the appropriate solution to their problem. 'When I took on this project, I would not have thought that the solution provider would be found in a company like Sodexho... It was far outside my view range,' commented the Belgian Social Affairs Minister to the SPI area manager.

Success with organic growth is never a happy accident. The process performance played a central role in giving both more confidence to SPI's people and reassurance to customers.

CHAPTER 5

CUSTOMER PERSPECTIVE

Organic growth is also achieved by drawing benefit from intimacy with customers who are confident in the supplier's performance. It is based on the customer's willingness to bet on its supplier's ability to deliver a product or service that does not exist yet. In this context, the customer acts as a catalyst and may even dictate the company's growth policy.

One consequence of the customer's belief in its supplier carries an important implication: a challenge for the supplier to manage second-tier suppliers or business associates that have to be mobilized in order to meet the customer's demands.

THE CUSTOMER AS THE ESSENCE OF ORGANIC GROWTH

To illustrate this statement, we can take an example from the automotive equipment industry.

Rieter: Promoted to a higher league

Rieter is a Swiss-based company that is positioning itself as 'the acoustic integrator' for cars, trucks and even trains, such as the double-decker TGV. This global specialist is recognized as a world leader in its sector. Rieter manufactures components that impede noise entering the car. These include NVH (noise, vibration and harshness) materials such as carpet, head-liners and dampers, and components such as the undershield, heatshield and parcel shelf.

Over the last five years the role of the automotive manu-facturer has kept evolving from producer of cars to marketer of cars, thus modifying accordingly the role of the supplier. This new breed of partner was forced to adapt itself to the new role desired by the automotive manufacturer: from component supplier to full-service integrator with intermediate stages, supplying functions (a braking system) or modules (a fully equipped dashboard).

This is what Rieter experienced with its customers, in particular with a truck manufacturer. For instance, at one of its customer's premises Rieter's own staff operate the SAF (Secteur Avancé Fournisseurs, an independent and autono-mous workshop on the automotive manufacturer's assembly line), where it assembles the truck cabin that is then delivered as a single component to the truck manufacturer.

Because of this new business context Rieter is currently ranked among the largest suppliers, joining some sector heavy-weights such as Michelin and Bosch, a promotion to a higher league. It means also that Rieter is producing components that go far beyond those of its core business.

The customer offered this opportunity to its chosen supplier based on the latter's demonstrated quality and the uniqueness of the relationship. The client believed that Rieter could handle the challenge.

One question cannot be avoided: has Rieter taken on too ambitious a challenge? So far the answer is no. Nevertheless, its position is not permanent. Consequently, it must keep confronting reality through the relevance of its performance. One can also think in terms of missed opportunity: what would Rieter have lost if it had not taken up this stretch goal? This is what the next case illustrates.

CMD: Turning down a growth opportunity does not mean maintaining the status quo

CMD is a manufacturer of heavy mechanical components mainly used in steel, energy and cement processes. The company is known for its 'made to spec' gearboxes. Globally this is a relatively small business, with an annual value of $3 billion shared between a few players (Falke in the US, Flender in Germany, CMD in France and David Brown in the UK, which also produces Aston Martin cars as well as agricultural and military vehicles). This kind of gearbox is critical to a process. If it breaks, the line will stop for a very long time and cost an enormous amount of money due to lost production in a continuous process.

The cost of a lost day of production is estimated in the cement industry to be €150 000 for a small to medium-sized mill, but in the copper industry it rockets to €1 million. Consequently, design and manufacturing specifications for the gearboxes are set to meet an expected lifespan of around 25 years.

In this context, maintenance activities represent a substantial part of a company's turnover. Preventing a breakdown and organizing its resources to improve reaction speed when a breakdown or a problem does occur are a full-time job for the maintenance department. However, maintenance budgets are also subject to attempts at rationalization.

Fos-Sur-Mer is a steel mill near Marseille belonging to Arcelor, the French-based world-leading steel producer. The steel process uses many specific and standard gear-boxes.

CONTINUED . . . CMD: Turning down a growth opportunity does not mean maintaining the status quo

To maintain them, the various gears need to be hobbed periodically. The gearboxes that have to work under the most difficult constraints are manufactured out of case-hardened and ground steel, the hardest quality of steel available on the market. Very specific tools are required to cut and hob this quality of steel and these are only possessed by specialist companies like CMD. The price of these operations also reflects their difficulties. In contrast, hobbing the gears for the standard gearboxes does not demand the same price premium. In this context, CMD's maintenance job encompasses the characteristics of a niche operation, which is usually inaccessible to standard product operators.

In the early 1990s the heads of maintenance and procurement at the Fos-Sur-Mer steel mill agreed that they had to simplify the maintenance of gears and the associated hobbing activity. They decided to propose that this be carried out by a single contractor. They not only developed a rather sophisticated programme in terms of the financial objectives, but also sold the project at the corporate level. The idea was to run a pilot project, which could later be implemented at least in the group's other French steel mills. Then came a difficult question: who could do it? The answer seemed obvious: CMD, the company that could handle the most sophisticated products. The head of maintenance announced that he would finalize the deal in the following weeks, being absolutely confident of CMD's interest in this integrated maintenance contract.

Imagine his surprise when CMD tactfully rejected the proposal to handle standard product maintenance. Its answer was purely technical: 'It is too far from our core skills, you are sub-optimizing our resources, we can offer you more.'

This answer must be considered wise from a process point of view. However, from a customer relationship point of view

CONTINUED ... CMD: Turning down a growth opportunity does not mean maintaining the status quo

it sounds like strategic nonsense, which the new chairman, whom I was advising, inherited.

The client was unable to find an appropriate supplier and was obliged to revert to a less ambitious scheme. It not only split the contracts between standard and special products but also lost face in the eyes of its top management. Nevertheless, once the 'last resort' operator is in place, the scenario might take on a different light. Realistically, a couple of years later the standard product maintenance company might suggest to its client that it is also given the special gears to hob: 'Why not try us now to see if we are on a par with CMD?'

The lesson is clear. In oligopolistic or near-oligopolistic business contexts where there is a contest of which there can only be one winner:

It can be misleading to assess the supplier's position in the light of both the strategic value of its own product or service and potential substitutions currently observable in the sector. If your strategic value to the customer is high

> It is risky to operate beyond the limits of your own processes, but not to embrace a broader customer-conceived perspective of the relationship is even riskier.

and your customer will encounter difficulties in finding a new source of supply, it is easily understood that this customer needs to enter into partnership with you. Nevertheless, this is not a sufficient reason to limit the scope of your collaboration to the limits of your own processes.

By disregarding an opportunity for growth conceived by the customer, the supplier is allowing its customer the possibility of introducing a newcomer. Even if the customer is not precipitating the confrontation, it is an opportunity for a competitor to catch up or at least to stay in the race. Do we want to give this opportunity to the customer? To the competition? Obviously not, but the next question is at which cost?

Some managers will object that in their experience it is wise to let the competitor enter this new game and then fail in order to bring the client back to your point of view. This opinion is acceptable in only a few circumstances. I recently observed such a case with a leading American bank and its express shipment suppliers in Malaysia. The bank played two operators off against each other over the course of a few months. The area sales manager of the company that was eventually reappointed commented: 'They experienced the difference and they got an unambiguous demonstration of our superior performance.'

However in my opinion, relying on the inability of the competitor to fulfil its promises is a risky bet. More systematically, the first company to jump into a new business gets far ahead on the experience curve, even if the work has to be subcontracted to an associate, while maintaining an exclusive relationship with the customer. Therefore the competition can seldom catch up, unless it is at the price of a Pyrrhic victory, i.e. one involving great losses on its own part that it is not usually prepared to bear.

Organic growth relies on a rewired combination of marketing techniques to secure the current business and to create the future. Process-based marketing and permanent relationship marketing are the techniques that aim at achieving the first goal, while dialogue-based marketing focuses on the second. In both situations:

> **The ultimate goal is *not to sell* your services or products *but to be bought.***

The purpose of this book is to explain through practical examples a systematic way of improving corporate value. I want to draw on my current experience to address change and allow readers to draw unparalleled benefits from a clear-headed confrontation with business reality.

PART II

CREATING THE TECHNICAL CONDITIONS

*I*n the late 1980s I was visiting Japan to benchmark the design of a training session for 350 directors and deputy directors of the manufacturing division of the automotive manufacturer Peugeot Citroën. This top executive programme, called 'From Productivity to Competitiveness', was taking place in a company that was quickly recovering from a difficult business situation through the market success of one leading model, the Peugeot 205.[1] In 1987 Jacques Calvet, then CEO, was on the front page of *Fortune* above the caption: 'Peugeot coming back from nowhere'.

In preparation for this assignment I had the opportunity to meet a couple of times with Professor Robert Ballon from Sophia University in Tokyo. This Belgian Jesuit Father who landed in Japan in General MacArthur's footsteps was very keen to share his passion and help you understand some specific key characteristics of Japanese companies' decision-making process. One of these, *nema-washi*, was very interesting because it describes the amount of investment in discussion to prepare a decision based on consensus. The word comes from Japanese gardening vocabulary and covers the idea of preparing the soil to plant a tree. The problem is not to judge whether the Japanese economy is well off today or not with this kind of concept, but to recognize that creating the appropriate context is a critical prerequisite.

In organic growth we cannot escape the preparation phase, which is aimed at creating the appropriate context. A management concept is like an iceberg, so before climbing on top, a dive under the sea could be worthwhile in order for us to know where to put our feet afterwards.

To design a growth approach that builds on a company's existing strengths, the first step focuses on identifying what needs to be incorporated in the preparation phase to allow organic growth to be generated in a way that is safer, cheaper and nimbler.

I have structured this part, Creating the Technical Conditions, so that it zooms in from a bird's eye view to a very focused and practical perspective. In the first part I stress the idea that the arena of organic growth is the customer account. Based on what I have been able to observe and experiment in, my purpose is to propose what, in my opinion, is the best managerial toolkit for effectively implementing a growth policy at the customer account level.

I suggest starting from a high–altitude perspective in order to give us a frame of reference. My own frame is a detailed understanding of the company's competitive advantage with its associated strategic flavour. I believe that managers, like pilots, must have indicators that tell them if they are in line with their target, which is the purpose of the two ratios in Chapter 7. What a specific client receives from its supplier creates a set of expectations and the way the product or service is delivered positions that supplier in a particular way. This positioning is like a snapshot but is quickly transformed into the opening shots of a movie, and there are numerous pitfalls involved in making sure that our movie keeps on receiving rave reviews. Chapter 9 addresses the specific interactions necessary with the customer in terms of content and role to be performed. Finally, entering into the heart of a specific customer account, I discuss how to retain a perspective and avoid being flooded by information. How effectively you do this is translated into the accuracy of your sales forecasting.

Note

1   Currently Peugeot is the second largest European car manufacturer with circa 3 million units per year. In 1998 it achieved only 2 million units. Many analysts judged that this was below a critical size and claimed that it should merge with another manufacturer. Its success is all the more remarkable, therefore, and demonstrates that there is more than one way to do things.

CHAPTER 6

A WAY TO HANDLE STRATEGIC ISSUES

My purpose is not to develop a new strategy identification and formulation technique, but to explain which well-known tools will enable a company to keep a strategic perspective in the design of an organic growth approach.

Formulating strategy to uncover new areas of growth represents one of the missions of the executive committee. The following two propositions represent a caveat that any company needs to remember when it deals with strategic issues:

1   A relevant strategy cannot be developed solely by sitting in the boardroom. As John Le Carré comments: 'An office is a dangerous place from which to view the world.'
2   It is even more dangerous for an organization to rely on historical perceptions, true at some stage but no longer relevant to business realities.

Therefore, the most straightforward approach to strategy is based on the active involvement of the executive committee in tackling a reality-based understanding of the company's future by answering two interrelated questions regarding the key ingredients of a strategy:

- What is the company's *competitive advantage? and*
- What are the *means* to prolong it?

COMPETITIVE ADVANTAGE – A HACKNEYED CONCEPT?

Competitive advantage addresses a simple idea:

> *A competitive advantage is a combination,* which can be described along three axes, not only one:

How, through the way a company is dealing with its market's key success factors, is it perceived as bringing more value to its target customers than the competition does?

- Product.
- Service.
- Organization.

The relevant combination

Product, service and organization are three possible generic dimensions. Through experience I have observed that they can be tailored to the particular situation; I always come back to managing this combination or a reformulated one but with the same flavour. It

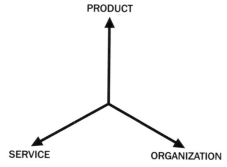

Figure 6.1 The combination. Step 1: Drawing the reference frame

represents a meaningful training aid to help people realize where to find the most suitable areas of progress for their own competitive formula.

Consequently, the appropriately named dimensions are a question of context where no universal answer is available. By attending to the selection of the words the strategist demonstrates his or her intimacy with the sector. Nevertheless, to be effective and avoid the risk of being paralysed by research, the generic dimensions are perfectly suitable for initiating the first rounds of the investigation.

In support of the importance of this combination, what is generally observed among family-owned businesses as a typical pattern of development reinforces the idea of relying on a combination rather than on a single dimension:

- The first generation champions either the product or the service. The rationale is clear: you need passion to start a business.
- The second generation goes to business school and therefore wants to apply what they have learnt to consolidate and structure the business to squeeze out more profits.
- Finally, the third generation wrecks the whole system or reinvents it to enter a new stage.

In 1996, for the 50th anniversary of IMD International in Lausanne, Switzerland, Professor Neubauer, a leading authority on family-owned companies, explained that this pattern could be observed over 20 to 25 years.

It is fair to say that this used to be presented as a sequential process, which is relevant for understanding the main stages, but at the same time we are running the risk of over-simplification. We are no longer in an either/or context: an organization can be at all three stages at the same time. Consequently, in order to survive two types of information need to be known:

- What is the minimum performance imposed by the market in each dimension – product–service–organization?
- Which dimension is perceived to be dominant in the company?

Heytens, mass market furniture fabrics producer

As we have seen, under today's competitive pressure a corporation must be able to address all three dimensions – product, service and organization – at the same time. The Belgian decoration solutions distribution chain Heytens (already mentioned on page 13) offers a good illustration of this proposition. In Belgium over eight years, between 1987 and 1995, its founder developed a way of delivering unparalleled value to customers due to a unique combination of competitive advantages, and opened around 60 shops in Benelux, France and Germany.

Its unique selling proposition includes:

- *Product design*: once a year the company issuing a new collection of fabrics to meet customers' expectations ranging from ultra conservative to trendy. The collection is supported by an IKEA-style catalogue.
- *Awareness of the customer* signified through a strong message: no charge for making up the curtains of your choice in any fabric above €11 (at €11, this represents 85 per cent of the products in the collection, which carry a maximum price of €30).
- *Organization*: average time taken to deliver made-to-order curtains is two weeks. This company cuts and sews 400 000 pairs of curtains each year in its facilities in Belgium and Tunisia.

Even though this strategy was designed to be excellent in all three dimensions, the results of various focus groups into the market perception were even sharper: Heytens was seen as having a product line style. This represented the distinctive quintessence of the competitive advantage, its dominant flavour. But what is the range of the impact of this uniqueness that the market recognizes?

Attempts at development

Moving to the south of Europe, Heytens discovered that the pattern of development needed to be revitalized. Other com-

CONTINUED ... Heytens, mass market furniture fabrics producer

panies were jealous of its success. One of its competitors was advertising a 'me too' offer in 115 out its 160 shops in France, while Heytens was still in the emerging phase of its development with 25 shops. The competitor's offer was a mere imitation of the original concept so one could conclude that it should not matter, but that is not the case. Customers who have never experienced either company cannot make out the cosmetic message. Consequently, the original competitive advantages could become less effective than in the past, unless a situation of parity in terms of infrastructure with the usurper can be reached quickly.

From a geographic point of view, Heytens is embracing an additional category that could radically reshuffle the cards. Consequently, its competitive advantages will not be able to generate their associated benefits in the same way, because the qualifying criteria for this new geographic area are under the influence of a competitor's message. Before it is able to deploy its original combination of competitive advantages, Heytens will have to overcome an attempt at concept hijacking by the competitor. In this case we can observe a lack of points of sale, which in global terms represents a handicap. The trap can be even more dangerous if one does not recognize where to fight in order to make Heytens' competitive formula shine. The nature of confrontation is not at all global but local.

Therefore the clearly recognized challenge was to be diligent at finding premises next door to those of the competitor. This is not merely opening new shops, but doing so with a twofold strategic objective:

- Give prospective customers the opportunity to make comparisons in order to challenge the competitor in your field of structural strength.
- Keep pleasing the fans with an offer that continues to mean something unique.

This case represents a good reminder that your approach to development must be effective. Even though the intrinsic relevance of a business model may remain the same, its impact can nevertheless be temporarily affected by a competitor's opportunistic announcement. This demands a threefold reaction to reach a business context as close as possible to the initial one with its associated level of success:

- Revalidate the relevance of your competitive advantage, both through internal benchmarking and testing that the competitive model is not encountering a weakness in one area (product–service–organization) while maintaining excellence in the other two. The goal is to be sure that there is no weakness in the model before promoting the uniqueness of its value, because a weakness represents a free gift for the competition to catch up (see Figure 6.2).
- Force the 'jeopardizer' to play on your own field of strength. By selecting a few well-gauged spots, provoke doubts by exploiting the competitor's own internal benchmarking to your advantage.
- Then, announce your next development steps.

Consequently, each time you plan to enter a new category you need to be realistic and remember that it won't be a walk in the park, unless the business is booming so fast that nobody will even

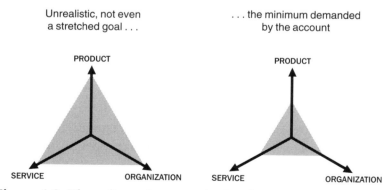

Figure 6.2 Three dimensions constituting the minimum perimeter of competitive advantage

pay attention to your presence even though you will be protected by some form of unique value in your selling proposition. Salomon, initially a ski bindings manufacturer, benefited from a similar situation when it entered the ski boot market in 1979. The current leader of that market, the Italian manufacturer Nordica, did not react fiercely because of the growth of the market and because of Salomon's innovation, the first ski boot with a rear entry.

A RELEVANT COMBINATION TO CONFRONT REALITY

This question of competitive advantage can be restricted to so-called strategic or marketing experts' concerns regarding its technical side, running analysis and formulating recommendations. However, very quickly the competitive advantage concept comes to belong to a corporation's collective knowledge. Consequently, one should be sure that top management's actions stay in line with what the market perceives to be the quintessence of the company's strengths.

I have often seen top managers, even CEOs, with a few words on a piece of paper, against which they systematically test any suggestion for the development of their company. This is a good method, even a kind of trick, that can easily and clearly be explained. It pays off by reinforcing the coherence of strategic thinking in a team.

This leads to an important question: are we addressing competitive advantage with enough pragmatism and care in our organization? To answer this, we must dare to conduct a simple acid test at executive committee level. Can each member of the executive committee and some key field personnel answer two basic questions?

- Do we have a competitive advantage?
- If so, what is it?

This sounds obvious, but imagine the faces of the executive committee members when they are asked to scribble a reply on the back of an envelope and then take three minutes to synthesize their individual formulations of the company's competitive advantage. Some may even wonder what the boss had been smoking the night before. The aim is not to assess the benefit of such a surprising test, but to be sure that when the company addresses the topic of competitive advantage, the whole organization is singing off the same hymnsheet.

The purpose of this exercise is to make the executive committee aware of the strategic reality in their market and to break mental representations, which are too often mainly driven by a past perception of performance.

To sum up, I have explained that a *competitive advantage is the combination* of three disciplines (product superiority–passion for customer–organizational effectiveness) that offers the ability either:

■ *To perform the same thing in a different way to the competition.* We are more effective, more systematic, quicker, our attention to detail is sharper and so on.

Or:

■ *To offer different things.* This means that we are able to answer needs that customers did not even know they had; we are able to anticipate appropriately.

In this context, the organization is just trying to test a common internal perception about its ability to be different. To do this I suggest the following test.

Step 1: On the back of an envelope

Start to answer the two questions regarding the company's perception of its difference or differences. One can also formulate the question in a more straightforward way: why is the company beating its competitors? Why does the customer like us?

Step 2: With the help of Figure 6.3

Help the audience improve the quality of their spontaneous answers by introducing the idea of the three dimensions: product–service–

organization). A second list of dimensions can also be introduced to give a more dynamic perspective: for example innovation, sense of customer, low delivered cost.

Give a graphic representation of the company's competitive advantage by plotting the current internal perception of the current situation.

Using Figure 6.3 one can identify the level of alignment of the executive committee on the dominant characteristics of the company's competitive formula. Discuss with the group the dominant characteristics and allocate 10 points between the three dimensions.

To push the relevance of this exercise further, it is wiser to confront the internal perceptions with the market's assessment, account per account (see Figure 6.4 for an example).

The 'validated' profile can then be compared with a profile for a competitor (see Figure 6.5). The dotted line represents Rieter's recognition that one of its challengers is trying, by competing on price, to undercut its leading position. This result warns the organization about the priorities to implement in order not to fall foul of the economics and to keep playing with the white (a chess expression meaning keeping the advantage of playing first) in other areas of the game.

When a customer is using two different suppliers to fulfil his (or her) expectations, he is almost certain of getting different results

EXECUTIVE COMMITTEE MEMBERS' OPINION	PRODUCT, INNOVATION	SERVICE, SENSE OF CLIENT	ORGANIZATION, LOW DELIVERED COST

Figure 6.3 The dominant characteristics of the company's competitive formula

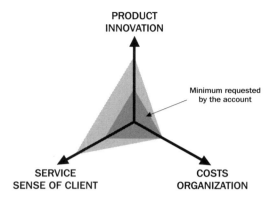

Figure 6.4 Rieter's perception of its relative competitive advantage on one specific customer account, compared to the minimum imposed in this sector

from each of them, although there are areas where the supplier's delivery profiles will overlap. Either of them can be recognized for product or service excellence and so on, but *neither is below the minimum qualifying performance in terms of product, service or organization* (that is, there is no weakness according to the standards of the customer). However, the customer has recognized that to fully achieve his expectations he might want both. The customer knows exactly what each supplier can offer; he also knows how and in which area to gain the most from each of them.

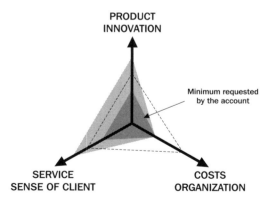

Figure 6.5 Rieter's perception of the dominant characteristics of its competitive advantage compared to the suppliers involved on a specific account

I am convinced of the managerial benefits in terms of clarification and consistency of searching for the most appropriate formulation for each customer situation in terms of competitive advantage. This effort has educational consequences that can help a company avoid fooling itself. The purpose of the next story is to remind us of the benefits of confronting our own perception of competitive advantage with the customer's.

We are the champions of quality

In the late 1980s two executives from Paribas (a French merchant bank that has since merged with BNP and is operating as BNP Paribas) left the bank to operate a leveraged buyout of a small electrical components company manufacturing plastic shelters. They became joint CEOs and struggled to turn the company around. The key customer was EDF (France's electrical utility). The company was a little rusty, but with their skills and their willingness to succeed, and a very demanding and innovative quality improvement programme, they quickly improved its manufacturing performance.

Confident in their new know-how and reinforced in their conviction by the judgements of leading quality experts, the executives decided to invite EDF to a presentation of their reengineered development approach and manufacturing process. This turned out to be an objective success and the location of their manufacturing premises, Saint-Malo in Brittany, was the icing on top of the cake, with seafood and fine white wine wrapping up the show.

Shortly after this promotional event, I had a discussion with these executives regarding how to exploit strategically what was considered a new competitive advantage: superiority in product development and product quality. Moreover, this advantage was not merely a perceived one, the customer formally admitted it during its visit to the new premises.

I always consider it worthwhile to double check, to cross-consult, and I like to use the common-sense expression true

---

CONTINUED ... We are the champions of quality

---

anywhere in the world: 'Hurry up slowly', or 'More haste less speed'.

I convinced the joint CEOs that it would be wise to interview managers from EDF's central purchasing department. The main topic of the meeting was the respective positioning of the four suppliers operating on this market. I asked the purchasing manager to express this in one phrase:

- The first-mentioned supplier was termed the 'manufacturing process expert'.
- Then came the 'innovator'.
- The third seemed to be good news, 'not met in the last two years'.
- Finally came the turn of my customer. I thought I already knew the answer: they had told us the week before in Saint-Malo that it was the 'product quality champion'. I was astonished, therefore, to hear the word 'banker'. I tried to come back to the previous week's comments, but this executive stuck firmly to his beliefs and commented that he and his colleagues were impressed by the quality of this company's financial results when they compared them with the average in the sector: 'twice as much as the second best is currently achieving.'

So this purchasing manager, to use Al Ries and Jack Trout's expression in *Marketing Warfare*, clearly has a positioning 'ladder' in his mind. Unfortunately I didn't like it too much, nor did my customer, because it meant that, with this customer's power of negotiation, sooner rather than later it will consider that there were productivity gains from this performance that should be shared.

The lesson was simple: *we had not yet addressed the true nature of competitive advantage*. Doing so allows the company to articulate a consistent approach over a substantial period of time. And we can conclude that some of the time the true formu-

CONTINUED ... **We are the champions of quality**

lation of the competitive advantage remains hidden. Consequently, there is a bonus in not satisfying oneself with a blurred perception. We need tangible facts not only for the analysis but also for their value in communicating with and motivating the company's staff.

I did not stop at this answer and I came back with another perspective of business reality. What fits best with the customer's expectations in terms of supplier attitude and behaviour? How is this reflected in the respective market share allocated to each protagonist?

Figure 6.6 illustrates the answer. This demonstrated that we were clearly *confusing* the product selection process and the business activity target with the business reality. In some counties the so-called banker's market share was far higher than 25 per cent. So what were these other facets of the customer's systems crediting to our banker? I don't think it was the superiority of its financial skills.

So far we had not yet touched on the tangible aspects of its competitive advantage. I had got a customer's opinion: the banker. It certainly meant that my client must learn how to manage the information available to EDF. On the other side and more frustratingly, we had not yet reached the point where the customer had recognized the company's difference and clearly credited it through its behaviour.

STATUS	RESULT
PROCESS CHAMP	25%
INNOVATION CHAMP	25%
'ABSENTEE'	25%
BANKER	25%

Figure 6.6 Market share allocated to each supplier

> ### CONTINUED ... We are the champions of quality
>
> A few weeks later I conducted an additional interview with a lower-level procurement manager in order to carry on investigating tangible facts that could explain the nature of the competitive advantage. The eventual solution was not exclusively a product-related one but a combination service and organization. The 'banker' had inventories in a couple of strategically critical places in France. The clarification case took place in Marseille – the reason for the success in this area was the flexibility given to the customer to allow last-minute orders, which compensated for its inaccuracy in planning for product availability at any time. The next question was how long this was sustainable.
>
> One should always keep a sharp eye on competitive advantage based on a customer's sub-optimized process. If it improves, we need to know what to do next. However, at least we have a clear representation of the starting situation on which to capitalize.

By recognizing the true nature of its competitive advantage, a company becomes clear about what it must do in order to prolong it. Its actions become more consistent. This corporation can be considered as effectively acting strategically because the difference it was able to achieve is recognized by the market and the organizational consequences will become the reference point for the whole organization in order to perpetuate this perception.

What I have outlined so far might seem to be a simple reformulation of something that is already very well known. Rather, I suggest considering it as an appropriate reminder for a general management context. Too many concepts that are no longer at the top of the current hit parade of management techniques are taken for granted because we think we know them. Consequently they are very often not fully mastered, start to lead us astray and do not provide effective support to managers. The risk is rocketing, because we are confusing speed and haste, focusing on the tree, the latest managerial technique, and missing the forest, the whole toolkit.

One can observe the same phenomenon in sport. How much training do you need to play golf or tennis well? A great deal. Our environment (particularly our media culture) contributes to everything but only shows us the visible part of the iceberg. In our zapping society people want to be on the course, on the fairway, on the slope even before they have started. There is a price to pay to avoid frustration. It is called training – but not any kind of training, as this relevant observation from Harvey MacKay[1] reminds us: 'Do you think training is good? Wrong, only *perfect training* is good.' I don't see why the challenge should be any different in management.

CONFRONTING REALITY WHEN CORRALLED BY A BUSINESS FORMULATION

Our next goal is to provide you with a trick to judge if you are a true 'difference addict'. We outlined above the critical importance of recognizing the competitive advantage and its dominant nature. We need to reach a further level of accuracy in its representation to align the organization accordingly.

Two weeks

While writing this book I was also preparing a seminar for a medium-sized European group, AFE. This company has a sales turnover of €320 million and employs 3000 people in 30 countries. Its core businesses are cast iron and plastic products and systems, where it holds in various specialities European or global leadership. The subject of the seminar was 'Under which conditions can the manufacturing process become a sales and marketing tool?' This is the kind of subject I like because there is always fun and challenge behind it.

In preparation I met the manager of a business unit manufacturing components that are integrated into truck trailers. In

CONTINUED ... Two weeks

his business unit he had a management committee that gave me clear evidence of its field involvement, calls with sales reps and accuracy of knowledge regarding each key customer's current situation. This management committee had been allowed to get close to the customers. The question is: what can they do with the knowledge they have gained? Of course they can come closer to customer needs, but there is another high-value dividend from this policy on which I want to focus.

Market involvement pays off because it offers the management committee the opportunity to reconfirm two key points:

- Why was their company chosen by the customer?
- Why is it allowed to charge a 10 per cent premium in a price-sensitive context?

The answer is *speed of response*. This company is the most responsive in the industry in terms of not only delivering on its promises but also leadtime. Leadtime is even becoming a milestone: AFE can supply whatever the customer wants in two weeks. This not only beats the industry, but is also a very relevant source of difference for a sector that is structurally in search of flexibility.

Very often AFE has to deliver to the haulage contractors a trailer that does not exist when the order is placed. Consequently the competitive advantage takes the form of a milestone, a reference point that the whole organization has to live up to.

The company works in five shifts over seven days. The weekend shift works for 24 hours and is paid for 35. The business unit is organized as a profit centre.

The 'consistency acid test' for competitive advantage can be formulated as follows:

This justifies decisions that might appear to be paradoxical.

In this case, as everywhere else, the business experienced ups and downs. However, when the size of the team had to be adjusted, naturally the management team started by reducing the week shift, while common sense might have suggested starting with the most costly one, the weekend shift, although that would have removed the means of its flexibility.

> **When an organization is clear about its competitive advantage, it will recognize organizational priorities that may even go against short-term common sense to protect the consistency of its strategic perspective.**

Not acting in a way that is consistent with competitive advantage represents the most effective approach to wreck the company's competitive advantage and give an opportunity to the competition to catch up. As a final point, this kind of practice does not happen without good internal communication regarding its rationale.

The result of this exercise is to enable a company to understand its strategic style, to check that there isn't any weakness even before drawing benefit from its relative strengths. In summary, strategy is not a game of pluses and minuses. Consistency is one of the most critical words to keep managing strategically.

DIFFERENCE IS THE STRATEGIC GOAL – PROCESS EFFECTIVENESS IS THE MEANS FOR PROLONGING IT

The executive committee's managerial toolkit must include a reflex that allows it permanently to act strategically by simultaneously possessing:

- The presence of a market-validated competitive advantage, *and*
- The means to prolong the validated competitive advantage.

In the AFE example, there was a link between competitive advantage and some critical organizational consequences. Now the question is becoming precise: which effectiveness in its portfolio of skills must the corporation deploy to secure the market relevance of its competitive advantage?

In this respect, an article by Michael Porter in the *Harvard Business Review*[2] provides a major clarification to avoid confusion between what is strategy and what is operational effectiveness (OE). OE can apply in each functional area of the company with a champion and it represents the expression of the means for prolonging the initial competitive advantage. Too often, over time, OE absorbs the strategy and the critical distinctions between the two areas disappears. Then, 'in good faith', the company ends up in a strategic cul-de-sac.

This corporate rhythm or sense of creativity for rejuvenating competitive advantage, associated with operational effectiveness to secure the relevance of competitive advantage over time, is not represented by distinctive activities by separate people or entities. In organizations with superior performances, it is the responsibility of the same people but acting in different contexts, at different times, with different intensities. This is why, according to my observations and experiences of companies' strategic efficiency, I consider that a famous sentence from the founder of Matsushita, Konosuke Matsushita – 'Big things and little things are mine, middle things can be delegated' – needs to be reformulated in the light of this research. For the executive committee member it becomes:

> **Big things and little things are ours and I am accountable for my own middle things, my area of functional expertise.**

The game in operational or process effectiveness is about *becoming excellent*. However, the danger is that your competitors can reverse engineer the nature and characteristics of your competitive advantage and then allocate resources appropriately, learn and catch up. This usually leads to a situation of parity, because you can't overtake a walker by stepping in their footsteps in front of them. To surge ahead you need creativity to break the rule that the strategy of sector 2 is dictated by that of sector 1.

If your competitors are able to imitate you, it is partly because of their talent but it is also mainly because of your own behaviour. When your accomplishments become known through publications (perhaps by your own managers or business school professors), competitors can not only understand the current state of your art, but also what you intend to do.

Consequently in any industry there is, over time, a diffusion of knowledge through training, publishing, consulting and eventually imitation that leads to a convergence of practices and is followed by a parity of performance among the members of a particular sector. In such a situation two consequences can be observed:

- The customer's power of negotiation is reinforced.
- Price wars often take place.

PROCESS EFFECTIVENESS IS YOURS, SO BE SOLID IN ITS DEFENCE

I agree with Michael Porter, who wrote that the ultimate strategic innovation in the context of parity is acquisition by those who are financially more nimble. However, if a company does not wish to be bought, it must recognize that the two aspects of strategy have two different masters. OE is the preserve of the functional areas, while creativity, which is the essence of strategy, is the collective responsibility of the executive committee. Superior creativity is the company's route to rejuvenating the nature of its initial competitive advantage and to creating the future.

The unsolicited guest

To illustrate this point about convergence, I would like to summarize an article from *Républicain Lorrain*, a local newspaper in north-east France. It reported that a tyre factory had opened the previous weekend for public tours in order to integrate this new industrial facility more into the local community. During this event, security personnel were obliged to seize rolls of film from visitors who were too interested in some specific aspects of the company process. It appeared that these people were engineers from one of the leading companies in this sector. The comments of these 'Sunday competitive benchmarkers' were very straightforward: 'If you

---

CONTINUED . . . **The unsolicited guest**

organize such an event, you should be prepared that some unsolicited people invite themselves to the party.'

This might sound somewhat cynical, but in fact it translates the reality of competitive observation; I do not like to use the word intelligence because there isn't any in this context. Your competitors are keen on discovering your best-demonstrated practices and ready to uncover the unexpected because they already know a great deal about you. Consequently, I agree that such an opportunity cannot be missed. It is the rule of the game, but you shouldn't help it along.

This is in fact what many people involved in business-to-business operations have done through their websites, offering great opportunities to anyone to discover even more precisely where they operate. As the newly appointed development vice-president of Philadelphia Gears commented, 'I am not a gear man, so I browsed on websites and I discovered things that the old company vets did not even know.' But he added an interesting restriction, 'Now I am so much involved in the business, I am always telling me that I need to find the time to keep browsing, but it remains a pious vow.'

Your process effectiveness is yours, so be solid in its defence – but you must be ready for the unexpected, so be fast in your speed of reaction.

> The idea of not missing a competitive benchmarking opportunity represents a cultural mindset. The question is one of momentum, how permanently your team and even yourself are on alert. The relevant information is never announced.

Oh s***!

I remember wandering around a packaging exhibition in Milan with the head of product development of a packaging

---

CONTINUED ... Oh s***!

equipment manufacturer and one of his subordinates. We were passing the booth of one of his competitors when he started to become very excited. He noticed the presence on the booth of one of the company's key clients, but the discussion did not look particularly friendly. He quickly told me that they had recently lost a bid against this Italian competitor for price reasons. Moreover, he qualified the reason as 'dumping'.

Then the unexpected occurred. The client on the booth demanded that its new supplier should open one of the machines. Some excitement occurred in the booth, the guard was taken off, the machine opened and its inner workings were available for anyone to see. Luckily enough we were there.

The product development manager's answer was a spontaneous 'Oh s★★★! They are using chains instead of gears... I understand why it is so inexpensive, it is more simple to manufacture and assemble such a product.' Other comments kept bursting out.

The tension eased and I suggested going for a coffee. I observed the two engineers as they kept talking. The head of engineering told me that we still had many visits to make. I agreed, but I asked him if he could draw what he had been able to observe with his colleague. 'Obviously, I am a development engineer,' he answered, a little offended. Then I added, 'The visit can wait, we have better things to do' and we spent a good hour making sure that the unexpected opportunity was not sub-optimized, converting a happy competitive benchmarking observation into information.

Once again our experience in Milan showed us that 'an office is a dangerous place from which to see the world'. From an office we would not have been able to manage such an opportunity. The trick is to be able to grasp it. To some extent it represents a part of the rejuvenation process for corporate creativity, but it is not enough. Consequently from the very beginning of this process, we must think of the organizational tools necessary to share this information.

The rejuvenation process can involved very sophisticated areas of the business model, as the following example illustrates. During an interview about marketing effectiveness in a business-to-business context, one of my IMD MBA classmates, Thierry de Kalbermatten – currently general manager of Bobst, the Swiss-based world leader in cardboard packaging equipment – reminded me of the importance of extracting the critical or relevant information at the correct point of observation in order to stay strategically creative:

> We are obsessed by our competitors' products performance. Not for their characteristics, our reverse engineering practices perfectly fulfil the task. But we are very eager to understand the way customers can use them and to know what validated yield they can achieve with them.

This last observation underlines the fact that this obsession to confirm and then renew the relevance of one's own competitive advantage is a never-ending game. Once one is well aware of product characteristics, as in the above example, one can pass to the next level, like in a computer game.

Summary

Competitive advantage, which represents the reasons for a company's market success, is a combination of product–innovation, service–passion for the customer and organizational effectiveness–cost performance. The comparative weights of these dimensions expresses a form of company competitive signature that is recognized and valued by a share of the market. The executive committee must be able to evoke this in a homogeneous way, in order to compare its opinion with the customer's perception, account by account and including that of the competition. This competitive advantage offers a recognized and appreciated difference whose sustainability is due to the effectiveness of the process, which will prolong its impact in terms of customer perception.

Action point

Check with the executive committee members how far they have a common vision regarding the firm's competitive advantage (see page 36).

Notes

1   Harvey MacKay (1989) *Swim with the Sharks without Being Eaten Alive*, William Morrow, New York.

2   Michael Porter (1996) 'What is strategy?', *Harvard Business Review*, November–December.

CHAPTER 7

KEEPING TRACK OF BUSINESS REALITY

*I*n Chapter 6 I stressed the idea of competitive advantage validation and its associated process effectiveness requirements as foundation bricks for a strategically minded organic growth policy. I will keep strongly underlining throughout this book that this combination is based on an eager sense of collecting the relevant information in the appropriate place where the added value of a service or product can be discovered and appreciated by the next customer in the business system. This allows us to check not only that the corporation is well in line with the expectations of its market but also that the organization is behaving accordingly.

The purpose of this chapter is to fine tune this sense of alignment, both externally *vis-à-vis* the customer and internally *vis-à-vis* the employees. This two-pronged system, customer satisfaction and customer perceived value, will allow us to have more control over the effectiveness of our customer account management.

RATIO NO 1: CUSTOMER SATISFACTION

The idea is to focus the corporation's attention on being market driven, not broadly, but accurately. Consequently, the first step is to introduce a reference point on the customer side. I think it is relevant to address this from a broader perspective than *needs* by taking careful consideration of *customer expectations*. This challenge forces us not to lose track with the idea of innovation by addressing needs that the customer does not even yet recognize.

Awareness of customer expectations leads to recognition of the critical importance of the process

How many organizations – or, more precisely, sales or marketing departments – can date to say that they are not carefully tracking their customers' expectations? None, very few? This is again an issue of confronting reality. Below is a series of four questions that immediately give a good estimation of how far a particular organization is plugged into its customers' expectations.

1   How are the expectations of the customer formally collected? Who is supposed to do this?
2   Does your company recognize the critical importance of customer expectations by giving appropriate training in listening and observing to those in charge?
3   Is information about customers' expectations regularly updated?
4   Who is involved in sharing these results? How often?

Addressing this subject takes us into the first step of a realistic customer information system. I very often get questions regarding the design of an effective questionnaire to collect these expectations. That is not the question. The issue is to recognize the importance of the idea of customer expectations. It is about creating the conditions for a relationship that allows customers to express their expectations, keeping in the back of our mind that they will have to do it over a short period of time. So asking about the questionnaire is like putting the cart before the horse.

Consequently, one appropriate way of discovering customer expectations has always been to discuss with a customer their own business performance. Sometimes it takes time to reach this context, but if you leapfrog the necessary leadtime it will be to the detriment of the customer's expectations. If the answers to the above questions do not sound favourable, your progress at entering into customer intimacy will be due to your systematic approach to collecting expectations, not to the brilliant architecture of your management information system. That helps only once you have got the correct information.

The challenge of the customer satisfaction ratio is to assess if the company's performance can match the customer's expectations. Consequently, this first ratio is as follows: customer satisfaction = performance : customer expectations (see Figure 7.1).

The interest of this ratio is that it strikes a corporation with a very forceful message, which says that the target is only one value: 1. What follows is even more demanding:

- *If the value is below 1, the company is already effectively out of business* and it is risky to bet on its future unless a massive change occurs that is credited by the customer.
- *If the ratio is above 1, the company will end up out of business* because it is wasting resources.

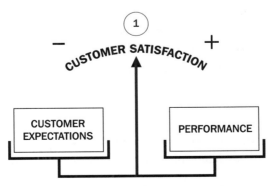

Figure 7.1 Customer satisfaction, the starting point

It does not even take off!

The management of expectations is a subject that demands attention. I was witness to a delightful experience in Rovaniemi in Lapland, the town where Santa Claus is supposed to live. On New Year's Eve I was outside in the polar night following a kind of Disneyland electric parade and suddenly Santa Claus appeared behind a curtain of fir trees on a sleigh drawn by elks. Two children next to me became very excited, shouting 'Santa Claus, Santa Claus!' This boy and girl, who were between three and five years old, kept looking at Santa Claus full of delight. They both asked to be lifted up on their parents' shoulders so that they didn't miss the sleigh full of toys.

The show went on and I noticed that the boy was expecting something, almost holding his breath. Then Santa Claus disappeared behind the fir trees. The show was over. I could read the disappointment on the little boy's face as he looked at the little girl and said, 'It does not even take off!' He was there in Santa Claus's home town and he could visualize what he had seen in books and his parents had made him believe, and there had not even been the smallest flight. He started to cry, followed by the little girl. The analogy with customer relationships is not difficult to draw!

I like this idea of a ratio equal to 1. It goes against some form of conventional wisdom that says, 'exceed, beat customers' expectations as a way to differentiate'. I do not consider this approach to be the most appropriate or sustainable. Over-consumption of resources does not build up a superior credit in the long term. It merely sticks to the idea of achieving a *coup*, nothing more. This is why, in order to operate strategically, the essence of the approach is to carefully stick to customer expectations, which raises the question of the quality of the associated information-collection system. That justifies the acid test discussed above regarding customer expectations and the associated collection and management.

We can encounter difficulties in tracing or controlling customer expectations. Consequently, this ratio can run the risk of being perceived as too conceptual, even too theoretical, which it is not. In my efforts to render it more practical, I have discussed it with many sales people and marketers. One of them, the marketing director of UPS Europe, gave me a good insight to put us on the right track.

His idea was that in commodity products, where the vast majority of companies operate, 'We are successful if we deliver what we have promised' and he added 'systematically'.

To confirm the business relevance of this point, we can observe what is happening in terms of interaction with a customer. The company is supposed to achieve what the sales person has promised to the customer on behalf of the company. Consequently, all the added value of the sales person is to match the most meaningful range of customer expectations with the company's feasible performance.

> **Consequently, the customer satisfaction ratio reminds us of the critical importance of operational performance or the effectiveness of the process.**

Therefore, one must avoid the well-known trap of over-promising and under-delivering. The challenge is to be able to do this with a strategic approach, which means staying in line with your competitive advantage and your core skills.

The answer is people mobility, not size

In the truck industry a trailer outfitter, the European leader in this sector, offered a good illustration of this point. This organization manufactured a kit allowing a bare trailer to be equipped in one operation. The trailer company orders out of a catalogue or to its own specifications. The managing director claimed that the reason for his company's success was:

> We are the only one which is able to offer a mass customized solution. Our competitors adapt their product lines to the market. We react faster than anybody. Our commonly recognized main

> ### CONTINUED ... The answer is people mobility, not size
>
> difference is the substantial size of our design department, but in fact it is misleading. The nature of the advantage is not in terms of structure but of skills. Those who are now in the design or the sales departments had spent a couple of years in the manufacturing department. Consequently, we all precisely master what the company is able to accept or not in terms of stretched goals.

This example suggests a simple warning and a practical consequence. Developing solid awareness within the company of its performance ability:

- *demands careful design.* The company must keep checking that it is not relying on an organizational trick that only used to be true. To confront business reality, one must measure how much time the sales people spend formally with the product development and manufacturing process side of the company. A good acid test to avoid delusion!
- *generates a virtuous circle in terms of organizational effectiveness.* Sales people with a permanently updated idea of what their own company can achieve put the company in a better position to consider a stretched goal. Moreover, the company gets rid of mediocre beliefs, such as that the sales force is the advocate of the customer, which means accepting everything under the reasoning 'if we don't do it the competition will'. This does not happen, because the corollary of the transparency regarding the company's process performance is the sales people's competitive benchmarking of competitors. By doing so, the company avoids the risk of running at two speeds.

The idea of the company's performance may remain conceptual if one does not propose a means to express it in a practical way. To recognize the various levels of performance one can consider the business as made of building blocks describing the critical steps to be taken into account from the conception of the product or the service to the completion of the business cycle. They must be recognized as the key steps in the company's operating process or business system. The goal is to find a means to prioritize the answers in order to be able to manage a scale of sophistication, ranging from a generic answer to an advanced one, which is generally where the competitive advantage lies if one is able to manage it consistently. The answers can be unveiled in a consistent way if one uses Figure 18.2 and the associated comments, page 228.

THE IMPORTANCE OF THE PROCESS DEMANDS THAT THE CUSTOMER EXPECTATIONS DIMENSION BE REVISITED

Sales people give practical relevance to the customer satisfaction ratio by transforming expectations into *promises*. In fact, this represents the added value of sales people on top of the company's reputation. This transformation is not automatic. It can take place if the sales person can exploit to their company's advantage the credit they have acquired with the customer. Consequently, the nature of the relationship can be termed consultative selling.

During any well-managed discussion with a customer, one can observe that their expectations are divided into three categories:

1 Needs.
2 Wishes.
3 Dreams.

In this context an obvious trap is being led by our spontaneous reaction, which make us think that customers are only ready to pay for their needs. I am convinced that the relationship with a customer is more subtle and customers' expectations more complex. Customers hope to be satisfied in a broader range of expectations than exclusively needs. This is a situation that fashion experts have recognized for many years. This point can be illustrated by one of the favourite comments of one of my former MBA students, currently a marketing manager for a luxury brand company, claiming that they have to manage a new breed of customer whom he describes as having 'Hermes bag and Primark scarf'.

Through this process the sales person is transforming customer expectations into promises, which the company can keep. In this context, the goal is not to exceed the promise but to be *in accordance with* what the company has announced. This changes the rule of the game and introduces a new twofold challenge:

We all know that any company can be taken unawares sometimes. An organization is made up of fallible human beings. This does not represent a problem if one is on the lookout for the next opportunity, fully dedicated to satisfying the customer.

> ■ Be *systematically* in accordance with what is announced to the customer.
> ■ Promote a quick *means* to *restore* conformity with customer expectations – just in case!

I would like to illustrate the idea of conformity using the experience I gained with an express shipment carrier that is competing in imaginative ways in order to be perceived as different from other such companies. This kind of programme, too often based on marketing gimmicks and able to be imitated overnight or within a short space of time, is more an unquestionable source of margin reinvestment in the market price rather than an effective customer loyalty builder.

For instance, one of these carriers picks up a document in Europe before 6 pm and delivers it the next morning to Park Avenue, New York before 8 am. What an achievement! The customer's judgement will be very straightforward and summarized by: 'This result is just what the carrier promised.' The customer does not care about the difficulties of the supplier's business; the responsibility, planes, hub, vans, tracking and tracing system are the carrier's job characteristics. One must pay attention to not trying to get gratitude for something that is merely perceived as normal as long as it has been announced, although difficult to achieve.

In the vast majority of businesses that are only dealing with commodity products or services, one must stop the spread of expressions such as 'delighting the customer' or 'an experience with us should be legendary'. The point is that one can express it the way one wants, but should beware of sacrificing the substance of the service or product content to provide an easy cosmetic substitution.

Being in accordance with promises to the customer will be good enough (see Figure 7.2). The customer is an adult and does not need bells and whistles to decide if it should keep giving its business to the same supplier.

This is my proposition at this stage. However, I can immediately add that it is counterproductive not to draw benefit from one's own process effectiveness. It remains to find the appropriate way to do it.

> **The rule is straightforward: either you are in accordance with your promises and survive, or you under-deliver and you are quickly out of the game. Consequently, the customer loyalty builder is the operating process.[1]**

EXPECTATIONS, PROMISE, CONFORMITY – WHO IS THE TARGET?

Being in accordance with promises to the customer is not as easy an objective as it might appear when one takes into account all the care necessary to manage this form of information system. A second step in the scale of difficulty occurs when you add the need to do this systematically. However, a third level of challenge must then be addressed. The purpose of the customer satisfaction ratio is to measure the company's effectiveness at retaining its customers. The proposition says that if your process allows you to deliver in accordance to what has been promised to the customer, the customer

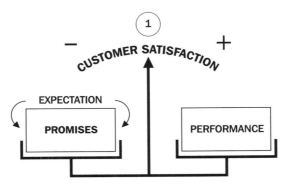

Figure 7.2 Customer satisfaction is about conformity

satisfaction ratio is equal to 1 and you are entitled to take part in the next round. Pushing further the accuracy of this observation naturally leads to a new question: who is concerned by this conformity?

A satisfied individual does not necessarily mean a satisfied client

I was visiting a French customer of Sodexho Pass International researching how we could find insights for our organic growth rules. With the account manager, we arranged to meet a female clerk from the human resource department of a medium-sized telecommunications equipment maintenance company.

The customer's employee unambiguously described the relationship with SPI over the last five years as exemplary. There was nothing to add, it was 'fine tuned like music paper', as we say in France. We could have stopped our investigation at this point, confident in the quality of our findings. However, due to her professionalism, the sales person mentioned the range of new services provided for free by SPI. For instance, a company can tailor its monthly order and its staff will receive in their own envelope a personalized cheque book of meal vouchers for the month with the company logo on it. This is not a gimmick, it has some clear benefits in terms of speed of delivery at the end of the month. To be fair, one must add that the competition can offer the same service. To implement this service the EDP department merely have to download the application, which will be combined with the payroll software.

After this brief presentation the clerk did not look interested at all. She started to explain how well oiled her operating process was. It was a quarterly order and each month she cut the meal vouchers from large sheets, prepared the appropriate number of vouchers per employee, formed each cheque book, stapled them and put each of them in a named envelope. All of this took her approximately half to one day.

On the way back to the office, I challenged the sales person on how she assessed the risk on this account. 'What

> **CONTINUED ... A satisfied individual does not necessarily mean a satisfied client**
>
> risk?' she asked, surprised. Simply put, this account was open to the competition because the conformity concerned a person and not the account. This is a very serious challenge to conformity, not only with individuals but also at the whole account level.

In this case SPI was clearly delivering a performance below the generic level of the state of the art available in the industry. This was not due to its fault, but because one person at the customer's premises had decided to use the supplier's performance to fit her own needs and not exactly her employer's. Consequently, it is very easy for the competition to play the game of 'you don't get that and you are paying that much'.

The next question naturally emerges: how many accounts are in this risky situation in your own customer portfolio?

In this case the decision taken was to plan a call with this clerk's manager to present what was available. Some readers will object that we are creating problems with the person we are working with on a day-to-day basis and even sawing the branch on which we are seated. To some extent I agree, but we face a more serious issue if the status quo represents a threat. Consequently, the objective is to satisfy the customer and not only a few individuals working for the customer.

GIVING THE COMPETITOR ROOM FOR MANOEUVRE

Assessing customer satisfaction at a meaningful level in the customer organization and not limiting one's own relationship challenge to one individual, even if they are presented as the decision maker, is a very sensitive subject for sales forces. It is rather seldom that we observe a sales force that dares to challenge the idea that reaching conformity with an individual working for the customer is not the same as reaching conformity with the customer, unless it is validated for the whole decision-making system. This observation brings us to the next case, in Japan, with a very large sogoshosha or trading company, Itochu.

Hit them where they ain't

The express mail business in this firm was split among four operators according to the destinations where they were assessed to be the most effective. The leader was achieving a turnover exceeding €4 million. The customer had two main offices one in Tokyo, where the above-mentioned turnover was achieved, and one in Osaka, with something also substantial, around €1 million.

The leading carrier's account manager managed this account very carefully. In Tokyo, he reported that he visited the mailroom manager every day. The latter reported that he considers this care as proof of the quality of the relationship and as the best means to prolong it. Nevertheless, over the years the relationship has become entrenched in this pattern, which has ended up representing an opportunity for a clever competitor.

The plan of attack was very straightforward. It would be ridiculous to try to convince the mailroom manager that he isn't receiving the best service from his current leading supplier. However, what would happen if he received a directive to work with somebody else? This is what happened in Osaka, where FedEx met a finance vice-president of Itochu, competed purely on price in the context of savings and immediately got the contract. The mailroom manager was unable to play the role of ambassador.

In fact this kind of relationship, which over time becomes restricted to a very limited number of people in a company, generates its own insidious inefficiency in an appearance of customer management effectiveness.

Once the competition has understood the trick, the risk rockets of encountering a large number of strategic breaks in your customer portfolio. You were not managing your competitive

> **The longer you haven't been challenged, the more fatal even the slightest attack can be.**

space, but at this stage of the relationship it is too late to react, you can only count the casualties.

RATIO NO 2: CUSTOMER PERCEIVED VALUE

The first ratio had a narrow, quantitative target, but with the second there is no quantitative objective. The purpose is to enter in the details of the dynamic that contributes to prolonging customer satisfaction through careful monitoring of customer-perceived value.

At this stage the current proposition is simple: the customer has bought your promised difference and it was delivered accordingly. Over time, what can threaten this well-balanced system? If the difference is no longer performance, then price might become a perfectly suitable threat. When price is involved one is entering into a zero-sum game, called a price war. The customer perceived value ratio encapsulates these warnings.

The ratio is as follows: customer perceived value = performance : price (see Figure 7.3).

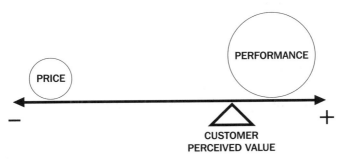

Figure 7.3 Customer perceived value

The purpose of this ratio is not to find a value, but instead to focus the customer's attention on the uniqueness of its supplier's performance. The question is, therefore, how can we achieve it? Before trying to attempt to find a formal answer, we should avoid the trap of fooling ourselves into believing that 'satisfying customers' is enough to assure a sustainable position in the customer's mind. To prevent this, we should satisfy two conditions:

- Communicate effectively and regularly the uniqueness of the company's value proposition at each opportunity for customer contact.
- Benchmark the company's performance against both the competition and the evolution of customers' expectations set by outside influences.

Many examples can illustrate the point that a satisfied customer does not systematically become a recurrent buyer. The striking point about this observation is the importance of this proportion among satisfied customers. The airline industry and the automotive industry gave us large numbers of examples.

In the mid–1990s, British Airways observed more than 10 per cent of its satisfied customers announcing that they were no longer willing to fly with the company. A Japanese manufacturer encountered a similar phenomenon in the US. This automotive brand was known for its high level of customer satisfaction in the classic automotive manufacturer survey. The questions are well known:

- Are you satisfied with your new vehicle?
- Would you buy one of the same brand when you change to a new one?

Out of the positive answers to the first two questions, only one-third of customers effectively do this three to four years later.

The question is what has happened, why do we observe such wastage? Two main explanations can be proposed:

- Inappropriate communication.
- Insufficient attention to benchmarking.

Familiarization ruins a customer's memory

Repurchase must not be considered as an automatic consequence of a positive experience with a supplier. So it is wise to argue that repurchase demands a level of active involvement from the supplier in order to develop a reflex of spontaneous collaboration in the customer's mind. This raises the question of what the supplier is doing to reassure the customer that he or she made the right choice in deciding to deal with this specific supplier and that continues to be correct. Consequently, a supplier should monitor how it is reiterating its value proposition to its portfolio of customers.

The challenge is a communication one with a two-pronged area of attention. First of all the quality of the communication, does the message received make sense to the customer, but simultaneously what critical mass is created in terms of communication. This means:

■ How many contacts are required with the customer actively to maintain this reflex?
■ Does the supplier possess the resources to reach the critical mass?

To give an ideal figure for the customer perceived value ratio would not be in line with the philosophy of this book. What it is for is to remind you to put this question at the top of your customer relationship discussion agenda. A reasonable assessment varies from case to case, but I can mention a fatal trap in this approach:

> **Do not rely on customers' memories to keep active a positive perception of your performance.**

Not to be paid

In the mid-1990s Martin, the French subsidiary of Bobst (mentioned on page 50) decided not to accept the proposal of XES (Xerox Engineering Systems) for the renewal of its plan duplication equipment. The reasons given were simple:

■ Lack of attention.
■ Insufficient contact over the previous seven years.

CONTINUED . . . Not to be paid

The situation was characterized by a kind of U-shaped customer relationship management style, where following signature of the contract interest in the customer starts to fall, staying low until it rose again shortly before the time for renegotiation. This context was reinforced by the fact that the customer, instead of changing its equipment every five years as was normal, did so after eight or nine. Consequently Martin was not a hot target for XES's account manager.

Needless to say, once XES's sales team knew about the new project, Martin became the centre of attention. Overnight the account shifted in the account manager's SPANCO (Xerox's term for Suspect, Prospect, Approach, Negotiation, Conclusion, Order) from cold to very hot. This sudden excess of attention turned quickly into irritation and more.

XES benefited from privileged access to the company's operators but did not draw any advantage from its relationship. There were no XES fans at Martin. Over the seven years of the relationship XES had become a 'necessary evil', if not less. So for the next deal XES started not only with no advantage but even with some handicaps due to its ineffective maintenance support during the previous two years.

Such behaviour from XES is characteristic of a lack of sense both of the cost of acquiring a new account and that of maintaining an account in a portfolio. It does not mean that top management is not aware of these concepts. It is here as a general warning, intending to remind us that:

- The gap between concepts and their operational effectiveness can be huge.
- Even a good company can always be taken unawares.

The meeting at Martin's premises with XES's managing director and his team could have sounded like an indictment against my customer complacency management style with this

---

CONTINUED ... Not to be paid

specific account. As usual, in the tough context of failure there is something substantial and positive to harvest. Martin explained how it would have managed a similar situation in its own business of equipment lasting longer and longer on customer premises.

Martin's products and systems are positioned as a sophisticated piece of equipment with very special support from the manufacturer. To do this and to remain perceived as a 'fixer' or a 'solution provider' by its clients, Martin must permanently reiterate in the customer's mind the uniqueness of its value proposition. The Martin way of doing this is periodically to send an invoice to the customer consolidating the list of services delivered with their unit value and their total 'virtual' price. The price is virtual because the second page of the invoice is crossed out by a red note saying: 'Not to be paid.'

The lesson is simple. Martin does these services for free, which is consistent with its 'fixer' positioning, but they do have a cost and the customer must at least be fully aware of their value.

This example represents one of the possible options for reiterating the uniqueness of our own value proposition delivered to the customer. We must stress the following sequence:

- Step one: Inform the customer of the attention it received.
- Step two: Choose the most appropriate unit in which to express your customer commitment.

One further need must be satisfied in order to keep control of the customer relationship. We may imagine that we have found the appropriate way to remind our customer that we care, but are we doing so tactfully?

The challenge of the appropriate unit

A key account manager from an express shipment company was seriously threatened by his main customer's increasing power of negotiation. The situation combined the result of a price attack orchestrated by his arch-rival competitor and some feelings of frustration. He described the case in the following way:

> This customer really has no memory, they are now asking us to slash our price by 20 per cent but they forget what we did for them. For instance, last year they demanded to re-open the hub in CDG, three Saturdays, we did it and we did not even charge them even though it did not cost us nothing, let's say €25 000.

In the previous example we observed that it was critical not only to demonstrate one's own sense of customer attention, but also to keep the customer informed about its value. The price or the costs of the service or product are merely an intermediate step to draw a more substantial value from this practice.

For instance, in the express shipment context, if you try to remind the customer of the €25 000 expended on its behalf, its answer will only remind you of the duties naturally associated with a contract with a €4 million sales turnover. Consequently, the point is about the relevance of the unit used to refresh the customer's memory.

My suggestion is:

In this specific case, might achieving end-of-quarter Saturday shipments and being able to benefit incidentally from the associated billing have allowed the European subsidiary to achieve something? It would have been better to know the full picture. I can imagine that

> **Systematically think in terms of benefits, meaning the impact on the customer's business, to guarantee that you get the credit for your customer care activities.**

it was able either to come close to a quarterly target or to beat it, but not knowing is like throwing the margin out of the window. Consequently, the key point is not only to make superb efforts to delight the customer, but also to keep a careful track of their impact on the customer's business. In summary, a superb performance cannot be articulated without an effective combined information and communication approach.

By combining performance and appropriate communication the company is preventing itself from failing due to its own behaviour. I started this demonstration by discussing the importance of the customer satisfaction ratio. Then I stressed the performance side and especially on maintaining the perceived value of the performance on the top bar of the customer's 'ladder'. Finally, I added the crucial importance of making it known. So three integrative steps must be borne in mind when one enters this game. These three steps are sequential and represent a score if they are all played together. We cannot play only an overture or the melody if we do not want to run the risk of spoiling our efforts at maintaining and consolidating the relationship with the customer.

A last trap must also be discussed. This lies in over-focusing one's attention on the quality of one's own behaviour and attitude relative to those of the competition. You may retort that what is suggested is already enough. I think it is enough, but the customer relationship may reveal surprises such as a change in the customer's expectations under the influence of a supplier outside your range of products or services.

I have deliberately not mentioned the competition in this discussion so far. If your company is one that is able to maintain its performance in the condition I suggest above, then you have very little risk of being taken unawares by the competition, which you are certainly scrupulously monitoring. Nevertheless, the threat might come from beyond the classic range of view of your particular sector. This is the purpose of the next example.

We are not concerned, it is not a competitor of ours!

In the mid-1990s Tetrapak France (at that time the unquestioned leader in brick form liquid packaging equipment and consumables) was attacked by International Paper at one of its top accounts in France. It managed to resist the competitor's attack, not losing accounts and also not slashing prices. The effectiveness of its business-to-business marketing approach apparently worked well, but Tetrapak decided to revisit completely its permanent relationship marketing programme and allocate a large amount of resources to it.

Aware of these efforts, I shared this information with a company who is involved in the same business system but not at all in competition with Tetrapak. This French-based company, Japy, is now a subsidiary of the German world leader in agricultural equipment, Westphalia. Japy is a leading company in milk storage systems to store and preserve the milk between the milking of the cow and the arrival of the dairy truck. Both Tetrapak and Japy were quasi exclusive suppliers of the number one French private milk collection company.

I called the chairman of Japy, whom I have known for a very long time. His reaction expressed surprise: 'Thank you, that is interesting, but how does it affect us? We are not concerned, Tetrapak is not our competitor.'

Objectively I must agree, because these two companies are not competing for the same euros. However, simultaneously I disagree regarding the absence of concern, because this situation represented both a threat and an opportunity.

A threat

This kind of approach will not change the ladder in the customer's mind, but it will alter the range of the customer's expectations.

Somebody is telling the customer that it merits being treated differently and here is the new tempo for the relationship. It is less threatening than if it were orchestrated by a competitor, but it is nevertheless threatening. Consequently, the appropriate management attitude would be not to react, not necessarily to do anything, but at least carefully to assess the consequences of this new deal.

To measure whether this new relationship tempo will become the reference point, sales people must pay attention to the content of their discussions with the customer: 'Who is the customer speaking about most? In which terms?' An indistinct answer will give you the first signal of potential risk in the relationship if you do not adapt to address developments outside of your range of products or services.

This warning introduces the need to master account per account who is considered by the customer as the most influential supplier in terms of customer relationship management. Is it the largest or most technologically advanced supplier? Whoever it is must be recognized with a functional benchmarking attitude.

An opportunity

When the best in class is identified, it sounds like a good idea to enter into discussions with it in order to exchange our respective best demonstrated practices. By doing so, one is preventing a possible case of failure due to insufficient attention. This example shows us that customer attention is a set of skills that brings a company far beyond the limit of its own sector. If you do not do this, you are running a double risk:

- You face reinforced negotiating power at the customer because you have not reacted sufficiently quickly to its signals.
- You are offering a golden opportunity to a challenger who can reshuffle the cards to its advantage.

Summary

The trick of maintaining a customer satisfaction ratio equal to 1 reminds us of the great importance of managing customer expectations. This first ratio makes us enter a virtuous circle, of which the goal is to be systematically in accordance with what has been promised to the customer through the effectiveness of the company's processes. In customer satisfaction the process is a critical topic that governs the credibility of the promises made to the customer.

Satisfying the customer is not enough to offer sustainability in the relationship, so the second ratio stresses the associated means to maintain the customer's attention on the superiority of your own performance, in order to avoid falling into the trap of differentiation based on a price war. The first ratio has a strong flavour of customer information management, while the second is more customer communication oriented, thus creating the appropriate conditions for a mutually supportive and consistent development system leading to well-managed growth.

 ## Action point

Check the effectiveness of your customer expectations management with your top 10 accounts (see page 54). In the light of this chapter, are you effectively securing today and preparing for tomorrow?

Note

1   At the end of this book you can read a story called 'Killing your ambassador', which describes the birth and death of a customer relationship in a commodity service. One possible reading focuses on the poor attention given to the customer. However, one former business development manager of one of the sector leaders commented on this story by saying that as long as the overnight delivery rate does not fall below 95 per cent, you have the most effective customer loyalty and satisfaction builder. The rest is important, but it is not reasonable to consider that it might work as customer retention insurance if we are below the target figure.

CHAPTER 8

YOUR ROLE IN THE CUSTOMER'S MIND

*I*n the two previous chapters I attempted to address what a company must achieve to strategically manage a positive perception of its performance. This represents one of the main foundations of an effective customer retention policy. My research and consulting projects also brought us an answer regarding how customers can formulate their perceptions of the company's performance. I was trying to answer a simple question: what role is the company fulfilling in the customer's mind?

This question slightly changes the focus, in order to avoid confusion between the perception of the performance and the role of this performance in the client's mind or even in its own business system. This can be explained as follows.

Performance is unique but is perceived as a side issue by the customer. Consequently, it must be regarded in a twofold way:

> **First, the driving dimension in the relationship with a client is the role associated with the supplier's contribution. Then comes the perception of the performance of this contribution.**

I have often thought about this twofold approach, but I received clear input toward reaching this conclusion during a discussion with the managing director of Technomed Medical System, a company at the forefront of research into liso therapy in the treatment of kidney stones. He explained the role of one of his service suppliers:

> To help us focus on the critical challenges of our sector by securing the facility management of functional tasks of the organization, which do not represent a source of added value for our company.

In this case the role of the service suppliers, including Sodexho Pass International, was clear: the supplier was a 'necessary evil', not regarded as critical but as mandatory, allowing a particular task to be achieved.

Being a 'necessary evil' does not mean, however, that the supplier's performance is not superb. Consequently, *role* and *performance* demand two separate sets of assessment in order to avoid the nightmare of *perceived performance parity*, a business context where no strategic advantage can be expected. Understanding on which side it is located, 'necessary evil' or 'fixer', is only half the effort; the company must also simultaneously assess the perception of its performance and follow the two-step proposition mentioned on page 69.

The manager's objective is to prolong the benefits associated with a particular positioning. Whether you are a 'fixer' or a 'necessary evil' is not the issue, which is rather whether you operate in a manner that is appropriate to your status. The role is a critical element that governs the nature of the relationship, but it is the supplier's responsibility to achieve the appropriate fine tuning through its performance.

FIXER TODAY, NECESSARY EVIL TOMORROW

We have observed that over time companies lose their aura, their good positioning in the customer's mind, if they don't have effective means to prevent this. A 'fixer' role is associated with the idea of being first, opening up a new category.

For example DHL was the first express shipment company to offer its express mail service in downtown Amsterdam. Then due to sloppy management because it was comfortable in the position of leader, the carrier saw its leadership contested. In a seminar I run at Cranfield Business School in the UK, a Dutch express shipment company station manager reported that the performance did not live up to the duty imposed by its initial positioning.

Any 'fixer' status can be threatened in two ways:

- *Lack of operational effectiveness*, which allows the emergence of the idea that better performance could be obtained from a competitor.
- The *routine* into which the customer falls because he or she becomes familiar with, and then accustomed to, what had been initially regarded as extraordinary performance.

The cause is deeply rooted in an erosion of talent at the company meaning that it is unable to anticipate this threat arising, one that is endemic to any business operator. If we do nothing then by the very nature of the threat we are heading towards an ocean of perceived performance parity.

NECESSARY EVIL TODAY, FIXER TOMORROW

Life in a 'necessary evil' context is characterized by a permanent risk of strategic breakdown. In principle, the supplier is protected by the quality of its performance. However, there is a risk of convergence (see page 47) because of the spread of best demonstrated practices through benchmarking and because hostile competitors headhunt your top executives. Consequently, we can easily imagine a risk of inflation of performance leading to the trap of perceived performance parity, where the differentiating characteristic among potential suppliers becomes the price.

Before addressing how to leave the 'necessary evil' status, one point of clarification. *Perceived performance parity* represents either:

- An *objective assessment*, which results from the supplier's inability to cope with the new tempo imposed by the competition.

Or:

■   An *unfair perception* of the situation. The supplier's objective performance is not fully credited by the client. It appears as the result of the customer's power of negotiation. However, experience suggests that the customer's power of negotiation is an argument used by suppliers who can no longer cope with the evolution of the rules of the game imposed by the client. I can add another symptom characteristic of such a situation: companies caught in this trap start thinking about new niches.

In order to leave 'necessary evil' status and become a 'fixer', the supplier needs to deliver to the customer or the market a significantly advanced answer, which does not usually happen. Two examples follow of the evolution of this role, one at the market segment level and one at the customer account level.

Canal boats in Amsterdam and double-deckers in Tokyo

Even though DHL was the first company to enter the express shipment business in Amsterdam, in the late 1990s it became stuck in cut-throat price competition between the sector's four leading operators. A new station manager took charge and his goal was to find a way to exit this vicious circle.

DHL broke the rules of the game by introducing an environmentally conscious way of achieving its business in downtown Amsterdam. Caring about the environment is not a marketing gimmick but a way of reaching this relatively inaccessible area. Instead of using vans to deliver and pick up downtown shipments, DHL was the first to use boats on the city's canals: a new way to reengineer its operations in traffic-congested areas. In Tokyo a similar solution employed double-decker buses.

This innovation clearly positioned the company as a 'fixer' or 'solution provider' at the community level. Solution provider status is given to a company that is the first to implement

---

CONTINUED ... Canal boats in Amsterdam and double-deckers in Tokyo

something that appeals to customers as meaningful and novel. Therefore it creates a new category and the company, as the inventor, benefits for a certain period from the customer's preference.

To prolong this period of time, we come back to the means of prolonging the initial advantage. In the case of DHL the goal was practical: impose this new way of operating on its competitors in order to keep leadership in this area of operations. The best means was to lobby for the common interest by supporting initiatives demanding that vans be banned from downtown Amsterdam.

I shared this case for the first time at a seminar at Cranfield in 1998. I liked this example for its comprehensive approach. We can observe not only a creative idea but also a system for prolonging the benefits of its relevance. Creativity without operational effectiveness is not a guaranteed way to thrive.

Charleroi Hospital

A similar situation can occur at the account level, where the 'necessary evil' supplier finds a way to solve a problem that is more difficult than the standard characteristics associated with the service itself.

Charleroi Hospital in the south of Belgium, near the French border, wanted to give its staff meal vouchers as fringe benefits. These can be bought from either Sodexho or Accor. The hospital faced a specific constraint, the need to deliver the meal voucher books over a period of three days to individual staff working in shifts. The challenge posed unusual logistical difficulties. Coping with this specific challenge represented an opportunity for Sodexho Pass International (SPI) to beat Accor and to reset the perception of performance to its own

---

CONTINUED ... **Charleroi Hospital**

---

advantage. It also represented a way for SPI to create a new category based on the ability to individualize the monthly distribution of meal voucher books.

The next question is: what was done with this fixer status? Was it used to get a leverage point for the development of a new category in the hospital sector, simultaneously avoiding sub-optimization?

FIXER TODAY, FIXER TOMORROW

From shipping documents to spare parts

DHL started its express shipment business in Norway. Its main activity was the express delivery of shipping manifests. DHL has held a dominant position for years but, although it was initially perceived as the innovator, that position was threatened by the arrival of other world-leading companies. This situation was imperceptibly but surely moving towards parity until the mid-1990s, when the local management of DHL benefited from its broad access to the shipping sector.

DHL invented a new service: delivering express spare parts, covering everything necessary for ships, ranging from a microwave oven to an engine shaft. Whether this was ingenious or not is not the question, somebody was inspired to develop this service because the benefits were unquestionable. The absence of a spare part can cost a lot of money or create frustration among the crew if the ship leaves without a critical detail resolved.

I like this kind of innovation because it appears as the result of a deep intimacy with the customer's business model (see Figure 8.1).

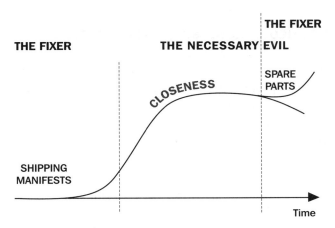

Figure 8.1 Rejuvenating the fixer status

This is another perspective on operational effectiveness, regarding the speed with which the innovation spread at the level of a world operator. The purpose is not to address at this stage the cross-fertilization techniques available in these groups. This example, like the canal one, was presented in the UK during one of my training sessions with an express shipment company. At the end I observed a French manager from Marseille in discussion with a colleague from Oslo. You can imagine the topic of their conversation.

In summary, the Norwegian example, and the following case from the heart of the Italian leather goods industry, Caserta, demonstrates a virtuous combination for business-to-business situations based on the intimacy of the relationship.

Leather goods samples

A brand such as DHL, because of its generic value, offers the foundation for an initial 'fixer' status. In Italy DHL was the first to open a dedicated station in a leather goods cluster, Caserta. For a while nothing of note happened. However, as in Norway, we can observe that the rejuvenation of the initial status is in the hands of local people who will invent an even

> ### CONTINUED ... Leather goods samples
>
> more appropriate answer. In Italy, the issue was developing the appropriate packaging to ship samples. With this combination of being first to open an agency and the ability to design answers that are well adapted to the business context, the early mover remains the local leader.

Consequently, we can formulate a consolidating rule:

Following the customer's suggestion

A frustrated customer makes a phone call to a supplier: 'We really need this done, could you do it for us?' The customer knows that what it is asking for is not among the supplier's core skills, but the latter's reputation as a fixer precedes it.

> **The strategic health of the business is proportional to the speed at which the local structure contributes to raising a barrier of access to the competition by demonstrating a company's superior understanding of the customer, thus leading to the appropriate actions for the benefit of the customer.**

How can this situation be managed? It is like riding a bicycle with a fixed gearwheel: you can't stop pedalling, condemned to permanent innovation.

The following are critical in this approach:

- Recognize your current positioning.
- Monitor the perception of your performance.

The fixer today–fixer tomorrow challenge is unavoidable if one wants to keep justifying a premium price, as in Figure 8.2.

Failing to keep focusing customer attention on the uniqueness of your performance leads to the 3Ps of perceived performance parity. Consequently it reinforces the customer's power of negotiation and makes it shift to a stage of risk-free substitution of suppliers, where the differentiator will be a fourth P, price. The game

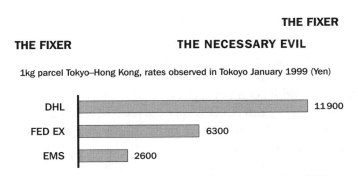

Figure 8.2 What do you invent to justify your premium? The various shipments might even travel in the same plane

becomes 'more for less'. Before blaming the customer for its blatant power of negotiation, we might wonder whether the supplier's own behaviour is not the cause of its difficulties in justifying its margin.

If the situation reaches this point, the company's situation can become even worse and fall into a classic trap: how can you exit from the vicious circle of the price war, where improving performance without identifying poorly satisfied or unknown customer needs leaves you in a position where you cannot charge for that increased performance?

INCREASING PERFORMANCE IS A HIGH-RISK CUL-DE-SAC!

Sticking to the principles observed in the customer satisfaction ratio (see page 55), if the corporation increases its performance, the customer satisfaction ratio will exceed 1. Consequently, the company is over-consuming resources while the customer's expectations remain the same. Because of self-indulgence, people consider that ratcheting up performance is worthwhile.

I cannot share this opinion if this supplier wishes to act strategically or build something different in its customer's mind. It is, in fact, a clear confession that the supplier has lost and this represents its only way to stay in the game by reinvesting a share of its margin in the market price. Engaging in a strategy of increasing performance while simultaneously on another front supporting a price war is tactically a Pyrrhic victory and strategically fatal.

The customer perceived value ratio (see page 65) gives us another benchmarking opportunity. In the customer's mind, both the supplier and its competitors can fulfil expectations at the same level. The supplier can never forget the level of resources needed to reach the targeted results. If it finds that it is consuming more resources than its competitors, it must be conscious that it is also cannibalizing its own future if it does not quickly find a way to improve its operational effectiveness. This situation does not lead to too many headaches for the executive committee because its members do not consider it important to have a good idea of the level of resources competitors are mobilizing to get the same result.

One, two, three – back to business reality

During a seminar with one of the four world-leading operators in bottling systems, we came to the conclusion that the competitive advantage for a specific division was its process control people, who are able to develop the most advanced systems to the greatest benefit of the client. I observed the audience, where a feeling of self-satisfaction was growing. What they knew intuitively was being confirmed by a rational management technique.

In this relaxed end-of-session atmosphere I ventured a question: 'Do you have any idea how good the process automation department is at your fiercest competitor?'

The answers were generic observations such as 'certainly not as good as us'.

I asked a second question: 'Do you know how many technicians and engineers there are in this department?'

There were similar answers, so I followed this by a last question: 'Do you think that X (one of the fiercest German competitors) knows this information about your organization?'

I was not expecting an answer, but noticed that it created a shiver in the audience.

You must be conscious that your competitor might be more eager than you at extracting the relevant information. If that is not the case they are like an archivist, accumulating documents or data with very little added value. If so that would be good news, but it is extremely unlikely.

Summary

Do not confuse the quality of your performance with the impact of your contribution to the customer's business model. It is in the light of this contribution analysis that the status of 'fixer' or 'necessary evil' must be recognized account per account.

A status or positioning is like a snapshot. What is more appropriate from a management point of view is the movie that can be shot reporting the means uncovered to maintain and improve the initial status. Moreover, this role must be systematically addressed from the point of view of relativity. A perceived status is based on a process performance associated with critical core skills. Recognizing it internally is the first step, but being able to observe its current stage among competitors also represents an information priority for an executive committee.

 Action point

Assess into which category – fixer or necessary evil – you fall with your top 10 accounts. Then take the fixer status list. What has been done to maintain and rejuvenate your positioning among these accounts? Do you assess it as appropriate for a sustainable customer relationship? Why?

CHAPTER 9

THE RELATIONSHIP WITH THE CUSTOMER – A STRUCTURAL TEMPO

*I*n the first three chapters of this part the importance of the customer information system was addressed from many angles:

- To validate the company's competitive advantage.
- To monitor the perceived impact of the company's performance.
- To assess the company's positioning.

If customer information is the critical raw material for an effective customer relationship programme, the first issue regards the nature of the times when we can collect this information, and the second who can be involved at the top level of the company.

TWO DISTINCT PHASES: WHICH ROLE FOR TOP MANAGEMENT AND EVEN THE BOSS?

In the relationship with the customer, it is wise to recognize two types of interactions:

- The time of *final negotiation* for the next contract.
- The time for *discussion*, which lies in between.

The desired outcome of a negotiation is clear: to get the deal. The challenge lies in optimizing the time for discussion. On occasion, companies may feel that putting the boss in the field, at the forefront for the final round, is a worthwhile tactic. I agree, but it depends on the philosophy behind such behaviour. If the goal of a field assignment for top management is to reinforce the company's customer intimacy and its value proposition as a means to assure the client that it is in good hands, this approach should be followed.

On the other hand, is selling to the customer an appropriate role for the CEO or an executive committee member? An unequivocal 'no' was the reply of the ex–CEO of Grand Metropolitan France, a former British-based food conglomerate: 'I don't see the customer, each time it costs me a 3 per cent price reduction.' If one follows this logic the boss should stay in his office, but once again we all know that 'an office is a dangerous place from which to view the world'.

Consequently, the above observations raise the questions of when and how the boss and the executive committee can be involved in the customer relationship.

The boss is not welcome even for a large order

My experience suggests that you should systematically avoid involving the 'boss' in the negotiation stage for an order, even a substantial one. If the boss deals with orders, it signals that the opposition is too much for this organization. To support this proposition, we also consider it wise to warn bosses not to be tricked by their own sales force.

Do not allow your sales force to make you play Rambo

In the mid–1990s at Xerox Engineering Systems (XES), Xerox's subsidiary dealing with plan reproduction and technical data management, at a standard prospective order review meeting a substantial prospective order appeared on the SPANCO system (see page 68). The name of the customer, the size and the competitive context naturally drew the atten-

---

CONTINUED ... Do not allow your sales force to make you play Rambo

tion of top management. To simplify the discussion, the next questions were:

- What is the percentage chance of success?
- When?

A month later the perspective on the deal remained the same, with some hints that it might be tougher than forecast. Two months later the conclusion of the deal was still pending and the boss, a former sales star, agreed to join the sales team to unlock the situation and finalize a deal, which should not have taken so long.

This turned into a disaster. The deal had been so poorly handled that the late arrival of the boss, rather than being perceived as a mark of consideration, catalysed the acrimony against his company. Consequently, he was unable to counterbalance the accumulated liabilities of the previous negotiation period. He commented, 'I have been shot like a rabbit in a wide open field.' The customer admitted, with some amusement, 'When we knew that their boss was coming we prepared the welcome committee.'

The boss must stay out of the final negotiation phase because:

- Either the deal is won and the boss has something more important to do than settling the final details. I recognize their operational importance, but there are other people empowered to do that task.
- Or if the decision is still pending, keep the white knight for Hollywood.

You may disagree with my suggestions, but some additional observations should convince the most reluctant. The (boss) wizard's magic wand has a name: *margin reinvestment* in the market price, as the following case illustrates.

The boss cannot lose

A project manager was complaining to his boss, the CEO of an electrical installation company, at that time a subsidiary of Compagnie Générale des Eaux, that the Toulouse rugby stadium was not willing to accept its proposal for a public lighting renovation programme. The project manager considered that the discussion was really tough, especially when one considered that the company was an official sponsor of the rugby club. Consequently, he asked his boss to activate his network of relationships.

The boss's effectiveness exceeded the project manager's expectations. Late that afternoon the boss came to see the project manager in the office he shared with a colleague and left on his desk the order for the public lighting renovation contract. Both the project manager and his colleague were astonished and left the building with no doubt why the boss was the boss.

The next morning the project manager could not believe his eyes when he read the details of the order. He had fought for many weeks to protect the company's margin centimetre by centimetre, and the boss had given it away. It was too much and he rushed into his boss's office: 'What did you do? You gave them everything for nothing!' He went on commenting very excitedly on the details of the contract.

The boss reminded the project manager that he had asked him to do something when there was only one option, to bring back the order. 'The boss cannot lose face,' he added. The boss's conclusion remained a long-lasting lesson in the annals of the company culture: 'I brought in the order but now the margin management is your problem.' The boss wasn't asked any more to be involved in negotiations with customers, which did not prevent him from being an effective part of the company's customer relationship policy.

This situation where the boss was able to overturn the sense of the deal is characteristic of a poor managerial process. The team in charge failed in focusing customer attention on the benefit or performance dimension of the perceived value ratio. Consequently, in this context the customer was waiting for the boss to concede what the troops had not yet conceded. The key question then becomes: the next time a deal needs to be finalized, should the organization once again call in the boss?

Creating the future is the boss's appropriate place

Therefore we should recognize the critical limits of an approach that involves the boss in the final phase of negotiation. However, in the continuum of the relationship with a customer, there is a time between periods of negotiation. The opportunity and the challenge are to use this time to the company's best advantage before the hot period of the next negotiation. Consequently my proposition is:

Consequently, we should recognize that there are two times for managing the customer relationship. In the negotiation phase, a responsible organization will stick strictly to the rule that the leader for this phase comes from the sales

> **The conditions under which negotiations are kicked off largely depend on what has been done in the preceding discussion time.**

and marketing side of the company, because it is part of their mission to defend the firm's margin. The boss should never participate in negotiations where it becomes his role to defend the margin. If this were to happen the company faces two problems even if the deal is obtained:

- The risk of becoming the customer's hostage.
- Destruction of efforts to empower sales people in any future negotiations of this sort.

We still need to answer the question of which kind of negotiation the boss should take an active role in.

10-5-1-50-1: An unwitting business lottery

The following example might help us to decide on some key principles. As a member of the board of a medium-sized manufacturer of passive electronic components, I was meeting its main customers in order to prepare a report on the company's perceived performance for the next board meeting. This analysis and survey are conducted every year. Consequently, the relationship with the customers, as well as with the sales force, is pretty familiar. In 1998 I visited the sales manager of one of the largest companies in the European defence sector.

The electronic company's positioning has been rather favourable for many years. It is the main supplier for a specific type of electronic component, with a yearly market of around €10 million, and it considers that it holds a fifth of client market share. The meeting started in a very straightforward way: 'I am happy to see you. I need to share with you our new supply policy... We are currently paying the equivalent of €10 million for these components. Three years down the road, it must cost us 5 million, we shall buy from three suppliers instead of fourteen, the leader will achieve 50 per cent of the total business and our target price for 1 w is 1 Euro.'

Then came a pause and the sales manager resumed: 'Considering our network of suppliers, my colleagues and I are unanimous that the reference supplier is *you*.' That was followed by a very long silence.

I am not very keen on this 'I have a proposal that you can not refuse' style of relationship. To summarize his proposal, we are covering 20 per cent of the volume for €2 million and tomorrow, because we are the most likely to achieve the productivity improvements expected by the customer, meaning slashing the price, we are now entitled to get 50 per cent of the business for €2.5 million. I was surprised by the sales manager's attitude. I suppose I was rather livid after this 'cold shower'. As for him, he looked pretty cool. Was this the professionalism of a tough negotiator? Not exactly.

CONTINUED... 10-5-1-50-1: An unwitting business lottery

The meeting came quickly to an end. Walking back to the car, I asked the sales manager his opinion. The discussion went as follows:

'It is like last year, he certainly has crazy pressure from his management to achieve substantial savings. He has limited means to achieve it, so he is trying to believe that he can play the same game as in the automotive industry or in mass distribution. These guys went to a training session and they think that they are Carrefour. He wants our margin without offering anything in return... He tried last year and I didn't give him anything.'

'But now he is mentioning this extra volume for the reference supplier.'

'Something interesting if he can substitute a supplier with another one. Are we accredited for the parts he has in mind?'

This new client's claim really struck me and shortly after leaving the client, I called the CEO. His attitude was less radical than his sales manager's. Like me, he found the proposal unacceptable and not very encouraging. Our conclusion was to ask for a second meeting, which I got within two days. So the subject sounded as if it was pretty hot.

The second meeting changed the perspective. First of all, it confirmed the hot nature of this new prospective relationship. However, I made a critical discovery: routinely, for many years, the supplier had been assimilating purchase and consumption. In fact, the volume of consumption was four times as large as the size of the outside purchases. Moreover, these components did not belong to the client's key technical issues. Consequently, it was wise to bet that the way they were produced was quite far from the current state-of-the-art methods of the leaders of this sector.

Thus from a simple issue of negotiating power to slash prices the question shifted to a strategic one. Who should be in the most favourable position to take a substantial part of the

---

CONTINUED ... 10-5-1-50-1: An unwitting business lottery

spin-off of this business when it occurs, certainly sooner rather than later.

Having been able, luckily enough, to extract this relevant information, the physiognomy of the relationship changed radically. Therefore the boss should take an active role in the process and even appear at the forefront of the negotiation phase. The risk of being hijacked by the client was consequently becoming a minor one compared to the possible missed opportunity of competing for a new role. As a side output of the meeting, I also got the information that the client's capacity to identify an alternative option was very limited.

Shortly after this event we were confronted with a similar situation at Schneider Electric. From the lessons of these experiences I have been able to suggest four significant areas regarding the CEO's or executive committee's involvement in the final phase of negotiations with a client, and these are detailed below.

Step 1: Quality of information system for anticipating

This concerns the ability to collect information to assess the company's perceived performance and correctly gauge the customer context. In this respect, I want to make a specific point about the effectiveness of the system of cost analysis.

Chasing margin to reinvest it in the market price

APM, the French Association for Management Development, is networking French managers through 140 local clubs and each year organizes 10 monthly meetings on a management

---

CONTINUED ... Chasing margin to reinvest it in the market price

topic. At one of these in the Vosges mountains, an interesting informal discussion started at lunch between a few members on how to deal with the negotiating power of the automotive industry when one is a medium-sized (130 people) manufacturer of steel-based components. William, a retired engineer with 40 years' experience in manufacturing management systems, quickly answered, ' "Sharp" information systems.'

'We all have information systems,' replied his colleagues and friends.

'Yes, but mine allows me to chase the margin,' he added.

His colleagues thought that they did not correctly understand, but he followed up with, 'To reinvest it in the market price.'

The group started to become more and more astonished and wondered if he was not pulling their legs. He carried on, 'For some components we have achieved huge productivity improvements. The client is not even aware of these results, but when the competition discovers them it is too late. It is a gift, so I do not want to give them the opportunity to outpace us. I anticipate.' His peers looked at him sceptically, thinking that what is taken is taken. Then he clarified the confusion, addressing the idea of the consistency of his approach: 'A few months ago, the purchasing people of our main client came to tell us that we should achieve a substantial two-digit percentage price reduction based on productivity improvement. I asked them how I could do this because when they don't even ask us for anything we come up spontaneously with savings, so we would have to see what we could do. I gave them 6 per cent and they accepted it satisfied, but I have heard how tough they were with some of our competitors.'

Information systems are also a means of anticipation to manage the customer's power of negotiation. Faced with the relevant information it becomes a top management decision. But it is a comfort. At this stage, the issue is not to be right or wrong in terms of the decision, but to have the problem set up in front of you early enough.

Step 2: Speed of analysis

It is not the purpose of this book to review top management's analytical toolkit. We take it for granted.

Step 3: Consideration given to the customer by the presence of the boss in the discussion

If the boss attends the discussions too often, his or her presence will be perceived as routine and lead the market to wonder with what level of autonomy people are operating in the company.

Step 4: Boss's speed of withdrawal

The agreement with the defence company was subject to a unit price reduction based on the invoiced volume. Six months later the situation turned out the way the sales manager had anticipated it. There was not enough volume to be consistent with the initial claim. So the purchasing manager wanted to meet the supplier's CEO again to renegotiate the deal. That did not happen this time, it was exclusively the sales manager's responsibility and the CEO added, 'Now I don't appear any more... I can tell you that they are making pressure to see me again but I resist, it is no longer my role.'

THE THREE FACETS OF THE DISCUSSION PERIOD

A customer relationship is like a time sequence, with peaks and troughs in terms of confrontations between the two organizations. To keep improving the effectiveness of the management of the customer relationship, we can move to the next topic: how to structure the discussion time in order to have a fruitful relationship. Many experiences lead me to propose that an unusual combination of individually well-known marketing tools should be used:

■ Process-based marketing.
■ Permanent relationship marketing.
■ Dialogue-based marketing.

The idea is to consider that a customer relationship has a life cycle. It begins, for instance, with a cold call from a sales person or spontaneous consideration for the customer due to the reputation of the brand or the services of the supplier, and it is perpetuated after it has successfully passed a customer satisfaction conformity test.

This integrative marketing management perspective on the various phases of an account's life cycle was suggested by many sales experiences with customers. The two following stories underline the difference in the nature of the customer relationship in reference to very straightforward criteria before and after the signature on a first deal.

U-shaped relationship

In the presence of the account salesman, I met a purchasing officer of Petronas in Kuala Lumpur, Malaysia. She was presented as the decision maker. The idea of the decision maker is well entrenched in the mind of sales people, but it needs to be radically reconsidered. It leads to a too narrow perspective in the management of an account. The decision maker is important, but he or she can receive influences that can affect his or her decision. So while the decision maker needs to be considered, the supplier's ability to gain confidence in the management of the decision-making process is even more critical to achieving a consistent job.

The relationship with Petronas was considered from the supplier's point of view as good, even excellent, and not much needed to be added. However, since the last yearly contract

> ## CONTINUED ... U-shaped relationship
>
> signature around six months ago, there had been no meetings and this meeting had been organized due to my presence in the country.
>
> Before the meeting, the salesman gave me objective evidence that a good job was being achieved with the client's operational people. Despite this, because of the client's current management style, the purchasing officer's assessment of the relationship was rather poor: 'We know that when you come, it is for a rate increase.'

In fact this assessment was incomplete if one objectively considered what was happening in terms of service and the ability of the company to keep its promises. It did not reflect the operational performance. Why was nothing factual reaching the purchasing officer's door? The process-based marketing was ineffective. No news is good news, so being good did not work positively to build a sustainable relationship, where the supplier can leave a customer-perceived transactional selling status – based on price and product availability – to enter into a form of tighter links. To be fair, we should also note that the purchasing officer's comment did not evoke any negative aspects in operational performance, because if there were any we would have known about them immediately.

The absence of a consciously deployed process-based marketing report deprives the supplier of the development of sustainability in the customer relationship.

> ## It took me nine months to decide
>
> Another observation took place in Belgium. The marketing director of SPI was meeting the HR director of a very large Belgian public utility to get his approval for an advertisement, which was supposed to use the client's name as a reference. The message was: '10 minutes each month to order indi-

> **CONTINUED . . . It took me nine months to decide**
>
> vidualized meal vouchers for 7000 people.' The HR director read this, read it again, took his time and finally looked at the marketing director with the following comment: 'It is fine, I like this message but that was not the problem, it took me nine months to decide.'

When I heard this I was delighted by this crystal clear marketing insight that we were receiving. This person was pointing out what had been done during the nine months prior to the signing of the deal to monitor and positively influence the selection process. In fact, this was certainly not enough to guarantee a happy ending. Some will consider that I am a finicky person and what counts is that SPI gets the deal. I agree that this doesn't happen by pure chance. The purpose of this observation is not to diminish the value of the team's effort, but to stress that companies must be more demanding in assessing their objective chances of success. By consciously reducing the space left to luck a company builds its future. Leaving the situation as it is, is as ridiculous as expecting to secure the outcome of the negotiation fully.

The lesson offered by this HR manager is to enjoin us to improve our assessment of how convinced we are that we will get the deal and to translate that into visible actions that the prospect can credit. The issue is to be fully convinced of one's own success, not a cosmetic announcement. The advertisement message was process oriented, while the human resource director reminded us of the importance of focusing our attention on what was happening before the deal through an appropriate dialogue-based marketing approach.

MILESTONES FOR DIALOGUE-BASED MARKETING

The appropriate marketing approach depends on the stage of the relationship. The area of focus in a business–to–business situation is signature of the contract, which becomes an obsession and the subject of too much impatience. Consequently it is worth proposing a change to the nature of the mission to discover rejuvenated customer care. The next proposition is:

From the initial contact to the signature of the contract, the supplier's

> **Don't sell, be bought – but do it tactfully.**

purpose has been to raise the interest in its solution in the customer's mind. Addressing the issue from this angle means that the goal is to convert the customer to the benefits of the envisioned solution, not to sell him or her anything. Once the client is converted, he or she should want the solution. The issue then becomes over which period of time it should happen and with how many customer contacts.

Doing this does not mean that the sales person won't be obliged to deploy reserves of talent to defend his or her company's margin. This subject must be considered as independent in a sequential context. First the goal is to fill in the hole in the customer's mind corresponding to the targeted needs. Then a sales discussion can take place and it would be unfair not to mention that its tempo will certainly be more gentle than in a hard sales context. Nevertheless, my objective is to avoid the sales person reducing his or her vigilance.

The Belgian public utility case demonstrates that this takes longer than expected. Although the customer is not yet ready, the supplier's people are far in advance and are impatient to finalize the deal as soon as possible. I remind them that it is wise to 'hurry up slowly', which means not being obsessed by the conclusion but by the appropriate tempo. Moreover, monitoring the tempo is the supplier's responsibility, which means that it can be accurately achieved by managing the customer's effort. Positive feedback in customer effort management will contribute to increasing the probability of a favourable outcome and confirm to the supplier's people that their investment is not in vain. Therefore, the next question is how we manage customer efforts.

3, 30 or 300?

An experience at China Steel Corporation (CSC) in Kaoshung in the south of Taiwan was typically illustrative of the customer effort approach. I was visiting this company, which is a client of CMD, which manufactures gearboxes for heavy mechanical applications and was mentioned on page 21. In 1998, the last time I visited CSC, the general superintendent explained that the vast majority of the heavy specific gears had been supplied by Flender, CSC's German partner. The reason for this dominant position was the effectiveness of the supplier's behaviour. For instance, each time there was a bid, Flender did not answer the bid by mail or fax but despatched one of its technical stars to validate the technical aspect of the client's expression of its needs.

My guest justified this approach: 'Our experience in the steel process is not yet on a par with that of the American, the European or the Japanese steel manufacturers. Here 30 years ago you would just have found a village of fishermen.'

Do we surmise that Flender's success is due to its physical presence? To a certain extent yes, because the company is achieving the same as its competitors but differently, by the specific way in which it promotes its technical competencies. That is a good strategy!

However, there is something more substantial to mention. Later on, a discussion with Flender in Germany brought me back to one of the critical steps of the approach: boosting operating margin by diminishing the amount of proposals without a positive outcome. Consequently, before deciding if the company must invest 3, 30 or 300 hours of technical people in elaborating the proposal, Flender assessed the customer's commitment by measuring its level of effort. This meant that before writing a proposal, Flender contacted its prospect for a discussion based on a document describing Flender's current understanding of the question after their first meeting.

The customer's attention, enthusiasm and availability, for instance to correct inaccuracies or mistakes, represent means to gauge the real willingness of the customer to deal with Flender. Therefore we suggest checking through the appropriate customer signals which potential supplier is holding the preference. That is the expression used by a foundry plant manager at AFE (mentioned on page 43) who was discussing with his sales colleagues the organization of a plant visit for a prospect:

> After the visit, we should be clear that we must still have the preference. But to do so one must be sure of what you (salespeople) have promised. Consequently, we shall be able to organize the tour accordingly... to stress what will be critical for him.

I like this very relevant proposition because the factory manager considers that he can give a *merchandising dimension* to the company's manufacturing tool by pushing what the customer must see. It is a combination of what the client is expecting to see and what the company knows will spark their interest. Managing this tool tactfully is one means of keeping the customer's preference on its side.

French factory workers speaking English to the Japanese prospect

Merchandising the factory is a team effort. The factory manager cannot achieve it alone without clear and transparent communication with the people negotiating the project. On one occasion the prospect, a Japanese company, was visiting the European foundry to assess the technical skills of this new potential supplier. Because of the objective of 'maintaining the preference', the factory manager stressed that the sales people did not consider this tour as a mandatory, routine step.

From the discussion with the sales people, the factory manager extracted a very interesting observation. The prospect was not so concerned about the technical skills of the company but about working with a continental Europe-based operator, which represented some hassle in terms of future

---

CONTINUED ... French factory workers speaking English to the Japanese prospect

communication. The Japanese believed that the company's staff did not speak English. They were not referring to the engineers but the workers, who represented a critical part of the quality requirements in the prospect's assessment. 'We do not want to encounter difficulties in communicating,' warned the prospect.

Then the merchandising exercise was completely clarified. The Japanese prospect would start the factory tour by a foundry yard where, believe it or not, some of the workers at this foundry in eastern France spoke enough English to communicate reasonably with the potential customer. That was enough to exhaust the subject of communication and return to the critical technical issues.

If the factory manager had not discussed very seriously the context of this visit with the sales people and merely organized a standard tour, he would not have actively challenged the probability of a favourable outcome to this negotiation. As this example illustrates:

A supplier's efforts to keep the customer's preference can take many forms. One generic way consists of identifying the critical elements of information required to develop the offer that the supplier perceives as most attractive and

> **The meaningful difference is always hidden in the details, reserving a premium to those who can reveal them.**

to measure accordingly the help received from the client, not only in achieving this task but also in fine tuning the relevance of the supplier's best perceived offer. A generic list of questions can consequently be suggested in order to assess how effective is the management of a first level of customer effort:

- Has the list of critical information to be gathered been formulated?
- Have these questions been formally asked of the client?

- Did the client answer all of them?
- If you got the answers, did you exclusively get them?

In relation to these four questions the supplier encounters only one risk: not daring to ask them.

Finally, it is not because a supplier has correctly managed the efforts of the client in order to attempt to keep the preference that there won't be a serious negotiation on price. This point is structural: some sectors are cut throat, while in others the competition is more gentle. What is critical is not to try changing the inherent style of the industry, but to be the best-prepared candidate.

PERMANENT RELATIONSHIP MARKETING AND AMBASSADORS

If you have effectively implemented an appropriate dialogue-based marketing approach, the customer's interest in your solution is at its height. Once the final details have been set up, the deal occurs. Then the supplier delivers its promises and its process, and if manufacturing services operate effectively there is little to say about it. The performance conforms to expectations, so the customer becomes accustomed to it and the vicious circle continues round to reach perceived performance parity.

Usually at this stage of the sales process, sales people consider

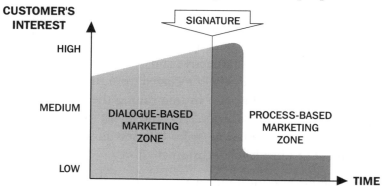

Figure 9.1 Two different marketing tools on each side of the signature

that their role is becoming very limited and they naturally fall into the trap of the Petronas situation (see page 97). The effective or perceived presence on the account falls below a minimum level. Consequently, the account can be considered as left open to the competition.

If nothing is done, this account will be either the location of a strategic breakdown or of a surging in the customer's power of negotiation. Consequently, the current supplier will be obliged to suffer in order to keep the account in its portfolio. What you sow so shall you reap. You therefore need a specific set of marketing tools for this stage of the relationship with the customer.

What is most commonly named permanent or constant relationship marketing generically fits well with the intended goal. The purpose is to keep alive the customer's interest in its relationship with the current supplier. Consequently, the challenge is to imagine the marketing treasures that will fulfil this task. We are entering into the marketing techniques for the discussion time with the client.

My purpose is not to address the list of tools and techniques that can contribute to structuring this permanent relationship marketing time; we have all met very prolific organizations that can do this. What I do want to address are two warnings regarding the way to achieve this:

- *The permanent relationship marketing time is conditioned by the effectiveness of the process-based marketing.* This means that it is useless and a sub-optimization of resources to enter into the permanent relationship marketing stage if the process-based marketing does not give you the green light to move ahead.
- *The effectiveness of the permanent relationship marketing policy should have allowed the organization to structure a network of ambassadors at the account level.* An ambassador inside the customer's organization means someone who can permanently demonstrate the benefits of working with the current supplier. A company does not get an ambassador by chance; you get fans by chance. The challenge is to transform fans into ambassadors.

Ambassadors are not double agents: they are clearly playing on the company's side and must not be confused with spies. They

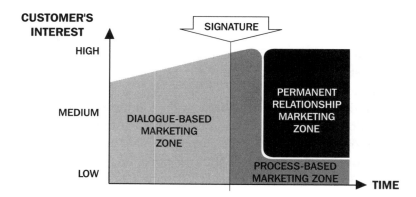

Figure 9.2 Three specific integrated marketing tools to conquer a customer account and make it thrive

always represent the interests of their company because they are absolutely clear about the benefits for their company of collaborating with the supplier. In addition they can also get a personal benefit, but it is the cherry on the top of the cake. I must stress this point, because it is on this basis that the ambassador network can last. If not, one day or another, sooner than expected and without prior announcement, you run the risk of being taken unawares. The great benefit to the supplier is that ambassadors protect the supplier because they want to protect the benefits for their company.

Consequently, one comes back to a communication challenge. The ambassador should be the recipient of your communication efforts because he or she represents the point of leverage for a specific account, sometimes even more.

An active ambassador deploying his or her full potential should be able to play on two levels simultaneously:

In the company

- *Protect your existing business* by demonstrating the many benefits of working with the supplier.
- Provide you with information enabling you to *create new business opportunities* for the future.

Beyond the company limits

■ *Prospect for business for the supplier* beyond the limits of his or her own account. Ambassadors can be of great benefit to the supplier not only in their own organization but also within their industry (see page 156).

■ Represent an element of stability in the relationship with the customer.

Consequently, the topic of whether or not there is an ambassador becomes one of the possible tests to assess how the discussion period of the relationship was conducted.

If an ambassador does not exist, you will notice his or her absence during the next negotiation phase because no one will be supporting your position. If the sales force affirms that an ambassador exists, it is the top management's responsibility to ask for evidence. I can suggest some specific questions to confirm your own opinion that the ambassador is effective:

■ Are we clear about the benefits the customer is drawing from its relationship with us?

■ If yes, can you document when and how you have shared this information about concrete benefits with the customer?

■ Is the ambassador effectively in place and who is he or she? What is our ambassador's specific track record? What is his or her interest in being our ambassador?

Finally, a top manager must keep thinking to discover a strategic angle. At the account level the ambassador is a means of prolonging the company's competitive advantage. Therefore there is a need to ask what you can do to keep motivating your ambassador tactfully. For example, you could organize a forum for industry colleagues on a specific business issue that might subtly reinforce your reputation.

Specifically how you do this is not important; I am convinced that it will be of good quality once it has reached our list of priorities. Not forgetting to ask the question is a more critical relationship management discipline issue.

Summary

To create a sustainable customer relationship two distinct periods of time must be recognized: time for negotiation and time for discussion. The first period is a functional responsibility area where the sales and marketing stars must exclusively operate. However, this negotiation phase inherits the collective investment by the executive committee and to some extent by the whole company during the discussion period.

It is over the discussion period that one can observe a three-fold marketing activity. For existing customers, process-based marketing and permanent relationship marketing are aimed at securing the current business, while dialogue-based marketing prepares the future in managing customer efforts and maintaining the preference in the customer mind.

The consequence of the effectiveness of these marketing approaches does not represent a waiver of potentially tough negotiations regarding the economic side of the deal, but the context will certainly be radically different. The customer unambiguously assesses the impact of the supplier's contribution to their own market success, and they may even already have become your ambassador.

 Action point

Consider carefully the context in which you are visiting a customer. Do not become a customer or a sales force's hostage.

Among your top 10 customers, what clear evidence can you observe of the presence of ambassadors? In these customer relationships what specific examples illustrate the characteristics of a good ambassador? (Compare this with the information on page 157.)

CHAPTER 10

THE 3CS

*I*n the previous chapter we stressed that the customer relationship is composed of time for discussion and time for negotiation. The top manager, CEO or managing director must not be involved in negotiations unless there is a strategic issue. In contrast, he or she must be personally involved during the discussion time in order to improve his company's effectiveness.

My research with an express shipment leader led to the conclusion that if we want to be accurate at the corporate level in terms of forecasting, it starts by accuracy at the account level. The rationale is simple:

In business-to-business situations a company observes its share of the customer, account per account. Success in account A does not guarantee success in account B. Consequently, the overall picture has to be reconsidered from an individual account perspective. In order to manage optimally at the account level the company's account information system must be organized in the most effective way to achieve this expected accurate forecast.

> **In a business-to-business context, the battlefield is the account, not the market share.**

In this context, the challenge is to gain in accuracy in order to reconcile the sales people's common sense and the corporate ambition. I try to find a way to achieve a clear and transparent reading of the competitive situation of an account. With this approach, any field person should be able to say: 'Next year, this account will achieve this much with us.'

The goal is not only to give a forecast, but to be able to support with any layer of management a contradictory discussion where both parties can conclude that a fair forecasting job has been achieved.

Account forecasting card

Our approach was to structure the practical information system in a manageable way. In this context, strategic forecasting at the account level is articulated in four topics and twenty questions (see Figure 10.1). The purpose of this model, which we named the account forecasting card,[1] was to find a systematic way to be able to deliver a strategic short story about the future of the relationship. This strategic story included the possibility of defending a certain figure of forecasted activity for the next period of time.

There is an important detail regarding the forecasting figures. In this approach we have definitely tried to prevent the money trap in forecasting by helping people think in terms of physical units, not currency, in order not to miss the true perception of the business reality. At the end of the process anyone can do multiplication, but only the account information expert can deliver an accurate estimate of the supplier's service or product consumption.[2]

To be effective, this approach must be able to be applied by sales people in the field in order to deliver sales forecasts, for which they can be accountable. However, the potential downside of the approach is that sales people may hesitate to establish stretch goals for themselves. Nevertheless, if the system is fully transparent and the reward policies are attractive and fair, the entire organization

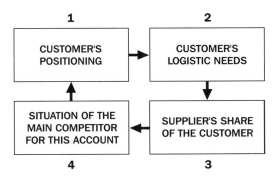

Figure 10.1 Four topics for strategic forecasting

will be empowered and remobilized. Moreover, by encouraging full transparency and availability of accurate data, the company's leaders do not lose control over its future but instead increase access for all personnel, which, in turn, enhances growth possibilities.

FROM 2CS TO 3CS

The practical information system was well received in the pilot phase but remains in limbo at headquarters. Nevertheless, we achieved great progress. I always like the idea of a structured story because it gives intellectual discipline to an organization.

A trip to Asia in early 1999 confirmed the importance of the approach. Few field experiences give me the opportunity to go one step further.

I normally summarize a business relationship with two main words: the *content* of the relationship and *contacts*, who you are meeting and what their position is. Contacts represent an important challenge because they stress the idea of formally drawing a map of the account. The educational value of this model can offer some help to an organization. As long as we can draw it (see Figure 10.2) we keep some common sense, which is crucial.

Managing the account battlefield was supposed to offer control over the competition's manoeuvres, but in Asia I discovered a situation that was not so encouraging because the competition could easily reorganize its movements (see Figures 10.3a and b).

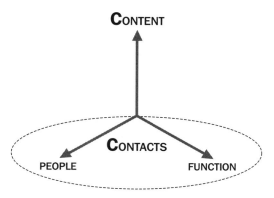

Figure 10.2 2Cs – a starting point

After this experience I moved towards an information system at the account level, which can be the synthesis of both approaches, the account forecasting card and the 2Cs. The first goal was forecasting, but we must also answer a second key question: can we prevent a breakdown in the relationship? We observed that it happened through lack of care to an area that is critical either for the customer itself or in the state of the art in managing a relationship with a customer in a business-to-business situation: the context.

The 3Cs are therefore the synthesis of our experience, a tool for approaching sales forecasting at the account level, with an idea of the sustainability of the relationship with the customer.

- Context.
- Coverage.
- Content.

Companies must pay equal attention to *each of the three elements* and must juggle the data and the interrelationships in order to obtain a full picture of the current status and of the future of each account.

Once we have recognized the opportunity presented by this approach, the question is to decide with which C to start the documentation of the model. Coverage will deal with a quantitative perspective of the relationship, while the two other Cs will deal with a more qualitative one. In summary, our objective is to analyse

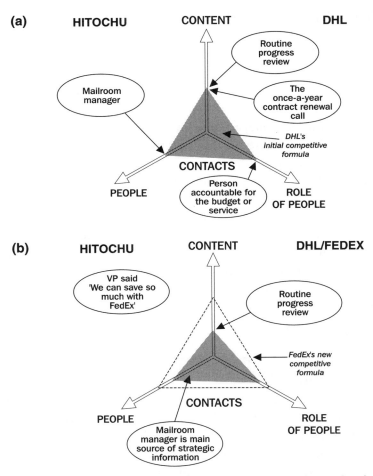

Figure 10.3 2Cs to explain where the customer relationship hurts

if we have enough (*coverage*) contacts at the account level with the appropriate persons (*content*), delivering a renewed and consistent sales pitch, in order to be able to write a synthesis of the perspective of this account (*context*), a short story saying where we are coming from, where we are, where we are heading towards. The last point represents our best documented forecast of the evolution of the business with this customer expressed as I like it in physical amounts (e.g. numbers of shipments of documents, computers, gearboxes or milk tanks and so on).

COVERAGE: THE CRITICAL MASS OF RELATIONSHIPS

Coverage represents an evolution of the idea of *contacts*, who we have met in the company and how critical their functions are for our future. The purpose of coverage is to recognize what *critical mass of relationships* has to be achieved with an account in order to reach a stage of mutual trust where one can start to have more control over the evolution of the account.

The idea of the critical mass of relationships came very early on in my research. We all know the finding that 70 per cent of breakdowns in customer relationships are due to a lack of care and presence.[3] It is an objective cause of interruptions in the relationship because too often a supplier considers its client as captive and not even deserving of the minimum: you may not even visit the account. An experience in process automation and electrical engineering gave us our first tool for managing the coverage of a customer account.

A sales whiz

The case took place in Marseille, in the south of France, where a former subsidiary of Vivendi, specializing in electrical and process engineering, operated in the petrochemical industry as well as in the civil nuclear sector for one client, EDF (already mentioned on page 90). On average, at that time an account manager was achieving a turnover of €3 to 4 million. However, in Marseille there was an engineer achieving €12 million, four times as much as his colleagues. In the consulting business, it is a mistake to pass up such a phenomenon, so the observations and the discussions were worth the trip.

The engineer was not only organized but very methodical. He considered that he was always playing with the white because he was even able to choose the deals he wanted to compete for or not.

His information system aimed at achieving the appropriate critical mass of relationships with the client's staff that was recognized as critical for his own employer's success. To replicate the creation of these conditions, I suggest following a five-step approach:

1   Draw a map of the account (see Figure 10.4), noting who is involved at each point of contact and explain the functions, the roles and the relative weights in the decision–making process.
2   Play a devil's advocate game: answer the question, are we dealing with the right people?
3   Include a process for updating the map in order to determine if the people who are the supplier's ambassadors and the front–line users of the company's products and services remain in their positions. In case of merger or restructuring, this document can allow you to track what is happening.
4   Set up a team, not just a sales person, to cover the account. With this approach you prevent many problems, such as who the account belongs to. What happens if the sales person leaves, can he leave with the account's business?
5   Establish yearly planning for contacts, involving the team members and their counterparts in the account. (Contact is not limited to sales calls and can take many other forms, such as email, phone calls, faxes, letters.) Finally there is an acid test: compare the ideal situation with the previous year's coverage.

This tool is a very good acid test to measure if an organization is as customer oriented as it claims. The test is the availability of the formal map of the account. If you don't have a map, you don't know where you are going. The army knows that pretty well. Between the creation of the French Military Academy by Napoleon in the early nineteenth century and today one teaching area has not changed: map reading.

Unfortunately there are no company maps available on the market or even on the Internet. Consequently, it is our responsibility as managers to verify that this tool is available and actionable. It is not a gimmick, it is a means to monitor if the deployment of our resources is in line at least with our common sense.

(a) **Draw the map of the account**

NAME	FUNCTION	DEPT	ROLE			WEIGHT			
			Info	Pres	Dec	1	2	3	4

Note: Info = Information
        Pres = Prescriber of appropriate actions
        Dec = Decision maker

(b) **Assess the critical mass of relationships**

CLIENT CONTACT Function	TEAM	Weeks Freq	1	2	3	4	5	6	7	8	9	10	11	12	13	14	15	16	17	18	19	20	21	22
	1......																								
	2......																								
	3......																								
	1......																								
	2......																								
	3......																								

Figure 10.4a and b Customer account map and critical mass of relationships

This idea of a critical mass of information for a carefully drawn customer map is not a panacea for customer relationship management, but it helps.

They don't like us

This tool for mapping a relationship and monitoring the volume of contacts particularly does not allow us to cheat concerning the reality of our efforts. It is also appropriate in project management. I was analysing a failure in negotiations where one of my customers had lost a civil maintenance project for a glass oven in a Saint-Gobain factory in the north of Paris. The project team members were convinced that they

CONTINUED ... They don't like us

had been the victim of a weird trick by the competition. The conclusion was simpler: once the map was drawn and the number of contacts with the client's decision-making team documented, we could all observe that some engineers and technicians were the object of specific care while some were left completely stranded. These people count nevertheless and they made us know this by saying 'No thank you'. When asking why they weren't given careful attention, I was glad to get a sincere answer: 'They don't like us.' It was too bad that we did not know this earlier, because it is not companies that like each other, but individuals. This information could have allowed us to anticipate a substitution and at least to address this issue actively, not just suffer it.

1000 contacts

At an automotive equipment manufacturer in Turin, I was preparing a presentation of a strategic plan regarding Fiat. We were reviewing the mapping tool, which the company did not yet use. The business unit manager proposed to construct a map with his team. On product performance the position was impressive: dominant. So far, the supplier's products were present in nearly all Fiat's product lines. Regarding the number of contacts I got the answer by phone: 1000 contacts for a team of 5, approximately one contact per day per person. In the quality of a result there is always a quantitative perspective that it is wise not to trade off.

CONTENT: DIVERSITY AND RENEWAL

The content of the sales pitch answers to two words: 'diversified' and 'renewed'. The content is there to offer customers the opportunity to speak about themselves. As Goethe said, 'If speaking is a need, hearing is an art.'

What are we telling the customer?

The content faces two structural threats: the customer becoming too familiar with it and the complacency of sales people in the case of acceptable process performance.

Sales people may consider that they have little to say because the company is uniformly delivering what it promised. Little by little one heads towards a U-shape style of relationship. The sales people often don't even make calls, because the nature of sales work is to talk and they think that there is nothing else to say than: 'Is everything OK?' Nevertheless, this represents a great message that can precisely reassure the customer on the validity of his or her decision to work with the supplier and represents a platform for leverage.

So what else can a sales person do? They can ask lots of questions and actively listen to gain a better understanding of the customer, but too many sales people seem to hear selectively and so are not able to decode what they are hearing.

In summary, the ingredients of a meaningful content comprise two basic dimensions:

■ To reassure the customer by systematically delivering what is promised with regard to process-based marketing.

■ If the above light is green, it authorizes legitimate promotion of a new dimension of the relationship: permanent relationship marketing. The nature of these actions is not only to focus on the customer, but also on its sector. It is a means to demonstrate the supplier's commitment to the customer's success. In this respect, I advised a supplier of breakfast products (Viennese pastries) to organize a yearly convention on nutrition, to demonstrate that it can imagine the future beyond the limits of the current relationship with its current clients (catering chain, mass distribution chain, wholesalers).

CONTEXT: THE CLUE TO NEXT YEAR'S SALES FORECAST

The last C concerns writing a clear story about our relationship, existing and future, with a customer. There is no ideal answer, but I would like to share the critical subjects that must be addressed to give sense to this synthesis. Below is a list of topics, which is not comprehensive. I want to address specifically how to develop an effective information system regarding an account.

Are we clear on what business the customer is in? Can we draw conclusions about our expected performance?

I was visiting a sales person at an Adidas office in Istanbul. This was a good customer, who since this time has centralized its operations in Hong Kong. We were at the door and I could read 'Adidas Mediterranean Basin Liaison Office'. I turned to the sales person and asked him what kind of activity they were fulfilling here. The answer surprised me given the appearance of the office: sports garments.

I asked to meet the boss for a short while to get an appropriate answer: this office used to prepare samples for the collection's selection campaign. They encountered peaks of activity in April–May and October–November. This had consequences for the way this account should be managed. The express carrier recognized seasonality in its business with Adidas but had not taken account of the criticality it represents for the customer's performance.

Have you drawn out the full potential of the account?

Too often the full potential of an account is considered as captured once that potential is reported over a long period of time in our books. SPI's new general manager for Germany and Austria noticed that by taking a broader look at the whole of Deutsche Bank he was able to generate additional meal vouchers worth €2.5 million.

Do you recognize changes in the customer's organizational structure?

SPI France lost its business with Volvo Truck Atlantique in the west of France. This was a dynamic, medium-sized customer. Not aware of the trend of the company's development, SPI's regional management tried to impose a new rate increase. This occurred when Volvo Truck Atlantique was passing from one to three facilities, doubling its staff and raising the value of the meal voucher by 20 per cent. Lack of information on the customer's potential evolution made the company miss a big deal, which ended up in a competitor's portfolio.

Do you have a historical perspective on the account: what has been done, with what results? Can you formulate the customer's supplier policy?

Customers announce what they are going to do, but usually people do not pay attention to their declarations. It is like a buzzing in their ears.

For instance, in the truck industry, one of the few world manufacturers announced in its plans that its goal is pretax earnings of 6 per cent within three years. My question to one of this manufacturer's partners was how much the current pretax earnings were. The answer did not come naturally, even though I was not discussing with someone on the loading dock but a business unit manager.

After some research, the figure was found to be 1.4 per cent. So the next question was also very obvious: what is the new tempo of the relationship? This was answered as follows: 'Our margin is part of their savings.' Call it productivity improvement if you like, but you still need to be ready.

Summary

The 3Cs is a customer account monitoring system. Without the appropriate number of contacts it is unrealistic to expect to develop a sustainable customer relationship. To reach this critical mass of relationships with a specific customer, a tracing technique must be implemented, which is the customer account map.

Organizing the content of discussions with the account is far simpler when one recognizes the sequential approach between process-based marketing and permanent relationship marketing, where there is always something worth sharing with the customer. Information is critical to secure the present and to create the future. With the first 2Cs we have been able to recognize that to get this information one needs to demonstrate enough care and commitment, through customer account presence and the quality of the communication with the account's decision-making team.

The acid test of this approach is expressed by the ability to synthesize the business relationship into a short story accurately expressing the account context, covering where the relationship is coming from, where it currently is and where it is going. This is finally summarized in a sales forecast for the next period, which an executive committee member without any specific intimacy with the account would consider well judged.

 Action point

Complete the map of your top 10 accounts and assess the respective critical mass of relationships.

KICKING ORGANIC GROWTH INTO GEAR AT THE CUSTOMER ACCOUNT LEVEL

This has been a long part presenting the technical conditions of organic growth, but reading it should lead to a practical output. To summarize what we have shared so far we could imagine completing the following exercise. If a manager wishes to write a specific customer account development presentation, what could be the structure and the content of the presentation according to what we have covered so far? For instance:

Step 1: The customer in his or her own environment

The presentation could cover the following subjects. What is this specific customer announcing in terms of its supplier or partner relationship policy? What is the customer's performance in its strategic group? Is this customer a winner for tomorrow? This might sound somewhat paradoxical, but have you ranked your customers? You should try to do this because your resources are not unlimited and the customer effort approach can help you recognize which customers to invest most in.

The first step must be summarized in three to four slides whether the supplier understands its customer strategy and assesses its associated role.

Then comes a straightforward question: is your analysis of your customer correct? There is only one way to answer: ask the customer and simultaneously implement your customer effort management policy. The time spent by the customer on the analysis will be a good test of its interest in the supplier's company. Be aware of the need to benefit from a critical mass of relationships. If you don't the exercise will be a little bold, but it is still worth trying.

Step 2: The supplier's perceived performance

Why stop in the middle of your efforts? Why not ask the customer to confirm how far your assessment of your performance is correct? This demands some homework, including a good deal of reflection on competitive advantage, customer satisfaction, perceived value and positioning based on an effective information system, which has helped us plot the customer map. This draft will be a wonderful discussion document, which can be tested with a few people along the decision-making process just for the sake of checking the homogeneity of the perception of the performance.

Step 3: Performance relative to the competition

It is very important to assess the competition's performance, not in your own words but in those of the customer. Given that a frame of reference has been proposed for the supplier's performance it would be constructive to have a discussion of the competitors' performance based on the same reference frame.

Using the tools discussed in Part II we have been able to write a presentation that is a solid analysis of the current business context at a specific account. The same manoeuvre can be achieved for any key account. I am sure that an executive committee would be keen on having this kind of presentation delivered on a regular basis, because it addresses the rationale of a business relationship, without any bells and whistles.

The structure of this presentation can be summarized as in Figure 10.5. The next two parts will allow us to fill in the missing block in this specific customer account development presentation.

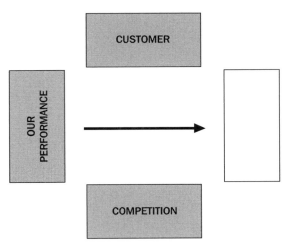

Figure 10.5 Structure of a customer account presentation, Step 1

Notes

1   Not to be confused with Kaplan and Norton's Balanced Scorecard. I chose
     the word 'card' in order that sales people will have all the questions
     summarized in a limited space to manage the exercise by priority.

2   I always bear in mind the example of a Japanese electronic laboratory equip-
     ment distributor in Europe, who during the due diligence of its acquisition
     justified its business plan figures. For instance, it listed the various depart-
     ments of GEC and then explained which one would need, for example,
     additional oscilloscopes, and it then passed to the next product in the line.
     This was a little slow but convincing!

3   This figure comes from a study by Professor Peterson at the University of
     Texas in Austin.

PART III

RECOGNIZE, UNCOVER, PRIORITIZE

*T*he management tools we addressed in Part II represent what I consider the necessary set to enter into the heart of the subject. The goals of organic growth are broad, encompassing many situations and helping organizations to:

■   find areas of growth when the overall business appears fairly stagnant.
■   keep facilitating an impressive growth rate.

For example, at Sodexho Pass International, Belgium has only a sixth of the potential of France but the Belgian subsidiary is achieving the same sales turnover as the French one. Has it found a way to plough the market more thoroughly? Belgian has a far broader product range than France, but why is this and how has it been led to operate in this way?

Organic growth also offers the opportunity for an accurate diagnosis before deploying the approach. Implementing organic growth provides us with the means to assess the strategic health of an organization. This measure is based on a comprehensive set of complementary and interrelated areas of observation, which should tell us unambiguously:

■   How does the organization secure the present?
■   How does the organization create the future?

The concept of organic growth is the result of collaboration with brilliant companies. An intimate $7S^1$ journey into these organizations – looking at the interrelationships between strategy, systems, structure, skills, staff, style and shared values – leaves you with some legendary experiences. Their financial performance is very often superior to the average performance in their sector. Consequently, their goal is to stay on the leading edge of their sector, which is why this kind of managerial innovation represents an area of particular attention for their top management. It represents one of the means to keep staying ahead of the competition for tomorrow.

Consequently, from my experience, I consider the organic growth approach will find its optimal relevance in three situations:

1   Organizations that are leading their sector and permanently revisiting and assessing the relevance of their business model.
2   Organizations that were unambiguously leading their industry sector and observed that their competitive edge has now become blunt while their market reputation still means something.
3   Organizations in turnaround situation that are beyond the recovery phase and in search of a reengineered approach to secure their future.

By implementing organic growth, these organizations will be able to uncover and prioritize growth opportunities *and* systematize a dynamic process for managing business and sales development.

THE ORGANIC GROWTH MATRIX

The organic growth concept is based on a four-quadrant matrix (see Figure III.1). This represents nothing intrinsically innovative from a graphic perspective, it is merely a means to support our search and exchange of ideas for more effective management practice.

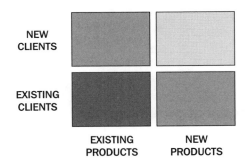

Figure III.1 The four quadrants of organic growth

> ### An early morning fruitful discussion with Pierre
>
> A couple of months ago, due to an inappropriate Thalys schedule,[2] I arrived in Brussels too early for a workshop regarding our efforts to structure sales forecasting in SPI. Pierre is one of SPI's area general managers and a group executive committee member based in Brussels. We started to discuss informally a list of services available in the portfolio and a number of recently signed contracts. Some of these were obtained from very old customers buying the same kind of services recurrently, some were from new customers and some represented additional sales to existing customers based on new products or products that the customer had not yet bought from SPI.
>
> Our main concern was the risk associated with each deal if we wanted to stick to the idea of a customer satisfaction ratio equal to 1. 'Can we try to sort these various business contexts according to their respective level of risk?' suggested Pierre.
>
> On the back of an envelope, we started trying to sort the data by drawing boxes and testing names for each dimension and we ended up with the very simple framework in Figure III.1 that has subsequently become so useful. This four-quadrant matrix will constitute the reference point for structuring the exchange of ideas regarding this management development research.

The three facets of organic growth

Organic growth has three sources (see Figure III.2):

- *Maintaining* the current portfolio of customers and products or services.
- *Developing sales*, either by offering new products to old customers or by attracting new customers with the existing product range.
- *Developing new businesses.*

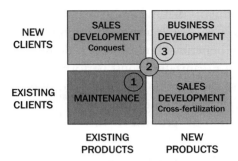

Figure III.2 Three games over four quadrants

The starting point of organic growth consists of remembering one fundamental of growth: *not to lose*. Therefore, it is critical to verify that the company is not losing sales as well as sales opportunities while selling existing products to existing customers.

The first situation was termed *maintenance*. Once you are confident that existing customers are satisfied (as outlined on pages 53–74), they can be approached with new products or services, an attempt that constitutes one of the two avenues for generating sales development.

Sales development is a traditional means that can be regarded as having two alternatives, either to acquire new customers or to sell a broader range of existing products or services to the existing customer base. So the first extension of sales development is a *cross-fertilization* campaign among existing customers where the company tries to expand the market for its products or services. This derives from the company's confidence in the benefits accruing to existing customers. This confidence also enables the company to try a second option by entering into new territory, proposing the same solutions to new prospects: *conquest*.

A third category naturally emerges from the sales development process, which I have termed *business development*. Here the company offers new products to new customers. This last area of growth carries big risks – and also large possibilities of reward.

Consequently, for a corporation the various growth options uncovered by the organic growth approach must be prioritized in terms of exposure to risk. The level of risk is determined by calculating the adjustments that the company would need to make to its current processes to snatch a growth opportunity versus the associated potential benefits. Here process is defined to include all the activities that an organization must perform in order to deliver the *promises* made to the market (the idea of promise is addressed in the customer satisfaction dynamic, page 59).

My definition of promise involves *customer satisfaction* and *customer perceived value* (these ratios are discussed on page 55 and 65). Higher risk is concentrated in situations of *business development* where potential growth would result from addressing both new customers and new products or services. On the opposite side of the scale, *maintenance* of accounts represents almost no risk in terms of adapting a company's process. Nevertheless, due to insufficient attention and lack of closeness to customers, corporations very often run the risk of totally wrecking their growth ambitions.

How to deal with each quadrant of the matrix

In a four-quadrant matrix common sense would suggest starting with what exists, the maintenance box. However, for tactical and objective reasons I suggest launching the organic growth process with sales development.

Maintenance is a critical challenge. Consequently, if a manager or an outside adviser comes to meet the sales force and marketing people with a message such as: 'We are not sufficiently customer oriented' or 'We do not pay enough attention to our most valuable goodwill, our customer base', the result is obvious – this organization is going to embark on a sterile process of self-justification, which kills change from the start.

To avoid this trap and to stick to the conquest mentality, one can legitimately expect to find in any organization an adequately energized sales force. If so, one must find a way to make the sales force rediscover and appreciate the intrinsic value of maintenance. While the approach primarily focuses its efforts on sales development, research into the development aspects will bring some unexpected opportunities for customer account maintenance management.

Notes

1   7S is a comprehensive concept for understanding the effectiveness of an organization. See Tom Peters and Robert Waterman (1982) In Search of Excellence, Harper & Row, New York, p 9, or in order to read the essence of this approach consult Waterman, Peters, Philips (1980) 'Structure is not organization', *McKinsey Quarterly*, Summer.
2   Thalys is the name of the TGV (high-speed train) departing from Paris Gare du Nord and reaching Brussels in less than 1 hour 30 minutes.

CHAPTER 11

CROSS-FERTILIZATION

As a starting point, we already have access to a customer account, confirmed by management of the account around the 3Cs (see page 109). We assess that we can potentially draw more substantial benefits from our collaboration if we manage this account more effectively. For instance, we might try to draw in our direction business for which our organization currently has a solution, but which is shared with our competitors, or which represents a need that has not yet been recognized by this customer. In sum, we plan to attack a structural source of sub-optimization.

In commodity products or services, we have observed that customer loyalty is structurally very low because the customer can shift from one supplier to another without any penalty or so little as not to represent any constraint. Thus the strategic value of the product is very low and substitutability is very high.

Diminishing customer volatility by 30 per cent

One of the studies run by Sodexho Pass International in South America demonstrated that the juxtaposition of two commodity products in a customer account leads to a reduction of

> ### CONTINUED . . . Diminishing customer volatility by 30 per cent
>
> 30 per cent in customer volatility, compared to a portfolio of customers with only one product. This result is confirmed in a portfolio of customers with three and then four products or services. In summary, loyalty is linked to the share of the customer in the targeted area of its needs.
>
> This example demonstrates the crucial importance of becoming dominant in the relationship with a customer to secure a better future with it. The associated situation of larger inter-dependence, even if substitutability remains high, creates a new type of business opportunity for the customer care specialist. However, this situation presents also a typical trap, that of believing that the relationship with the customer has then entered a value-creation stage. This won't happen unless the price is right.

Discussing this example with a French insurance group, Groupama,[1] I received an important adjustment to this cross-fertilization approach:

> We agree that three insurance contracts for a specific account develop more loyalty than one, but it should be three insurance contracts sold in three deals ... not a package of three contracts sold in one hit.

Effective cross-fertilization demonstrates the ability of the company's sales people to keep reassuring customers that they made a good choice by giving it their business. This skill is critical but not typical, which makes it one of the distinctive characteristics of a top-performing organization.

INHERITING FROM THE MAINTENANCE PERFORMANCE

This insurance group's observation clearly illustrates the link between cross-fertilization and maintenance. The reason is clear: we cannot expect to launch a successful cross-fertilization plan on a reassessed target without having monitored its potential success. To do so, we are obliged to run an account review, sticking to the account management techniques addressed by the concept of the 3Cs (see Figure 11.1 and also page 109).

Clearly the sales or marketing people will be able to demarcate the optimal target by answering the question: how is the competitive space in this group of accounts managed? This means what has been done in terms of effective management and monitoring of the perceived value ratio to prevent the customer considering the competition's sales pitch.

With this new product or service proposal, the supplier, through its sales force or any other means, has something to announce to the customer (*content*). This additional contact contributes to actively managing the principle of a critical mass of relationships and its associated criteria (*coverage*). Then the cross-fertilization programme should start to work, if the target is not in a situation of absolute solitude and structural lack of care from its 'partner'. This analysis raises a simple question: are the efforts already achieved by the supplier deployed with the best consideration of the *context*?

> **Cross-fertilization demands the recognition that the success of the sales development operation is conditional on the quality of the maintenance achieved so far.**

In summary:

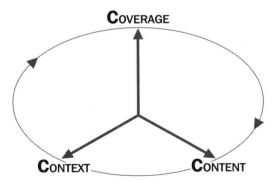

Figure 11.1 3Cs to organize information management at the account level

Then, on this selection of targeted accounts in optimal maintenance condition, the process can start to operate according to the following steps.

FIVE STEPS FOR BUILDING A CROSS-FERTILIZATION CAMPAIGN

Step one: Target group scanning

It depends on the quality of the database, but this kind of basic diagnosis cannot be postponed. The most appropriate approach consists of documenting a cross-fertilization matrix. We should be able to read from this the number of clients for the most critical product of the product line. Then we can consider another product or service.

To stress the importance of the quality of the database, I use the example of Sony Computer Entertainment, which has sold six million PlayStations in France and thereby developed a database of one million users. The French CEO, George Fornay, was at a conference of 1800 French CEOs in early 2002 focusing on conquering new territory. He explained that he spent around €600 000 merely on maintaining the database, adding: 'I am on the play list but I have not yet played.'

To assess the potential for development we should compare how many customers buy product or service A and how many of these are also buying product B; and vice versa for B. In order to measure the potential for improvement, the example of SPI in Belgium is illustrative of the magnitude of the challenge. There are two vouchers, the meal voucher (MV) and the training voucher (TV). Some 7000 customers are MV customers, 100 of which are also TV customers. There are 1200 customers for the TV, 100 of which are MV customers. There is no need to go any further. This analysis is intrinsically not brilliant, but it is detrimental not to get its results and behave accordingly.

This company is performing well, even very well, it has people of great talent and high professionalism, but there is a substantial amount of potential business just lying around. This is why I think it is worth starting with business that is not outside your own view range. This example demonstrates once again that the search for superior performance is in the detail.

Step 2: *Ad hoc* or formal network identification via search and validation of weak signals in house

Identification of the potential makes us run a second risk of sub-optimization: showering the identified target group with a message that is usually not accurate enough to raise substantial interest. This can be observed in mailing return figures below 1 per cent while, if appropriately prepared, this focused direct marketing approach should hit two digits or even more. Consequently, it leads to a situation of mediocre return on effort and inadequate conclusions regarding the relevance of the whole approach.

In sales development one great source of fuel for the corporate imagination is *segmentation*, which we can define as a way of uncovering unexplored routes for forming an attractive group of customers, something we could call a 'network of accounts'. The members of the network are all ticking at the same tempo, the art is to identify what that is.

In order to implement this process systematically, one must rely on a second concept, the *weak market signal*. This means identifying the appropriate key to define this network of accounts, whose common characteristics represent an opportunity to use our process in a distinctive way in order to be perceived as different. In this context, the sources of the weak market signal are more dependent on internal sources of observation and analysis. (The weak market signal will be discussed more specifically in relation to another aspect of sales development, large virtual accounts.)

In a small movie production company of fewer than 50 people, a sales representative and I were discussing SPI's quality of service with the client's female personnel manager. Frankly, the meeting was somewhat sterile. Eventually, reaching a conclusion while everybody was politely wasting time, the sales lady presented a new service, the service voucher.

The sales rep simply described the voucher's characteristics, without much conviction. It is a bonus of up to FF12 000 that can be given to employees once a year on an individual basis. In a company of over 50 employees this fringe benefit is managed by the work's council, but below 50 employees it is the responsibility of top management, who use it as a motivational tool based on individual criteria, something that is not possible when it is managed by the work's council.

We were able to recognize a weak signal in this HR manager's enthusiasm. In fact, it suggested that we should immediately organize the promotion of this new fringe benefit to personnel managers and top managers in companies with fewer than 50 employees. Paris would represent a first test, we merely required the willingness to do it.

Step 3: Formalizing a relevant selling theme with the sales force

A weak market signal is not enough; it merits being transformed into the appropriate selling theme. This means that the organization must be able to think in terms of customer benefits and stop being blurred by its product or service characteristics. The vast majority of organizations claim that they focus on customer benefits, but the issue demands a great deal of vigilance in order not to fool oneself.

Step 4: Assessing the attractiveness of this network

First, I suggest using criteria, quantitative and qualitative, to recognize the attractiveness with an integrated perspective. The following list of criteria seems relevant as well as manageable:

- Do we have the *numbers* (facts)?
- Are the numbers *attractive* enough (return on investment cost of acquisition)?
- *Operational* – is the customer ready to buy? Are we ready to deliver? It is commonly said that one dies more quickly from

cholesterol than from starvation, so are we prepared if our strategy works?

■ *Accessible* – do we know how to contact the decision makers?

■ *Winnable* – the unforgivable mistake, does the competition have a trump card that has not yet been recognized?

Secondly, I suggest assessing the relative attractiveness of your cross-fertilization operations. This means being sure that there is more than one account in the pipeline, because if not, you will always think that you are being effective and your analytical skills won't be employed to prioritize the targets appropriately.

Step 5: Articulating a market attack plan

When organizing a market attack plan I suggest paying attention to three critical areas:

■ *Legitimacy of the offer*. Access to the customer does not represent a problem, so when we offer a new product or concept it must be in line with our image or positioning. This point is very serious, because cross-fertilization is there to reinforce customer relationship sustainability, not only to do additional business. For instance, I always have in the back of my mind the story of the world leader in dental anaesthetics, a French-based company whose image is clear globally. However in France, because of privileged access to the dentist community, it has completely spoilt its image, for instance by selling disinfection products to dentist practices. When I asked why, I got as an answer that this is a big-budget item for the dentist. This may well be the case, but it does not sound very strategic and the lab was unconsciously diversifying, which was turning it into a distribution business.

■ *Godfather identification*. Do you have a powerful trendsetter or earlier adopter who can advocate the value of this additional product line development?

■ *Means of active support for godfather*. Think how you will facilitate the godfather's advocacy job and sustain his or her commitment.

■ Direct marketing actions.

In my efforts to structure this approach I have encountered one critical difficulty: shifting from preparation to selling in front of the customer.

Direct marketing actions need the support of an effective test. The quality of the prospective results depends on the availability of active references for the new service offered. The purpose of the test is to validate the real link between the supplier's hypothesis and the market reality.

Consequently, I decided to operate via an *active reference-building workshop*. In the SPI context, this involves the heads of marketing, sales and legal and takes 10 hours. The purpose is to test the relevance of the selling theme with the best resources available in the company in terms of product adjustment capacity and in-depth customer understanding.

The benefits recognized in this approach are as follows:

- Validation of the most relevant selling theme.
- Confirmation of the most suitable targets.
- Design of the best attuned direct marketing tools.
- Control of the cost of sales development.

The direct marketing actions themselves were conducted by telephone, supported by fax and email in order to arrange a contract signature tour for the field sales force.

The cross-fertilization cases discussed above address the context of optimizing an existing product in the portfolio. Another situation can occur, when the company possesses an innovation that could potentially be offered to its existing clients. Two examples follow that illustrate this second type of cross-fertilization challenge.

INNOVATION-BASED CROSS-FERTILIZATION

A smart prototype is not a market attack plan

On page 7 I mentioned a company in Alsace whose competitiveness was becoming blunt. A lack of innovation was part of the reason for this development. However, this only

> ## CONTINUED ... A smart prototype is not a market attack plan
>
> appeared to be the reason; more precisely, this company was very innovative, but its market-relevant innovations were not ready for enrolment in an effective marketing programme. This meant, for instance, that the commercial brochure was not ready, the characteristics of the equipment were still blurred and so on, so the sales force was unable to operate effectively.
>
> The sales force and the marketing department can become a source of sub-optimization of growth if they don't pay sufficient care and employ the most suitable techniques. Nevertheless, top management must also check that the cause of sub-optimization is not further rooted in the company's organization, representing a signal of more serious problems.

The innovation can be put into effect, so what should be done? My recommendation is still the same:

This should contribute to consolidate the business relationship and create the first platform for developing leverage.

Experience of organic growth reconfirms what Ted Levitt used to write about differentiation and consistency.[2] His theory says that a market answer is a multi-layered system that he drew

Resegment your target according to the company's maintenance effectiveness observed account per account in order to achieve the first orders quickly and with a minimum of effort.

through a combination of four rings. They describe the level of sophistication with which a market answer is designed. From the generic answer for the first one to the potential answer for the four together, Levitt advised adding one circle after the other in a consistent and controlled way, because he observed that marketers are obsessed by achievements on the outside circle while not being blameless on the first one. His message is that business is not about a positive sum of plus and minus – you must develop consistency if you do not want to reinforce the customer's power of negotiation.

An innovation is usually something taking place on the outside circles of Levitt's model, but it should not be penalized by poor performance on the more generic aspects of the supplier's solution. Consequently, even when dealing with a superb innovation, the challenge is what to do to avoid leaving a part, sometimes a substantial one, of the margin associated with the uniqueness of the innovation in the client's pocket?

An easy objection would be that this only happens when the value of the innovation is questionable. The next example, of unquestionable value, demonstrates the contrary. Innovation is one thing, but in customer portfolio management and especially in the business-to-business context, we must bear in mind that we inherit the maintenance performance. Trying to manage sales development based on innovation without considering the maintenance situation is like deciding how to dress looking outside through a window pane full of condensation.

The value of the innovation is unquestionable, but you are not heard

Rieter, the acoustic integrator mentioned on page 20, developed a new integrated solution called Ultra Light. Consulting for this client, I met the head of the purchasing department of the fastest-growing European automotive manufacturer. The innovation allowed a car manufacturer to save 15 kilos on a compact car at a cost equivalent to the previous solution: a win–win situation.

Over the previous three years, this account had been reconquered by a talented and ambitious business unit manager. The business context, in terms of customer care, was currently at its height. Moreover, Rieter had just organized a special one-day innovation session for this client to launch Ultra Light formally and present what was being developed in the company's various laboratories and research centres. The conclusion of this meeting was very favourable: 'Congratulations, keep doing it, but don't forget to keep us informed,

CONTINUED ... The value of the innovation is unquestionable, but you are not heard

although you are a Swiss company with its typical sense of secrecy.'

Then I met the alter ego of the above-mentioned senior manager at another European car manufacturer. At that time this account represented a larger sales turnover than the first company, but it was not being managed with the same style and effectiveness. This car manufacturer, two years before this meeting, had demanded substantial efforts of its suppliers and Rieter had not answered with the expected enthusiasm. A few weeks before our meeting, this manager had also personally received the Ultra Light presentation, delivered by the business unit manager.

When I met him he did not utter a single word regarding this innovation, but the whole meeting was taken up by discussing the past and the poor partnership-minded attitude of the supplier. However, the customer was not even listening to something that could clearly contribute to its own competitiveness. To take an analogy from chess, the supplier was at stale mate, which made selling even a superb innovation extremely difficult. Eventually there was a favourable outcome, but only with additional and demanding effort.

Clearly, this second account encountered a specific problem. Nevertheless, overall I would say that it was managed with insufficient effective care. The business unit manager was mediocre and unable to develop a critical influence on this account, so to justify his poor performance everything in the current business context was explained as a consequence of the confrontation between the two companies' top managements. This point was true, but then came the question of what he did to modify the business context.

The key point is that his talent was not effective enough to turn the situation around. Consequently, he fell into the classical consequences of insufficient attention described by Professor Peterson from the University of Texas at Austin, in research regarding the threat of customer defection:

- In 70 per cent of cases customers leave because of lack of attention or insufficient presence.
- In 15 per cent of cases because of price reasons.
- In 15 per cent of cases because of quality issues.

A critical observation when reading this data is not to confuse the cause of the defection and the alibi. To avoid this trap, a combined marketing approach involving process-based marketing and permanent relationship marketing (see pages 96–104) should be implemented and monitored at the account level. The power of using these tools together means that companies can simultaneously prevent customer defection and uncover growth opportunities.

Consequently, by focusing part of the organization's efforts on cross-fertilization, a substantial share of the maintenance programme is also treated. The reason is clear: we cannot expect to launch a cross-fertilization plan on a reassessed target without having monitored its potential success. To do so, we can use the analysis topic identified as meaningful to assess the quality of management of the competitive space (3Cs) in a network of accounts.

With this new product or service proposal, the organization, through its sales force or any other means, has something to announce to the customer (*content*). This additional contact contributes to actively managing the principle of a critical mass of relationships and its associated criteria (*coverage*).

Then the cross-fertilization programme will materialize if the target group is not in a situation of absolute solitude and lack of care from its supplier. This analysis raises the following question: are the efforts already achieved by the organization deployed in the best consideration of the *context*?

Summary

Cross-fertilization programmes represent a form of managerial common sense. If we do not want to run the risk of sub-optimization, the effectiveness of our own maintenance policy must be assessed among the most supportive customers, who are systematically delivered what has been promised.

Cross-fertilization is not merely a means of achieving additional sales turnover, although in fact that is a consequence of the approach. Cross-fertilization belongs to the set of process effectiveness tools that aim at prolonging a competitive advantage. The evidence is clear: 30 per cent lower customer volatility (see Figure 11.2). This observation is a strategic one.

 Action point

Assess the first level of cross-fertilization potential by crossing the way sales to your top 10 customers interrelate with your current range of products or services.

Assess the effectiveness of your competitive space management among your top 10 customers to recognize and gauge their potential for adopting your next valuable innovation.

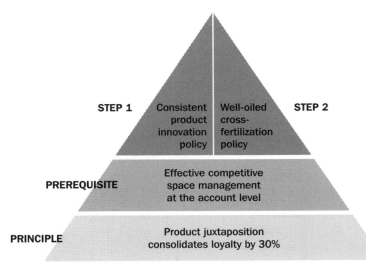

Figure 11.2 The key articulations of the organic cross-fertilization approach

Notes

1   This insurance group initially specialized in offering insurance products to the agricultural world, but since 1994 it has clearly broadened its customer scope.
2   See for further details Ted Levitt (1980) 'Marketing success through differentiation – of Anything', *Harvard Business Review*, February.

CHAPTER 12

THINK SMALL, WIN BIG

*B*efore thinking of conquering new customers, it is sensible to start by considering the sector's level of maturity. There are very few sectors where there is still enough space to develop by winning new customers that are not directly taken from the competition. Today, the vast majority of industries resemble a gangland where everybody is attacking everybody else.

In this context:

Attacking competitors' key accounts will almost automatically lead to retaliatory action, which will adversely affect some of your own key accounts. Such

> **Insufficiently articulated market attack plans result in a zero-sum game.**

an attempt represents, in the best case, a Pyrrhic victory, which under any circumstances not only provides the customer with a good way to reinforce its power of negotiation, but also diminishes the sector's overall level of attractiveness. Consequently, could small and medium-sized accounts represent an attractive growth opportunity if a reengineered marketing approach could be implemented?

FROM BREAK-EVEN POINT TO BREAK-EVEN DELAY

Customer loyalty programmes offer an economic dimension around two critical pieces of information whose effective use is not widespread among companies:

- Cost of acquisition of a new account.
- Cost of maintenance of the current portfolio of accounts.

Regarding the cost of acquisition of a new account, the question is to do with metrics: in which unit do we measure it?

The appropriate way to express it is as a *break-even point expressed in time*. This means the period of time needed to cover the fixed costs necessary for the acquisition of this new account. Many well-known examples have been publicized, for instance in credit cards the *break-even delay* is 36 months.

Sales development even better, losses worse

The full potential of this approach does not lie in the unit chosen but in the impact of the choice of unit on the organization. In 1995, I was tutoring a company consulting project with a team of MBA participants. The sponsor was an American-based express shipment company that had just arrived in continental Europe through a vast programme of acquisitions in France, Germany and Spain. In Spain development rocketed above 30 per cent between 1994 and 1995. However, the financial losses were abysmal and nothing seemed to be reversing this trend.

The explanation was pretty straightforward. In the portfolio of accounts in 1995, which had swollen in size from an index of 100 to 135, only 50 of 1994's clients were still present. Moreover, the break-even delay exceeded 20 months.

Consequently, the vast majority of customers were using the service once and then evaporating, for whatever reason. The main issue was organizational. Once the customer had

> **CONTINUED ... Sales development even better, losses worse**
>
> signed he or she was no longer the responsibility of the sales people, who operated as 'hunters'. The customer then became the responsibility of a desk account manager, a 'farmer', who had had no physical contact with the customer.
>
> When the situation was described to the sales people, their answers were unanimous: '20 months to start making money? If we knew that we would have been back at the account to promote repurchase. But our job and its associated incentive had not been designed that way.'

SMALL ACCOUNTS, INAPPROPRIATE FOR AN OPTIMAL PORTFOLIO BUT LEGITIMATE

The development of customer loyalty programmes leads to streamlining of the structure of the portfolio of accounts. In fact, with these new criteria, we can easily point out the most disappointing sales force performances. For instance, accounts where the break–even delay peaked above three years were absolutely astonishing for top management, but it was not unusual to find five years, even fifteen or twenty.

Nevertheless, this set of sound measures encompasses a more insidious consequence: the 'look-alike' or converging appearance of the way the portfolio is structured for all the actors in a sector of industry. Via consultants and training organizations good ideas are very quickly publicized and a fair amount of them implemented. It is therefore reasonable to imagine that one will quickly reach managerial parity. So the winner will tend to be the one that has the most brilliant key accounts and is not wasting its resources on small fry. There is a bonus for the early mover or the category creator, which is not good or bad but a business fact.

This opinion is acceptable, but is clearly associated with the idea of a zero-sum game because the sales people are dedicating the majority of their efforts to conquest, not maintenance. Consequently, deliberately or not, one can see the key accounts, which have quite substantial structural power of negotiation, becoming the arena of confrontation between the various actors.

It is clear that companies are not here to waste their efforts and to some extent they can organize a more gentle way to compete. However, in any sector of industry one can always find a 'mad dog' trying to bite anybody. This situation can be explained through management style, but the difference in the structure of the port-folio of accounts also represents a large part of the explanation. When an industry is converging in terms of the structure of the customer portfolio, the real danger comes from the company that possesses 'sanctuary' areas, which cannot be hit by retaliatory action by other competitors. These observations represent an area of competitive benchmarking that should not be neglected, because it answers the question of who is able to control their fellow competitors' cash flow.

> **Small accounts cost a fortune to acquire but focusing too exclusively on key accounts is not a panacea, so something else has to be found.**

Ready for a stretch goal, hitting 70 birds with one stone!

Consulting projects can encounter unsolicited delays. I was supposed to meet a particular sales person but the night before the meeting she cancelled. She had to travel in order to meet and sign a contract with a customer. Because of the com-petitive context, she was pushed to finalize without any delay. I decided to go with her and we would be able to discuss the topic of the meeting in the car. It was a really long discussion: 400 km return!

The idea of break-even delay was not widespread in the organization at that time. We were crossing a viaduct over the Meuse river, the landscape of the valley was gorgeous and I heard this killing comment: 'This customer is really exag-

CONTINUED ... Ready for a stretch goal, hitting 70 birds with one stone!

gerating, he could have sent us the contract by mail, we are driving to Bastogne for 10 users.' I didn't dare to imagine the break-even delay, which would be even worse if the client legitimately included part of my own fees in this deal! So this journey, to some extent, sounded like a waste, although the discussion with the sales person was fruitful. But two-and-a-half hours' drive for five minutes with a customer it is not optimal in terms of productivity conquest. On the positive side, it is a new account that might expand.

Then the unexpected occurred: the customer was the manager of an *Atelier Protégé*, a special workshop for slightly disabled people. While signing the contract he commented, 'A new *Arreté Royal* (law) is contributing to demotivating my 10 foremen. I need to find a way to remotivate them. Maybe among your vouchers I could find something appropriate. You should think about this.'

While saying the last words he handed the contract to the sales person, who ended the meeting by adding a couple of process operational details and finally we left.

In the car park I asked Murielle, the sales representative, if she had heard the same thing as I had regarding the foremen. She was not sure. I asked her to call the customer back, which she did in the afternoon and confirmed the point. Then the next questions came spontaneously:

'Who does this new law affect?'

'All the *Ateliers Protégés* in Wallonia.'

'How many are there?'

'I don't know.'

'Call him again and ask him.'

Not a small account but access to a large virtual account

The answer came the next day: 70. Consequently, we were in front of a potential opportunity of 700 users through those

> **CONTINUED ... Ready for a stretch goal, hitting 70 birds with one stone!**
>
> 70 accounts. Because of the maturity of the market, a competition-free account of 700 meal voucher users does not exist any longer. So the challenge was how could we hit 70 birds with one stone. Was this a stretch goal or a crazy idea?
>
> If we were able to do this, we will become able to manage a large virtual account (LVA) and consequently create a new category that should be worth investing our time in.

An LVA gathers small accounts that are encountering the same specific problem, which can be used as a common denominator to engineer a specific marketing and sales operation or solution. This network of accounts is characterized by three criteria:

- *Small* number of accounts (70 in this first case, 47 in another discussed below).
- *Substantial* number of potential users (700 users in the first case, 2500 in the second experience). This second criterion is critical to qualify as an LVA. For instance, in the second case involving airline companies operating in France, the size of the company is on average around 50 people. This profile of account ranked around 10 000 in the portfolio of customers of the French subsidiary of Sodexho Pass International, while the new LVA was among the top 50.
- *Accessible* – the network must gather decision makers for the product or service involved. If not, one runs the risk of entering a never-ending race after ambassadors. This game is called the oasis syndrome. Which oasis is the most beautiful? The next one! You are disappointed when you discover it because you idealized it so much before in order to keep your morale high.

Because of the structure of the service voucher sector, which is a duopoly, each time one of the protagonists dares to attack one of the highly visible customers in its competitor's portfolio, it is immediately followed by a reaction regarding another key account in its own portfolio. This finishes in a zero–sum game and, even worse, allows the customer to keep more and more of the margin in his or her pocket.

When both organizations are fairly alert, if one is attacked it reacts immediately; however, organizational issues (motivation of the sales force, ineffective information transmission between department or product quality concerns) can cripple the effectiveness of the reaction. You cannot build a strategy on this basis – it is tactical. Organizationally speaking, this situation is strategically unhealthy because it leads to mutual paralysis, which penalizes the capacity for reaction of both protagonists. Given that it would be unrealistic to expect that the competition remains limited to the current players, both of them are mortgaging their own future. Consequently, the whole organization's commitment to this approach is strategic and the goal is to invent a 'sales system' to leverage the effort of acquiring the LVA.

Therefore conquering a large or medium-sized virtual account is a programme aimed at uncovering gems, which are exclusively visible to those who have been able first of all to recognize the signals of their existence and then to circumscribe their specific perimeter. An LVA is invisible to others or visible too late, which does not allow an effective competitive reaction. This is a clear area of implementation for a stealth marketing approach. Implementing this technique in the case of the airline companies in France, when the competition was aware of the manoeuvre, once the vast majority of the members of this large virtual account had signed their new contract it cut its service price by an amount hitherto unheard of. This contributed to convincing the last remaining members where their true interests lay.

A WEAK SIGNAL BEHIND EACH LARGE VIRTUAL ACCOUNT

From the example we have been able to notice that the critical moment was the customer's comment about one of his current concerns. The key tool for this kind of sales development programme is the *weak signal given by the customer*. The question is: would Murielle have been able to pick up this signal on her own?

My current conviction is that she would not. If one remembers the atmosphere of this meeting, all her mind was concentrated on finalizing the contract, securing a positive first experience. Weak signals are not warnings, so one must stay intellectually nimble and focused from the moment one passes the company gate until one leaves it and even longer. Usually this is not the case, because sales people are preconditioned by the metrics of transactional sales.

It is not until the business card has been reprinted with business consultant instead of sales representative that the miracle will occur.

Chance favours the prepared mind

Another example was in a pharmaceutical company, at the same kind of meeting as in Bastogne with the human resource department. The result of this meeting was fruitful. The opening of new manufacturing premises, which will gather on one site three currently existing ones, represented a serious opportunity to consolidate and develop SPI's position. While walking back to the elevator with the client, my gaze was drawn to a picture of a factory. Instinctively fishing for information, I asked a question: 'Is that one of your factories in California?'

The company I was at manufactured vaccines using a substance from rabbit brains, and I was thinking of San Diego because of the biotech industry in that part of the US.

The answer came: 'No, it is our rabbit farm near Toulouse.'

This site had never been mentioned during our current negotiations and it must without any doubt be included. Was this an omission by the client in good faith or a tactic?

Relevant information does not announce its arrival. It just hits you, then it is up to you to draw benefit from it or to leave it lagging behind you due to lack of concentration.

Multiple occurrences, combined with your own perspicuity based on process mastery and a sense of opportunism, make you conclude with insight that there is something worth digging further for. Organization of the weak signal safari starts out of the office and will be addressed in detail in Part IV.

> A weak signal is not a customer demand, the customer is not even formulating it as a clear need to be satisfied.

FROM WEAK SIGNALS RALLY TO SALES

Once a weak signal has been identified, the next critical step is to transform it into an attractive *selling theme*:

This process is very similar to the one described in the cross-fertilization approach. It also leads to the design of a market attack plan in four steps:

> Meaningful benefits for a substantial, accessible, actionable and winnable target.

- Target group scanning.
- Formalizing a relevant selling theme with the sales force.
- Assessing the attractiveness of the *ad hoc* or formal network.
- Articulating a market attack plan:
  - Legitimacy of the offer.
  - Ambassador identification, selection and validation.
  - Active means of support.
  - Forum and workshop.

One can easily imagine that the process of developing large virtual accounts is more cumbersome than that used in the cross-fertilization approach. In attempting to manage the cost of acquisition of additional sales effectively, some form of leverage would be welcome. In large virtual account sales engineering, the principle is to use the market as the most powerful marketing tool.

Consequently, this organic growth sales development technique mainly relies on the influence of an ambassador.

In this process we have identified a weak signal, which has been assessed and transformed into a selling theme. The marketing talent consists in offering this selling theme or relevant message to an ambassador in order to give him or her the opportunity to broadcast it to his or her *ad hoc* or formal network.

THE CRITICAL ROLE OF THE AMBASSADOR IN THE NETWORK SALE

I have already recognized the importance of the 'influencing person' in the sales process. Here I want to go much further.

In order to achieve this, the ambassador becomes the central person in this approach.

> **Instead of selling the product or the service, we want to be bought by a group of customers.**

I want the same as Valéo

I decided to systematize this approach after an experience in the logistics industry. In preparation for a seminar I was interviewing the CEO of Nicolas, a family-owned logistics company in the centre of France, in Clermont-Ferrand, the home town of the global tyre manufacturer Michelin. The company operates 1400 trucks, warehouses and many square metres involved in just-in-time operations. This company had experienced excellent progress with the windscreen wiper division of Valéo, an automotive equipment manufacturer.

We were addressing the company's means of development and, after having covered the classic ones, the CEO mentioned an experience that he considered as a happy accident: 'One day I received a phone call from the head of logistics at Sagem (a large French-based telecommunications and defence group). And his question was very straightforward: can you do the same thing for us as you have achieved for Valéo?'

The point is that somebody sold the benefits of the solution implemented at Valéo. Who? Valéo's logistics manager! The nature of the conversation between the logistics managers was certainly like a consultative sale: there was a problem, its

CONTINUED... I want the same as Valéo

forumlation was validated, there were options for solutions, relative interest in each solution and the choice. However, there was a final and critical sentence from the ambassador: 'Our partner in this project was Nicolas.' According to the ambassador's credit in the sector, the colleague did not decide to reinvent the wheel. He might be willing to adapt but his goal was certainly to save time by benefiting from the accumulated experience of his colleague and he followed his advice.

Based on objective facts, the benefits of the current experience and the credit of the ambassador, the vast majority of the ambassador's alter egos would follow his advice. Consequently, by which characteristics should we recognize a true ambassador? Secondly, what means should we provide him or her with in order to reach the desired result?

A PROFILE OF AN EFFECTIVE AMBASSADOR

Who is the ambassador connected to?

The point is to recognize to which 'club' the potential ambassador belongs. This club should become a network of accounts. It can be formal, an association of logistics managers for instance, or completely *ad hoc*. In this respect, it represents a very powerful means of resegmenting an existing business and of becoming the first to create a new category based on the identification of a more subtle way to gather a group of clients.

What is the value of this ambassador?

The question is to assess the weight of the ambassador as an opinion leader. In this form of network sale, the art is to conquer without formally selling. And the appropriate person must be found; if not, one runs the risk of wrecking the whole process.

Why is this person interested in playing this ambassadorial role?

Suppose that the ambassador has been found and a couple of critical questions, such as why this person is becoming your ambassador, have been clearly answered. How can this role help the person selected? In a club of executives in the airline industry, we were able to identify a true ambassador, who was the treasurer of the association and wished to provide substantial evidence of his effectiveness to the group. By contributing to developing and making available superior conditions of service for the members of the association, he thought that he would have a good theme for being elected president of the association when the incumbent stepped down.

The caveat in this process is clear: don't run the risk of compromising your ambassador, because the club might not have the slightest idea that he or she is a hidden sales person for your company.

DESIGNING THE AMBASSADOR'S WORKSHOP

The very best way to ensure effective broadcasting of the message is to offer a forum to the ambassador, once we are sure that this person is an opinion leader for the whole network. While a qualified ambassador has not been found, it is a waste of resources to launch any formal programme. Once they have been founded and validated, however, one can start preparing an information forum for the selected network. The goal is to welcome new customers in a way freed from a conventional sales style.

The sponsoring company should give the ambassador the means to organize the promotion of the selling theme or the concept. This forum will provide unquestionable value if one can foresee benefits for three targets:

- The ambassador.
- His or her own company and network.
- The sponsoring company.

The forum has the following characteristics:

- *Purpose* – to present a solution to the problems of members of the network, so that they make the 'right' discovery.
- *Style* – the forum should be like a workshop, so that it is not a disguised sales event. It is even possible for the corporate sponsor to be absent.

The purpose of the approach is to give an ambassador all the necessary tools and means to lead their colleagues to think that they have found something

> **The two key words for the success of a forum are *preparation* and *control*.**

mutually beneficial for all the members. This goal satisfies two characteristics. The sponsoring company must:

- *Help organize the meeting in a transparent way.* Usually I suggest paying careful attention to the context of a premises visit, a group lunch and so on. The question regarding the product or the service to be promoted must be a clear point on the agenda.
- *Write the draft of the ambassador's presentation or case.* This must respect a key marketing technique for this kind of approach: rationally offering the choice of options to the audience in order to make the vast majority of participants follow the opinion leader's suggestion through their experience. By writing, you control. This is common sense. Each time I have written a draft for someone, he or she has taken it and made some corrections, but the main thread has remained.

Nemo auditur[1]

The presentation focuses on the problem confronting this network of professional managers. Consequently, the style is a workshop one, not a sales pitch. Beware of what I have called the Xerox Business Services/Crédit Lyonnais trap.

> ### CONTINUED... Nemo auditur[1]
>
> In late 1995 and early 1996, the facility management division of Xerox, XBS, had to present a proposal to Crédit Lyonnais (CL) concerning the outsourcing and spin-off of its internal printing facility, mainly dedicated to administrative documents and concentrated in a printing premises in a city along the Loire river. The challenge for CL was to achieve a yearly saving of $2 million.
>
> The sales representative, a business consultant, with outside help wrote a short 15-slide presentation for a 15-minute show. The structure was as follows:
>
> - What is the nature of the $2 million savings?
> - Why are these savings feasible?
> - Why is XBS the best option?
>
> The day before the presentation, I got a message from the XBS consultant in charge of the account: 'My boss is coming with me and he will deliver the presentation alone. He is OK with our presentation but he has found it a bit too short. Consequently, he wants to add three slides and change the structure.'
>
> I had no problem with the first point, although the art is to remove, not to add. On the other hand, regarding the structure of the presentation the challenge was radically different. The new structure was:
>
> - Xerox is a world leader in the document process.
> - Xerox is the best partner for facility management.
> - What benefits will CL draw from this collaboration?
>
> Unfortunately, the new structure did not aim at the same audience. The first document was customer centred; the second was supplier centred. Why? Although Xerox pins up on its walls large posters about empowerment, it is not so nimble at practising it. CL is a very big account so the boss felt he should be involved. And he delivered something standard

CONTINUED . . . **Nemo auditur**[1]

with which he was confident. However, it was not what the audience was expecting. In a workshop the problems are audience centred. The second presentation did address the audience's problem, but it made the audience impatient. Either you go immediately to the heart of the subject or you must expect to see the audience turning off.

The deal was postponed.

In this context it is critical to pay attention to details. As a last trick, the forum sponsor's logo should not even appear on the document that the ambassador will use. This prevents competitive reaction if the ambassador's document circulates afterwards. It keeps the ambassador's sponsor hidden and avoids the ambassador being alienated.

Robert Woodruff, a former president of Coca–Cola, used to say, 'There's no telling how far a person can go if he doesn't mind who gets the credit.' This beautiful concept was given to me by an American colleague and I would venture to add, 'as long as one gets some experience and does not remain naïve for too long.' I understand this to mean don't be too impatient with getting results. This principle provides means to avoid the common *faux pas* of calling attention to yourself and destroying your enormous investment in this ambitious reengineered sales system.

Fine tuning the ambassador's workshop is the target of the preparation phase. In specific circumstances, the sponsoring company will be invited to join the audience. It may even be asked to comment on the benefits of the solution offered or even to lead the workshop. This kind of event can always occur in a positive context, if one has prepared oneself for the tougher business conditions of a workshop exclusively run by the ambassador. On the other hand, if one starts with a sales pitch it is impossible to revert to a network workshop.

APPLYING THE LESSONS OF WINNING LARGE VIRTUAL ACCOUNTS TO SPECIFIC MAINTENANCE CIRCUMSTANCES

This approach of the large virtual account is presented in the context of winning new accounts. Starting from this perspective I have also found another way to draw benefit from these techniques.

A key account can be the object of a very difficult question: 'Are we sure that we have drawn out the full potential of the collaboration with this account merely by dealing with the current products or services before any cross-fertilization efforts?'

This question is the result of the experience of the SPI area manager for German-speaking countries, who did not stop investigations at the name of the account but wanted to explore the full extent of a German bank. This brought him DM7 million of additional voucher issues.

When a weak signal is identified and an appropriate selling theme formulated, the idea is then to find an internal ambassador and organize a workshop with the largest possible internal audience. The benefit is twofold:

- To reconfirm the benefits associated with our collaboration for those who are already in a business relationship.
- To discover the potential of new benefits with a set of strongly supportive references to those who are not customers during a problem-solving session.

This process is a clear permanent relationship marketing action. It demonstrates the ability of the company to revisit in detail the foundations of its collaboration with a customer account.

In Chapter 11 I suggested that it was wiser to start the organic growth process by attempts at cross-fertilization rather than strictly focusing the effort on maintenance. However, the importance of maintenance should effectively be rediscovered in the process of pushing sales development.

The large virtual account is a strong sales engineering process, which shares the same steps as cross-fertilization techniques once the selling theme has been formalized. Consequently, we can already imagine some means of organizational leverage in the organic growth process. In order to become more sensitive to weak signals, the organization can train its people to adopt and master large virtual account techniques by using them first in the context of maintenance of key accounts (see Figure 12.1).

These two options provide the sales force with a programme aimed at winning and brings back into the centre of the process the importance of account maintenance along its three dimensions: context, coverage and content, the 3Cs.

Summary

The large virtual account is a powerful management concept. It expresses the manager's ability to avoid a 'Catch 22' situation by rising from an ocean of competitive parity and insightfully offering a well-judged market answer based on weak signals, while the competition is still wondering what is going on.

In Part II I discussed the information skills that allow this multi-layered reading and observation of the market to be developed. The large virtual account is a dividend of having a good command of these skills. However, conscious of the interest in this way of rebuilding key accounts with an acceptable cost of acquisition, our talented managers cannot stop in the middle of the stream. On this occasion they must develop tools to leverage its effectiveness and draw benefits from the concept of network selling. In this context, they can count on the support of an ambassador who means that the company can be bought instead of selling. This opens the door

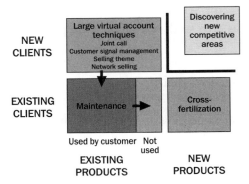

Figure 12.1 The dividends of the large virtual account approach

for partnership, a situation where the customer does not have any other option, reinforcing tight links between both organizations.

This multi-layered reading or observation system, which makes you discover a sales development opportunity, is a real challenge. Nevertheless, the challenge addresses a very serious issue: do we operate with the appropriate filters? We all start from the same raw material and some of us are able to draw the appropriate conclusions, while others are not. This makes a substantial difference. It is true in companies as well as in life, but in companies it is very difficult to confess that one is not able to apply the appropriate filters, which is why I think that daily life offers us more realistic examples.

I remember an experience in the Salvador Dali Museum in St Petersburg, Florida, observing two children less than ten years old commenting on how they saw the toreador in a painting by Salvador Dali called *The Hallucinogenic Toreador*. Both were describing the details of their discovery, one the bullfighter's hat, the second his nose. Next to them, an adult with the same tour guide was making a great effort to discover what the children had already become very familiar with. He moved to the left, then to the right and walked backwards, but nothing happened. This was not a matter of information but of how nimble one is with specific filters. In this case the important word is *specific*, because the adult could not see in this context but presumably had excellent sight in different circumstances. The point for a corporation is to be sure to be sharply focused in its own specific area to see where the competition is still wondering, or at least not to encounter a weakness in this area so that it remains on par.

 Action point

Test your skill at managing ambassadors among your existing customers to prepare your organization to operate a large virtual account, applying this concept in the first stage to a maintenance case.

Assess the effectiveness of your competitive space management approach among your top 10 customers to recognize the potential innovation launch booster that they may represent for your company's next valuable idea.

Note

1   The full Roman law expression is *nemo auditur propriam suam turpitudinem allegans*, meaning 'one cannot plead one's own turpitude'.

CHAPTER 13

DEVELOPING NEW COMPETITIVE HORIZONS – BUSINESS DEVELOPMENT

*T*he purpose of this chapter is to use additional experience acquired on consulting and research projects to outline how to foster sales development through the idea of a large virtual account in a business development context (see Figure 13.1).

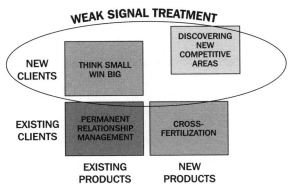

Figure 13.1 A weak market signal, the common driving force of business development and sales development

Again we are creating a new category, with at the back of our mind the simple idea of attempting to be first at opening it, in order to get the lion's share of new business areas.

The sales development challenge consists mainly of dealing with the conventional environment of the company's traditional product–client combination with the goal of avoiding sub-optimization. In this chapter I propose to challenge traditional beliefs in order to find new business with customers that are not yet served, with products or services that are not currently in the company's standard product or service lines but that will appeal to the corporate process in practically the same way as the traditional business. However:

> **Business development supposes a prerequisite: the ability of the executive committee to extract itself from day-to-day operations.**

WHAT BUSINESS ARE YOU IN?

The award for business development goes to – *who*?

Bearing in mind the challenge of business development mentioned above, I observed in the executive committee of SPI Belgium that the two champions of business development were not those traditionally expected:

- In first place the lawyer.
- Second, the information systems manager.

Why such a ranking? Some other functions would have been more naturally expected at the forefront of this mission.

First of all, it is important to observe that, in this organization, there are some business development projects that are not systematic and are subject to much confusion with sales development projects. Consequently, one must beware of fooling oneself about the goal.

> ### CONTINUED... The award for business development goes to – *who*?
>
> Secondly, the reason might become clearer if the end product, the voucher, is temporarily forgotten in order to focus on the traditional question: 'What business are you in?'
>
> The appropriate answer for SPI is 'social regulation-based information flow management.'
>
> It is not printing paper vouchers or anything else, which are merely a means to an end and the subject of day-to-day problems. Consequently, the critical skills in this area, which refer to the engineering of the service, are social regulation expertise and information systems management.

BUSINESS DEVELOPMENT: A QUESTION OF CORE SKILLS

SPI's lawyer Valérie's personal talent was unquestionable and her new ideas were unanimously considered as bringing rejuvenated oxygen to the whole system:

- *Her skills* in public law are perfectly in line with at least 50 per cent of the definition of SPI's business. The same observation can be made of the information systems star.
- *Her previous status* is the icing on the cake. She used to be an *attaché de cabinet* at the Ministry of Social Affairs in Belgium. This could have been considered as a hackneyed way of developing exclusive access to some political decision makers, but in fact the real benefit lies in her ability to reinforce the credit for her core professional skills in the people she meets.

This constitutes a unique combination, which brings a reengineered perspective to the customer relationship. She systematically operates at least one step in front of the classic product characteristics discussion, browsing through the jungle of social regulations on the simple but sensitive subject of 'allowed, not allowed, interpretable, at what risk' – in short, *value* for the customer.

Vouchers may seem to be pretty far from this context, but that does not mean that they are forgotten. They become a visible part of a process at the end and the paper voucher, smart card or software does in fact encapsulate the margin associated with the added value of this service.

Valérie's or Werner's (the head of the information system) success story could be compared to a soccer fan's favourite scoring goals in every match. However, beyond the goals, what must be underlined is the insight of the team builder who decided to hire these talented people to deal with the same things as its competitor but in a different way. This refers to strategy.

This implies a serious warning. Do not conclude that Valérie is a consultant and that SPI could have sold her services to cover part of her costs. That would have been a mistake. She is a fixed cost of the selling strategy, which should help develop the business. The story of a paper packaging manufacturer will illustrate this point.

From packaging to design studio and back

This company needed to reinvent its business because it was operating in a niche designing, cutting and printing vinyl record sleeves. Before the party was over, it entered a new business area. The opportunity was due to the CEO's relationship network. One of his friends, a top manager in the fashion industry, encountered a problem with carrier bags for his luxury brand. He asked a favour: 'Could you manufacture 5000 bags for yesterday?' The company was Yves Saint Laurent and this success was followed by the acquisition of other prestigious client names in the same sector.

The company thrived in this new activity, because the market liked the way it discussed, translated and adjusted the style department's brief and even exceeded its expectations. Reconfirmed in his beliefs by the tangible facts he could observe, the CEO decided to launch a packaging design studio.

He closed it six months later!

Again, the question remains the same: what business are you in? Confusion of the end product for which the market is paying with the sophistication of the skills you have to deploy to deliver the product or service is very painful. It costs a great deal and, even more, you can lose your soul. You are paid for the visible part of the iceberg. If you want to be paid for the submerged part, you leave organic growth and embark on diversification, which is a radically different subject.

Back to Valérie, her approach is clearly at the heart of what I earlier termed dialogue-based marketing. She has nothing specifically to sell, but her goal is to build the invaluable customer goodwill, the customer reflex that in a business-to-business context leads clients to be willing to share with their valuable partner their hottest business concerns.

In this context, the supplier is obliged to act in a proactive way to ensure that it will be bought as a result of a common-sense decision by the client. At the end of the discussion process, the customer will not be able to foresee any other way to get more value than from this specific supplier, compared to what the competition's pitch is offering. Finally, this situation does not necessarily mean that discussion of the economic aspects of the deal will not generate some tension.

Consequently, my suggestion is:

To some extent part of SPI's current success was favoured by Valérie's arrival and her style. Nevertheless, for organizations that have not had an infusion of new talent, we cannot accept as an alibi 'We need to hire new people to initiate some attempts at effective business development.' In fact, we don't need new people but rather new ideas, which in the above case are associated with the newly hired person. Even if this resource is not available, we must find a way to revisit and revalidate the meaning of our own core competencies to check that they aren't hiding gems that familiarity is tarnishing.

> **A fruitful business development programme can only be built if the company and its top management can demonstrate outstanding skills in the core competencies of the business that the company is in.**

We are the difficult content experts

A second example illustrates this additional possible way of business development. Recently I spent two days at a workshop with a bottling process engineering and manufacturing company (see page 7 for more details) in the Vosges mountains. We revisited the nature of its core skills and I considered the output very valuable. The audience was able to shift from its initial presentation that focused on its end product of high-speed conveyor lines, 'the Rolls-Royce of conveyor lines for bottling applications', to productivity improvements to the bottling process by advanced process automation regulation and effective organizational skills.

While SPI hired skills that allowed it to differentiate itself with the customer, in this second case the unique skills were made of jewels that were insufficiently well-recognized internally, hidden by the tyranny of the market served. However, the second case was also reserving an additional surprise for us.

This company was 'beer sector oriented' or 'mineral water sector oriented', representing roughly the same technical challenge. But we reached a point where we could also formulate another possibility for positioning. The company is also recognized as a 'fixer' by other mass consumer goods companies for what they call a 'difficult content' case. For example, how and at what maximum speed can they convey a plate of a ready-to-eat baby food. This was a challenge submitted by the Vevey-based world leader, which the company had successfully resolved, although it was hidden in the meanderings of the organization's information exchange system.

At the end of this approach we could at least map its results, as shown in Figure 13.2. To expect to get a harvest the suggestion is unambiguous. '100 per cent of those who have won, have played', as a French radio advertisement for the LOTO used to go, and one must periodically run this kind of executive committee workshop if one wants to avoid sub-optimizing one's own opportunities. There is no shame in confirming the corporate beliefs and lighting a new business opportunity from an unusual perspective.

The business opportunity will naturally emerge if the field is appropriately prepared. My observations and experiences make me think that this happens if professional expertise, combined with a context based on trust and confidence, is unambiguously and quickly created, as the first case illustrates.

However, quite often the possibility of an almost equal exchange with the customer, as Valérie did, might not come naturally and easily. Then another approach needs to be implemented. In this context, I suggest attempting to reach this target with a more didactic approach to avoid sub-optimizing the company's success and assets. Select the benefits brought to a 'pilot' client by a new specific application and describe them in a very short presentation, such as fewer than 10 slides delivered in less than 10 minutes. Then train the company's sales people to deliver this with enthusiasm. In this way it is possible to recreate the core skills context of the SPI case.

The merit of this approach is that it gives a favourable tempo to the dialogue-based marketing process, based on analysis and the choice of the most appropriate angle from which an organization would like to be considered. This contact will be addressed with a perfect strategic mind because strategy is about choice, which also means renouncing and that is exactly what this process is doing.

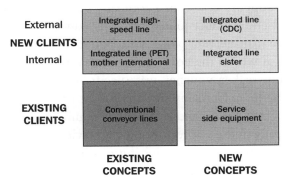

Figure 13.2 Partial results of a workshop regarding the company's core skills and their consequences in terms of organic growth

Consequently, the contact can start from something tangible, which can allow the accurate topic of consideration to emerge by analogy. Finally, as usual formalization also brings a valuable side effect, reinforcing the confidence of the sales person.

The cases and presentations are means rather than a lethal weapon, but they represent one of the ways to hook potential customers by addressing them with hard facts and tangible experiences. The goal is not to sell, although it is wise to expect that they will not remain insensitive to this.

A last detail for this first cast: you are not fishing for comments such as 'great, brilliant, spectacular', but for 'I did not imagine you had got this kind of competencies, and you have already experienced it with so-and-so'.

If you can do this the prize is won and you are on that customer's list. Now it is your turn to find an opportunity to test the effort this potential customer is prepared to put in for a potential supplier.

Core skills open doors and comfort friends

In this book I have often described the business of Sodexho Pass International. In terms of core competencies, this has been summarized as the management of a flow of information based on the enforcement of legal rules regarding labour law. This materializes in a first end product, the vouchers, which are the means to support aspects of a company's fringe benefit policy. A second end product joined the first, vouchers to support a social care management policy with public institutions, including cities as well as the government of a country. For instance, the asylum seeker voucher was specifically designed for the Land of Berlin in Germany and later for the British government. Consequently, the second end product family started to anchor the company in the vast sector of social services.

In Belgium, one of the institutions in this sector is called CPAS – Centre Permanent d'Action Social – representing around 600 accounts. It provides a wide range of services to the local population and in particular to senior citizens. Some

CONTINUED ... Core skills open doors and comfort friends

CPAS were already customers of the catering division of Sodexho. The food and management services division had in the course of its permanent relationship marketing actions been one of the sponsors of CPAS's annual convention for a couple of years. However, CPAS did not apparently need SPI's end products, the vouchers, because each of these institutions is the service provider itself.

Nevertheless, food and management services shared the sponsorship of a convention with its sister division. The goal was simple, to reinforce the visibility of the group over its range of services. The discussion with some CPAS officers and especially with some opinion leaders revealed some unexpected interest in further discussions with SPI. The interest was not in SPI's end product itself, but in the productivity improvement that the skills and technology mastered by SPI could represent for these institutions.

The meal vouchers used to be in the form of paper, but SPI considered the development of chips for smart cards as a potential means of substitution for the paper voucher. Conceptually the idea was very attractive because a smart card could become the new end product for many forms of vouchers. For instance, in South America, in Brazil or in Argentina, the diversity of vouchers is far broader than in Europe, ranging from meal to gasoline and even including pharmaceutical products. The idea suffers from a number of constraints, however, which the early movers such as smart card manufacturers Gemplus and Schlumberger, as well as banks and some service providers, had already encountered in the development of the electronic purse.

Nevertheless, a less ambitious application could provide an appropriate answer for some institutions. In fact, the CPAS was drowning under tonnes of paper for the data on the services it offered. Simplifying this represented a challenge that was worth taking up.

CONTINUED ... Core skills open doors and comfort friends

Consequently, some CPAS representatives saw in this card a means to get rid of the forms that social service providers were obliged to fill in, in order to trace the service provided, e.g. medical assistance, delivery of meals and so on. So the idea was to equip the people entitled to the service with a card with their personal details stored on it; the service provider clerk or professional, such as a nurse providing home care, gets a second card and a card terminal to register the transaction. When a service is provided both people slot their respective card into the terminal. The nurse keys in what has been provided and the patient validates the service.

In this context Sodexho will collect the data and consolidate the report for each CPAS institution and its employees, respectively 600 and 20 000 in number, and the independent service providers such as nurses and physiotherapists, around 15 000. The idea quickly reached a level of maturity because of the tempo given to it by the development team, where the only possible next step was to start a pilot project regarding one CPAS with 220 service beneficiaries and 17 service providers.

Regarding business development techniques, one can observe that the SPI team exactly matched the characteristics of a network sale with the purpose of creating a large virtual account. The techniques of sales development regarding the network sale were a weak signal that was recognized through the pressure on these public bodies to simplify the administrative process and their search for productivity improvement. After this instance, the selling theme was still making progress through a pilot case but was also developing an ambassador in the CPAS network. Finally, the CPAS represents an attractive large virtual account when one considers the leverage effect through the potential number of users.

Considering the characteristics of this growth option, one can observe that the driving force of business development is more often the core skills that have been mastered than the end product itself. In this context, the end product – the smart card – might be considered as a substantial new technological breakthrough, but in fact it is not, because it does not affect SPI's positioning on its core skills. However, by becoming an early mover in the possible trend of evolution of our own end product, we are both consolidating our own core skills and capturing the status of an innovative company.

An incidental lesson of this case must also be shared. This business development opportunity also brought a positive side effect in terms of cross-fertilization. The CPAS pilot led to the idea of offering a new service to its service beneficiaries: gift vouchers for Christmas.

SPI stopped the experiment in late 2001 after 18 months although the business relationship with the customer continues, bearing in mind that there is an area of so far unsatisfied need that must be readdressed as long as it is in line with its own core skills evolution.

This example is not characteristic of versatility but of advanced management skills, which recognize that success in business is conditional on the number of attempts and not on luck.

> **The early mover attitude goes hand in hand with the ability to withdraw fast in order not to prolong the pain.**

A final observation to be considered in reengineering the business development process consists of avoiding the so-called decision maker trap.

Too often I have observed sales people who are over-obsessed with developing a kind of exclusive relationship with the decision maker. They think that if they can control, meaning influence, him or her, they will get a decision in their favour. In my opinion this is a form of mental restriction that impedes recognition of where the appropriate efforts must be deployed. This suggestion immediately starts to come naturally as soon as the approach to business development is based on some of the formal tools mentioned earlier. For instance, one should observe the map of the customer or the prospective account and the associated concept of managing the appropriate deployment of the critical mass of relationships (see page 114). This test is very effective in assessing if too much emphasis or importance is being given to one part of an organization.

A business development expert cannot deprive current 'business doers' from making a functional contribution. By both focusing on the 'business doers' and keeping a sharp eye on the decision maker, one reduces the competition's ability to catch up.

In this first part of business development, we are describing a growth situation where the initiative is on the supplier's side. There is also an opportunity for business development organic growth that benefits from the customer as catalyst. A limit has already been observed to organic growth. Organic growth is different to diversification, but very often one can observe that customers are pushing their suppliers to address processes that they haven't yet mastered.

BUSINESS DEVELOPMENT OPPORTUNITIES IMPELLED BY THE CLIENT

Business development impelled by the client is a very specific situation. If you miss the boat your journey is over for a long time. In the automotive industry, components suppliers have been obliged to evolve from parts to modules and finally to systems in order for the luckiest of them to stay in the race.

What has happened? First, automotive manufacturers decided how they conceived the car of the future. Figure 13.3 describes the

---

Key for Figure 13.3

Co-design Systems

Sistema: insieme logico di componenti preposti a svolgere una determinata funzione del veicolo
SYSTEM – GROUP OF COMPONENTS AIMED AT A SPECIFIC VEHICLE FUNCTION

Alimentazione carburante: FUEL SYSTEMS
Climatizzazione: AIR CONDITIONING SYSTEMS
Insonorizzazione veicolo: VEHICLE INSULATION SYSTEMS
Sicurezza abitacolo: CABIN SAFETY SYSTEMS
Sistema elettrico: ELECTRICAL SYSTEMS
Sistema frenante: BRAKE SYSTEMS
Sistema di scarico: EXHAUST SYSTEMS
Sistema sterzante: STEERING WHEEL SYSTEMS
Aspirazione: INTAKE SYSTEMS
Audio: AUDIO SYSTEMS
Raffreddamento: COOLING SYSTEMS
Interni vettura: CABIN COMPONENTS
Informativo: HIGH-TECH INFO SYSTEMS

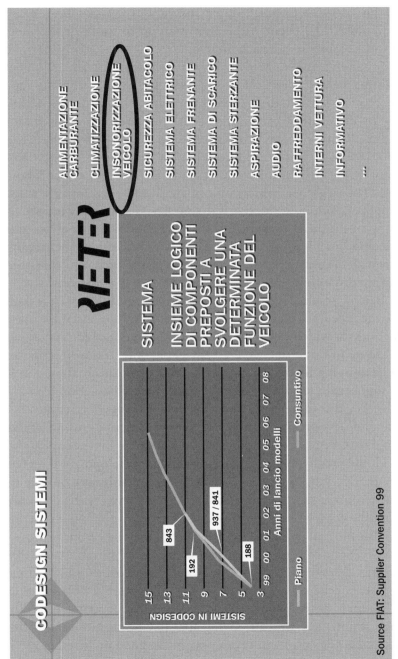

Figure 13.3   The system breakdown of a car, an example from Fiat

way Fiat decided to break down the various key functions of an automobile. The client is therefore starting to look for the most appropriate supplier for each function.

Secondly, due to the quality of their current and potential performance and their relationship with the customer, some suppliers have been able to seize the opportunity and anticipate a new way to define the relationship with the customer. This is, for example, what happened for Rieter (see page 20), which in the late 1990s became Fiat's acoustic comfort specialist. Usually this approach means a broader definition of the context for collaboration. The customer can rely on a single partner for a broader range of supplies. As long as the goal is to shift from parts supply to systems supply in the same technology, the challenge will not create real difficulties for a leading supplier. However, if the game is changing gears with the association of electronic or plastic parts, and your core skills are in another area, the challenge belongs to a higher league.

Being customer focused will lead to the acquisition of new skills and the need to take some additional risks due to these new processes for which one therefore becomes accountable. Very often the nature of this challenge is a managerial one. The new leader in the relationship must demonstrate its ability to manage the second-tier suppliers in its system. Then there is an economic hurdle, not a slight one, that of being able to achieve a level of effectiveness that compares favourably with what the automotive manufacturer would have been able to attain if it had not taken this system option.

Consequently, entering into this kind of development does not only require you to conceive of the idea, but also very quickly to align resources to cope with supplying something that previously wasn't the company's favourite cup of tea. In my opinion it is in this area that the real challenge lies, because at the end of this process a radically new company should emerge with a simple system for assessing its strategic health. The idea is to find projects in the four quadrants of the matrix in Figure 13.4. The presence of projects in the business development quadrant is a proof of strategic health. One cannot trade this off, saying that having no projects in this quadrant is not a problem because we are so good in the other parts. If you accept this complacent style of management, you miss the

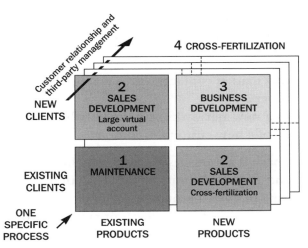

Figure 13.4 Four options for implementing organic growth in two main directions, one specific process and customer relationship

mission of the executive committee, securing the present *and* creating the future. It is only an active presence in each area that represents insurance to create a future for the whole organization.

Summary

Business development in the organic growth approach represents a twofold new development opportunity. These new opportunities are:

- Either the expression of a superior sales investigation talent, based on the strategic command of the company's core skills instead of the lure of the end product as a means to thrive in the business the company is in.
- Or the result of a customer relationship virtuous circle, where a systematically satisfied customer returns a dividend in the form of priority information, which is seized by a supplier or a partner taking on the challenge to enter into new businesses where it considers it has the skills to manage second-tier associates in order to supply the customer with a new function or system, but where it keeps control of an exclusive business relationship with the customer.

This demands a dialogue-based core skill mindset, as we observed above with Werner and Valérie (see page 168), who are keen on:

- Multiplying market contacts with a real orientation towards business doers.
- Envisioning new networks of partners who can be part of the design of a new customer solution.

This approach is a team-based one where the design involves players beyond the usual limits of the definition of a business unit, a company or even a group.

Here is an additional area where organic growth demonstrates its strategic perspective. In order to reach these new areas of customer satisfaction, this challenge will require further muscle being given to the organizational effectiveness dimension of the competitive advantage combination. If not, the company will stay at the cosmetic level.

 Action point

Ask your executive committee the question: what business are we in? The goal is to assess what dominant way of thinking is observable, end products or core skills? If the core skills reflex is not sufficiently present, the company will remain in the sales development area. This does not represent a problem, but signals that it is not preparing for the future with enough efficiency and care.

CHAPTER 14

THE ESSENCE OF GROWTH

I have deliberately positioned the maintenance chapter at the end of this part. Part II already covered this area in depth with the concept of the customer satisfaction ratio. Consequently, in the bottom left quadrant of the organic growth matrix involving existing customers and existing products or concepts (see page 127), the goal is, account per account, to get a customer satisfaction ratio, understood as performance divided by promises, equal to 1.

This result is based on an information monitoring system for individual customer accounts effectively managed through the 3Cs (see pages 109–123), which should allow the company to stay in line in terms of targeted quality of customer relationship. However, a ratio such as this is merely a concept to structure how to focus one's own managerial attention. The challenge is to transform it into a management reflex. Consequently, I want in this chapter to stress the practical management of the maintenance approach.

3Cs CAN HIDE 5Ss

It is not reasonable to imagine launching a revised maintenance policy for all the accounts in a portfolio. A pilot project is appropriate to test your own ease at dealing with this concept. The portfolio of accounts will be segmented into:

- Key accounts.
- Everyone else.

The 3Cs account maintenance approach should be applied to a few top accounts that achieved a substantial part of the turnover to quickly make this tool a best demonstrated corporate practice. To decide on the limit of key accounts in your own portfolio of customers, I suggest relying on the following criteria. Which are the accounts where it is considered worth writing an individual account development presentation, as I suggest at the end of Parts II and IV? This task represents a serious investment of time and consequently it cannot encompass all the portfolio during the first phase of implementation.

I dealt with this question of segmentation with AFE Metal, the steel foundry division of AFE (see page 43). It became clear that in its transportation segment the customer accounts were not as numerous in Europe due to the consolidation that had taken place in the sector. Thus Bombardier, Alsthom, Fiat and Siemens needed to be covered with a specific 3Cs approach. Then came the question of smaller accounts, which must not be disregarded and left as an unploughed field.

This means that instead of designing an account presentation, a technology-focused presentation will be more appropriate. The idea is to leverage the reflex to choose your company among accounts where the idea of managing the customer as a 'segment of one' would be excessive. In this respect, one of the foundry technologies is called 'lost wax'. I recommended writing a specific presentation regarding lost wax and communicating this to the smaller accounts with associated methods such as conference report mailing, or small reminders through web page updates to avoid ambiguity in the reflex of the company's positioning.

> For the *key accounts* the rationale of the approach is *information management* oriented, while for the *smaller accounts* the approach must be *core skills and technology communication* oriented.

The reflex of using the maintenance tool will then spread throughout the portfolio at a speed proportional to the efforts achieved by the management to enforce, in their own practices and exchanges with people in the field in daily contact with the client, a style of relationship where the key steps and articulations of the proposed tool are systematically used.

To shift from a customer account maintenance concept to a practical, hands-on approach, I propose regular assessment of the effectiveness of the account maintenance policy (at intervals depending on the industry's speed of development) through a discussion between the account manager and an executive committee member based on the 3Cs model.

Coverage

- Get a map of the account or have it drawn and assess the quality of coverage of the customer decision-making process and the potential presence of an ambassador.
- Gauge how critical the current mass of relationships is. Assess what is specifically done for the ambassador.

Content

- Have the account manager report what he or she knows regarding customer expectations.
- How has the company translated these expectations into promises? Are these specifically formulated for this particular customer? Assess the level of stretch goals the promises represent and qualify the sales-process people interaction in this formulation.
- Are the process-based marketing indicators favourable?
- What is specifically being achieved in terms of permanent relationship marketing actions? What customer efforts are observable on this occasion?

Context

■ As a result of this process, a short story synthesizing where the relationship is coming from, is currently and is heading towards should be available. Does it exist? Is it what you would have expected if the company had asked you on the spot to take charge of this account?

■ The sales forecast for next year should also be available. Does it exist? Can we get one? What is the unit used?

■ What is our judgment of our effectiveness in managing the competitive space? Are we in a situation where it is realistic to consider that the appropriate job has been done for the customer not to consider the competition's sales pitch?

To help assess the value of competitive space management, I suggest evaluating with the customer account manager his or her answers against the 5Ss of the following model. I formalized this 5S model as the result of consulting projects where I observed that suppliers in dominant and sometimes even exclusive customer positions meet these characteristics. The model is there to help in assessment and leads to a documented opinion.

■ *Skills*: Are the supplier's skills recognized by this client as superior in terms of product technology to its competitor? Here is an example of a positive customer observation providing a clue that the supplier is satisfactory: 'They have got the thickest catalogue in the sector and when one does not find what one needs a development engineer shows up.'

■ *Service*: I have not yet met any organization that claims that it does not care about service, even though sometimes one might doubt this. However, when one evokes the word service, the client tells anecdotes or impressive experiences that

> My experience in this area is that if you have to think about it for more than three seconds and you are still wondering, it means that you are not performing distinctively on the service side with this specific customer account. Distinctive performance does not need analysis to be assessed!

demonstrate how the supplier really cares. If the supplier only has a general idea, it is worth checking this out because it can reveal some surprises.

■ *Stability*: The business-to-business context is an area of consultative selling where market performance is based on a combination between a *concept* or sometimes a brand that generates the *customer's consideration* and a *commercial* person who reaches a positive *conclusion*. Consequently, there is a human side to this business relationship, which I like to assess from the angle of how we can express the customer's interest in the stability of the relationship. Stability is critical for the customer intimacy approach in order to avoid wasting a large part of one's investment.

In this respect it is important to hear from the customer's mouth: 'I have been working with Mr or Ms X for 8, 12 or 15 years.' I consider the stability of a relationship as a key point for a consistent objective in building a sustainable corporate relationship. Some readers will consider that in advocating stability in relationships, I am running the risk of the company falling into a routine. However, with the tools I am addressing in this book I doubt that this will happen. At the other extreme, I suggest being wary of unwittingly falling into the trap of seeing the customer as 'our most precious asset'.

Planning a visit to a German customer of a client of mine, I was not sure what he meant in our phone conversation agreeing to the meeting. He told me, 'It is good that you come to visit me, I will show you my card collection.' I have some doubt about my German language proficiency so I wondered if I had understood correctly. Then I met this client, who reminded me what was printed in the glossy paper supplier's brochure about the company's most valuable assets, its work force and its commitment to the quality of customer relationship. From his drawer he took a stack of business cards from his service supplier's sales people. He started to number them, stopped at eight and added, 'Over 36 months.' The supplier was not behaving in the way it claimed in its brochure. Stability is not exclusively on the client side.

A customer systematically reveals areas of stability

There is one final point about this characteristic of a business relationship. Stability is critical, so spending time looking after stability is a valid investment. A couple of years ago, I initially refused to conduct a management executive training seminar for a large bakery company present in many European countries manufacturing raw frozen bread. This company is the raw material supplier of products that allow a traditional bakery atmosphere to be recreated in the shops of a supermarket chain. In hypermarkets very often the distribution chain is fully integrated from flour to bread. My experience in the food distribution environment was so little that I was equivocating about the relevance of my contribution.

The CEO suggested that I visit the headquarters of one mass distribution chain, where I could meet someone who could give me some clues about this sector. I thought I was going to meet a purchasing manager, but in fact I met the distribution chain's chief bakery technologist, a highly knowledgeable baker. The discussion was delightful, I discovered the various levels of joint development that these two companies had been experiencing together, for instance what they call a 'bio' loaf. This type of development does not happen by accident. The distribution chain's baker explained to me that he remembered when the bakery company began in the late 1950s with *le père*. . . Since that time the two had been in an uninterrupted business relationship. This was in the context of a mass distribution chain where the volatility of suppliers is taken for granted. Why was the context so favourable in this instance? Sometimes one can uncover a happy surprise that must not be missed.

Even in areas where it is known that the mobility of people is high, the goal of effective customer relationship management is to find the hidden areas of stability in the customer's organization. This brings us back to the importance of the customer account map.

■ $: How does the customer assess the relationship from an economic point of view? What signals do you get that the customer is testing the competitiveness of the supplier's offer on the market? 'We are exclusively buying from X,' commented one customer, 'I know that I am not a fool paying the price I get for this service. Each time I meet a potential source of substitution, it gives me a means to keep my current leading supplier awake, and I tell them I have met the other company.' This is somewhat paradoxical, but this comment is positive because the customer is buying dynamically in a clever way – and he knows it. However, if you do not have the critical mass of relationships, this example can backfire against the supplier. The supplier does not have the clues to distinguish the kind of game customers are playing: are they challenging the terms of the relationship or reassuring themselves that they are in good hands with this supplier?

■ *Style*: How do we show our customer a commitment to the sector that goes beyond a simple supply relationship? For instance, a company such as AFE Technology, a division of AFE (see page 43), organizes a special event each year regarding the state of the art in heat treatment. The whole industry comes to this event to meet the leading authorities in the industry and also to socialize. It is perceived by the population of customers as a distinctive event that is the exclusive property of AFE. Once one operator has initiated this approach it is a waste of resources for another company to attempt to organize an alternative state-of-the-art heat treatment event. Something else has to be invented. A new category is needed because if not, you are reinforcing the position of the inventor of the category. It is a permanent relationship marketing event but it raises a critical question: what can be listed in your own organization in terms of permanent relationship marketing actions regarding your company's top 10 accounts?

The opportunity to have this kind of discussion with an account manager is to create a strong team spirit around best demonstrated customer management practices, where one can play without looking at the position of the other people on the court because we have repeated the combination so often that it has become second nature. Winston Churchill very often used an appropriate comment in this context: 'My best improvizations are those which I have rehearsed the most.' This is nothing new: management is to a large extent about tenacity and the art of repeating, repeating and repeating.

I stress this dimension of developing the appropriate reflexes because our sales and marketing teams are not systematically wired in the appropriate way. A signal from the customer is too often understood as a price cut. Repeating this question-and-answer exercise around the customer relationship topic makes company executives far more sensitive to the true meaning of a market signal.

What is behind the announcement of a 37 per cent price cut?

In late 2001 a process equipment manufacturer's marketing and sales manager reported to me that he was encountering serious concerns at one of his top customers, the European leader in its sector and one of the top few players in the world, to which it was an almost exclusive supplier. The challenge was straightforward: 'In Germany they have asked us for a 37 per cent price reduction on a particular product.' The discussion tried to forget the 37 per cent in order to reach an appropriate understanding of the context and extract the supplier from the 37 per cent trap.

The customer, a British-based holding company, had seen its stock exchange market value dive by half over the previous two years since its flotation. The product that is the object of the 37 per cent cut would be obtained from a former eastern bloc supplier whose expertise was not at all on a par with the European leader. A first reaction is to assess this opinion as arrogance in considering that a competitor cannot match your own performance. But at the same time, it is also clear proof of good management if the competitive benchmarking job has been done effectively and the evidence is available.

CONTINUED . . . What is behind the announcement of a 37 per cent price cut?

Assessing the value of the potential newcomer, it was clear that such a job with a 37 per cent price cut on the previous market price would generate nearly a one–digit figure for gross margin profit. Moreover, one could consider it is possible for the customer to benefit from this situation, so we did not forget to support our discussion with a drawing on the back of an envelope. In this case what we drew spontaneously was the matrix on page 204 recognizing where the negotiating power lay.

One of the conclusions of the discussion was that the customer was not managing the risk with the same care as in the past, there were very few objective possibilities of substitution and it was behaving as if substitution had become completely risk free for the company. Secondly, the potential new supplier could consider this account as strategic and consequently assessed the absence of appropriate gross margin as an investment. This raised the question of the company's financial health and local government subsidies. We agreed that the customer was trying to tell us something else. It had not been expressed in the expected form, but we should already have considered this as a priority dividend in terms of information because we were not in a situation where we had no option but to observe the substitution or were receiving this information very late in a discussion process. Then a simple question was addressed: how much is 37 per cent worth? In fact, it was 10 out of a total supply turnover of 110.

Finally after this contradictory exchange our conclusion was that according to the current business context the customer has certainly said: 'This whole supply must cost us 100.' It didn't want to change its leading supplier, so the poorly formulated question of a 37 per cent reduction became: can we achieve a 10 per cent productivity improvement, where, how, and within how much time? The relationship sky cleared up because the sales and marketing manager recovered the

> **CONTINUED... What is behind the announcement of a 37 per cent price cut?**
>
> feeling that he could regain the management of the customer relationship. The purpose of the discussion was to assess from someone else's perspective that we were not stuck in a Catch 22 position.

This short story reminds us that in customer relationships we can make our own this quality improvement suggestion: ask yourself seven times why, and you will act on the root cause. The goal is the same: an insightful manager must have tools available that help keep him or her thinking strategically with a bird's eye view over the situation. One must bear in mind that the beauty of such a tool is conditional on both the information system – intelligence or benchmarking – *and* the speed of analysis.

TWO RATIOS FOR A SOUND CUSTOMER MAINTENANCE APPROACH

I must agree that to some extent there is less glory in maintenance than in conquest, but there is a price to pay for failure: you cannot maintain the status quo, you can only lose. So what is the cost of losing an account? Answering this question requires two mandatory corporate performance indicators for effectively managing a portfolio of customers, which any sales person must have in the back of their mind to act strategically.

Cost of acquiring a new account

It has already been widely publicized that the most relevant way to address the concept of cost of customer acquisition is to rely on the idea of the break-even point (BEP). I suggested on page 148 that the most appropriate approach is to introduce the idea of break-even delay (BED), how long the product has to stay in the product portfolio in order to cover its fixed cost of acquisition.

This kind of figure does not need to be calculated for each acquisition, but I think that first it must be unquestionably known by anybody in contact with the customer base. Secondly, it represents an area of assessment of the yearly performance of the team managing the portfolio of customers. Finally, I think it worth repeating the limits I can see in this approach. It is easy to announce to corporations: 'Look, with this customer the break-even point is at 10 years, so part of your selling effort sounds like a complete waste.' Focusing on larger accounts that can generate a faster return on your commercial investment is conceptually correct.

However, the phenomenon of convergence must also be taken seriously into account. To a certain extent everybody, through the diffusion of managerial practices, receives the support of the same consulting firms or advisers. Consequently, there is a serious risk of convergence leading to a parity of practices. We live largely in a world of parity where everything is the same. Consider, for example, clothes from Gap or Benetton, or cars from Hertz or Avis. Imagine opening your eyes in a shopping mall without any customers and then try to guess which part of the world you are in. Will the names of the shops give you any clue to where you are? If an industry sector is giving its key account policy too much emphasis, it leads to a draw between players and a victory for the customer's power of negotiation.

The vast majority of players haven't used the challenge of reducing the return on sales effort investment to their advantage. My objective is to remind that you cannot be one of those. Consequently, it is mandatory to invest in managerial creativity in order to do the same things as your competitors, but more strategically, that is to say in a different way.

Cost of maintaining the current customer portfolio

In a study of the Scandinavian pharmaceutical industry, Cranfield Business School in the UK was among the first to show that these companies were, on the whole, spending 80 per cent of their marketing-related budget on customer conquest, while investing only 20 per cent in the maintenance of existing accounts. This sounds like putting the cart before the horse for people with solid common sense. In fact, it is to some extent evidence of unwitting arrogance, where we consider a sales relationship to be definitely acquired and consequently there is no reason for it to be lost, which justifies focusing expenses mainly on the acquisition of new accounts.

If you follow the advice in this book the cost of maintaining a portfolio of customers will certainly rise. Among new areas of expense you will find those regarding the development of combined information and communication tools, which must not be confused with the customer relationship management system. Have you drawn up the customer account development presentation, which represents the quintessence of this specific account information approach, or presentations on the state of the art of various company technologies, which allow the reflex of consideration to be maintained with a more scattered customer base. These expenses remain modest and their leverage, both in terms of customer maintenance and sales people's confidence, is very substantial.

Summary

To achieve an effective maintenance policy, sales and marketing management must be clear about the break down of their budgets between process-based, permanent relationship and dialogue-based marketing programmes.

At the end of Part II I stressed the resources issue because it constitutes an acid test for change. We must recognize that organic growth is a way to avoid sub-optimization of a company's growth opportunities. We have discussed a tool to sort the opportunities, then from opportunities we have shared experiences to transform them into businesses in each situation. However, one cannot expect to shift from concept to reality if resources are not reallocated in a different way. This means that the company's top management must be well aware of what it costs, how it should avoid losing, what level of investment a substantial sales development activity represents and, finally, the criteria for mobilizing the company's money for business development projects.

 Action point

Select a top customer account and run a 3Cs contradictory discussion with an account manager to enforce implementation of this way of dealing with information at the customer account level.

KICKING ORGANIC GROWTH INTO GEAR AT AN ACCOUNT LEVEL

After this part our customer account development presentation can go one step further by addressing the consequences of our organic growth analysis through the topic of our ambitions for this specific customer (see Figure 13.5). These ambitions are twofold: first, what do we forecast achieving in terms of maintenance and cross-fertilization respectively with this account? This step, systematically addressed, can be followed by a business development step where the supplier is discovering new competitive horizons impelled by the customer.

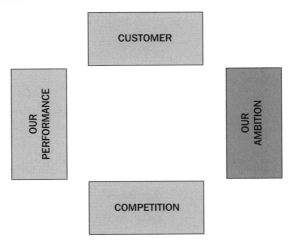

Figure 14.1 Structure of a customer account presentation, Step 2

PART IV

CREATING THE MANAGERIAL CONDITIONS TO SUPPORT ORGANIC GROWTH

*M*embership of the executive committee is not an honorary position where merely working with a will is sufficient; tangible and substantial results are demanded. Nobody can contest this obvious statement. Nevertheless, I want to address another set of results, which, conceptually, are included in many mission statements and which are not so easy to achieve. The reason is simple: the nature of the competitive challenge demands that we accept stretch goals, which force us to operate beyond our natural areas of expertise and even comfort.

In my consulting assignments over nearly 20 years, I am used to working for top management teams. I consider the first step of my role as the delivery to the CEO or executive committee a considered and appropriate formulation of the problem that I have been invited to discuss with them. Many times I have been invited to join these executive committee teams on a permanent basis. Consequently, when faced with a business issue, I consider myself as thinking in the same way as the vast majority of senior executives.

One of the goals of bringing the organization's most advanced talents into the marketplace is to *capture weak signals* that the sales people cannot hear, as the example on page 153 shows. This situation is the result of the nature of a sales person's job and the way they typically function in any situation.

In the case of the *Atelier Protégé* (see page 150), I met a prospect with the sales rep and was able to extract the relevant information regarding this potential large virtual account. In the case of ASE (see page 231), I met with one of the few top French customers of an express shipment company, accompanied by one of its leading sales reps, ranked third out of more than 100. I got a clear warning signal of a potential strategic breakdown on this account. In both cases, the sales rep passed along the signal without paying attention to it.

I am not at all intending to make you think that I am far more insightful than these people. I was simply acting as any executive committee member would have done. I was addressing these meetings from a far broader business perspective than the sales rep and the crop was pretty substantial. Consequently, my next point is twofold:

During these 'pilot' sales operations with the active field involvement of executive committee members, when I assessed what the crop was worth and its organizational consequences I wondered why so many organizations were missing these opportunities. The reasons are well known: *routine* and *institutionalization of managerial practices*. These lead

> **Don't only beware of changing the mission of the sales rep, but also find a way of not wasting these sales and business development opportunities, or more simply business warnings.**

to a context that makes you forget even obvious things.

The field involvement of executive committee members breaks institutionalization by bringing back relevant information to the executive committee level, where a member will not be allowed to lie around without running the risk of being judged as inadequate for the function. This is why a careful assessment of the appropriateness of the context must be carried out if one wants to enter this process with its associated characteristic of transparency. Each top management team member will quickly realize that he or she will be faced with an acid test, which will openly reveal to the whole organization the level of 'dream team' with which the company is operating.

CHAPTER 15

ARE YOU READY TO EMBARK ON THIS CHALLENGE?

*B*efore entering into the details of the approach, it is important to remember the goal, the main constituents of the expected return on investment and the role of the executive committee member in achieving the ambition effectively.

A story from Singapore will provide us with a fair set of illustrations of the benefits sought.

The crisis in Asia – an alibi or an excuse?

Preparing a seminar for DHL European station managers, to be held at Cranfield Business School in the UK, I seized the opportunity of a trip to Asia to illustrate this seminar with examples from another part of the world. This approach has always been a powerful means of supporting the idea of competing globally and surviving locally through welcoming any opportunities for internal benchmarking.

CONTINUED ... The crisis in Asia – an alibi or an excuse?

I visited the DHL regional headquarters in Singapore and received very effective support from the area management. This involved top managers ranging from the Asia Pacific chief operating officer to the marketing and sales managers for Singapore Island.

At the end of the 1990s Simon & Schuster was in their opinion one the best local illustrations of the development of a value-added service for the customer that went far beyond safely moving a document from A to B. Without having met the customer, I used this example in the seminar among many others and it was assessed as excellent according to the discussion it generated in class when it compared to an equivalent situation in Germany with a leading information systems company.

With this assessment in the back of my mind a year later, involved in a sales forecasting improvement project again in Asia, I thought that it would be a great idea to dig further into the consequences of this value-added service to analyse what lessons could be drawn in terms of sales forecasting.

My new contact with the local subsidiary began with disappointment. The Singapore manager had been promoted to Beijing, China. This was good news for him, but not for me because I would have to explain the context again to the new man or woman in charge. There was also very sad news: the brilliant marketing manager with whom I had had a very fruitful discussion had died in childbirth. The new people in charge were not as enthusiastic about Simon & Schuster as their colleagues a year previously. Nevertheless, I asked to meet the customer with the account manager. My mindset for this call was the same as an executive committee member.

The business context was not as favourable and the local management explained that Simon & Schuster was not hitting its business target for three reasons:

CONTINUED ... The crisis in Asia – an alibi or an excuse?

---

1 The crisis in Asia had reduced the volume dramatically.
2 The competition was becoming fiercer and fiercer.
3 The decision maker was a former FedEx executive.

That was DHL's view, but I had been expecting to hear:

- The customer's opinion of its own business context.
- An assessment of the relative competitive relevance of the service offered.

Some readers might think that this call sounds like a necessary evil with the presence of an ex–FedEx executive in the company and consequently it is fair to assume that the dice were loaded. It turned out differently. The crop was fabulous and many preconceived ideas were cast aside.

Poor express shipment performance? Not so!

The relevant answer referred to segmentation. The number of express shipments was at least equal to before, even increasing, because it concerned the shipment of samples and not regular deliveries. In crisis times or slowdowns in the economy, not shipping samples with the best care if not even more than during a boom is similar to sharply cutting the advertising budget at the first signal of a downturn in the economy.

Strategic group ranking

So the overall business context does not explain the evolution of DHL's performance. To get an answer about the relative positioning of the different express shipment operators was our next expectation. This materialized immediately.

In one sentence Simon & Schuster's director of operations summarized the respective positioning of the various players:

- UPS: on–and–off, bulk oriented.
- FedEx: eager sales force, but technical constraints.

> ### CONTINUED . . . The crisis in Asia – an alibi or an excuse?
>
> ■ TNT: eager to do business, responsive, publishing sector leader. The sector counts a great deal for them, certainly 50 per cent of their business on the island.
> ■ DHL: not responsive enough, number one in terms of network infrastructure but still dealing with an old rate structure (i.e. has not reduced its prices due to the crisis).

This kind of output is one of the central targets of any call in the field for an executive committee member. To render it even more effective, he (or she) must have in the back of his mind a model to map the relative positions of the players in his strategic group. To do so he can rely on a simple matrix (see Figure 15.1) combining an assessment of:

■ The perceived impact of the supplier's performance on the customer's business model.
■ The possibility of substitution among potential suppliers in this sector.

I saw this matrix for the first time in a meeting with the purchasing manager Europe for Caterpillar, who was explaining to me

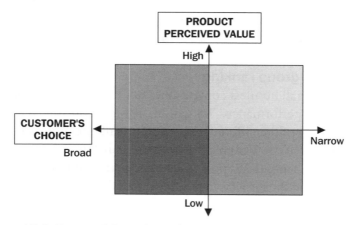

Figure 15.1 Recognizing where the power of negotiation lies

the structure of its suppliers for some specific parts on the back of an envelope.

I am keen on using this matrix. A serious answer along the first dimension is realistic only if one has spent a critical number of hours getting to know the customer to avoid too superficial a perception of the situation. Secondly, the idea of understanding how the customer can shift from one supplier to another is brilliant, because it forces us permanently to keep an eye on the competition with the following two questions in the back of our mind: what kind of value is the competition able to bring to the customer? What resources does it mobilize to do so?

These positioning answers must be understood as the information qualifying the nature of the service performed for a customer. The main interest is to understand how the customer is organizing its portfolio of answers according to its needs. The following example illustrates even more accurately the importance of extracting this ranking and keeping it permanently updated.

Dare to get on the customer's ladder

A purchasing manager for a European facility of a German brand of butterfly valves for cryogenic applications in the gas industry was positioning its current group of suppliers:

- AFE: the technical leader that has mastered the simulation of steel casting.
- AMPO: a very effective international Spanish foundry with 25 per cent of its turnover in US and Canada. As good as AFE but for advanced technical questions does not master the simulation of casting.
- La Cunza: does not play in the same league but outstanding in its limited range of skills and cost competitive, the supplier for cases where the technical dimension is not critical.
- Haut Sambre: not a twenty-first-century foundry, technically OK but depends on one man.

CONTINUED ... Dare to get on the customer's ladder

You can clearly observe two leagues in this portfolio. Then the answer to how to maintain the credit, to thrive and to grow becomes clearer.

The crisis in Asia revisited

Back to Singapore, where we are also able to map the respective players on the above matrix. Some readers may remain sceptical because this information has been given to us by an ex-competitor's executive. There is no doubt that he was playing a transparent game and that we can trust him. I always start with this mindset, ready to believe people whatever their professional career has been, even if it was with competitors.

The reasons are simple:

- First of all, if they try to build their future with their past they won't be able to get very far.
- Secondly, they are usually not very lenient with their previous employer because they know where its system was showing some weaknesses; if they buy the weaknesses they are aware that it might become prejudicial to their own success with their new employer.
- Finally, I am not completely naïve and do not rely on an exclusive source of information. I always welcome any opportunity of cross-checking that everybody is playing a fair information game.

Trying to push further the quality of our output, I asked if we could met the warehouse supervisor, the person in daily contact with DHL's process performance, in order to see if we could extract some additional insightful information.

The director of operations, who was more than friendly, offered for us to meet his subordinate. It was the first time that

CONTINUED ... The crisis in Asia revisited

the account manager had gone so deeply into the company. However, his competitor's colleagues were as unadventurous as him at scouting in the company's organization. We met a very open person who had barely received a call from the different express shipment sales reps. Again, we obtained a positioning of the different players, which was pretty much in line with that of his manager. 'Pretty much' in fact means an area of potential growth that is either under the control of the warehouse supervisor or managed by the operator who subtly occupies the field.

Well aware of the respective positioning of the different players, we could have got rid of any doubt regarding this assessment if we had been able to obtain a quantitative expression of this customer's opinion – for instance, the number of shipments per destination per company over the last week cumulatively for the current month and the situation for the year to date.

Were we pushing the bar a little too high?

In fact we weren't, because everything we could have been interested in was stuck to a pillar next to the supervisor's desk. When we started discussing the respective players' performance, he stood up, went in front of the figures and commented on them in a very professional and transparent way. I cannot promise the reader that this will happen every time I go in the field with a sales rep or an after-sales service person. Nevertheless, the goal is to create the conditions to receive the answers, so the first step is at least to raise the question. Too often sales people don't dare to do this and miss a critical signal.

When we got back to the DHL rep's Alfa Romeo in the car park, we were not the same people as those who had arrived. We had left the blurred stage of account management and new perspectives of development could start to be engineered. The sales rep has to some extent realized how the road that leads from Milan to Maranelo is paved!

No doubt there is something magic worth extracting from an executive committee member's field involvement. This story is an appetizer and my goal is systematically to benefit from such valuable dividends in terms of competitive information and the ability to design one's future with a specific customer. Moreover, this information must be collected, that means that effort must expended; it does not find its own way to the supplier's executive committee room.

The purpose of the next few chapters is therefore to describe under which conditions the involvement of the executive committee member should be prepared and run, thus leading to a recognition of what must be achieved to sustain the momentum.

CHAPTER 16

THE TRIPLE BENEFITS OF THE FIELD CHALLENGE

CLARIFICATION FOR THE EXECUTIVE COMMITTEE OF THE COMPANY'S POSITIONING AND ITS COMPETITIVE ADVANTAGE

A well-documented matrix is a good acid test for recognizing and sharing the company's current challenge. Moreover, this mapping can be achieved with the help of the power of the words used by the customer.

CONSIDERATION GIVEN TO THE OPERATIONAL STAFF IN THE FIELD

Montaigne said: 'To achieve great things one needs to be among people.' Whether we are talking about the new or so-called old economy, the business fundamentals have not changed and Montaigne's observation remains absolutely valid. Consequently, by involving itself in this field approach the company prevents the internal perception of operating at two speeds.

DEMONSTRATED CARE FOR THE CUSTOMER

Senior management involvement also provides a clear message for the customer. Nevertheless, this can lead to disastrous consequences if the executive committee member raises customer expectations that are not supported by subsequent actions. Field involvement demands that the company is aware of two traps and prepares itself accordingly.

The executive committee member can become the hostage of a customer wishing to solve a short-term issue regarding the current business context. An executive committee member in the field is inappropriate for this kind of discussion. It is the responsibility of a senior functional manager. Therefore one must help the customer not confuse the styles.

The customer can consider the sales rep as under observation, so he or she will play the role of sales rep's advocate, which is also not the purpose of the exercise.

The measures to be taken are simple: announce clearly the rules of the game to the customer's staff involved in the process.

CHAPTER 17

THE PREREQUISITES OF THE APPROACH

*T*here are two questions to clarify before launching the process of involving the executive committee in the field:

- Is the executive committee in line with its role?
- How is the company able to operate strategically?

At this stage, it is wise to refresh our minds regarding the executive committee's mission. This is twofold:

- Assure the present.
- Create the future.

If everybody agrees on this generic perspective, the point is to discover if the executive committee is effectively attempting to act on both dimensions and to make its members sensitive to its dominant activity.

By revisiting the agenda for the executive committee, the time allocated to the different topics on the agenda and the time effectively spent on the various subjects, the answers to the above questions will naturally emerge.

By their nature these two sides to the executive committee's mission are usually very well formulated. However, in a recent workshop with two executive committees, I had the opportunity to observe clearly executive committees that were merely limping along.

The first executive committee, which had gone through a turnaround period a couple of quarters before, was very focused on securing its existing business. This was easily understandable. In this executive committee, creating the future was clearly formalized on the agenda, but in reality it was only gossip, with some depth but nothing tangible that could be recognized. Consequently, be aware of a potential strategic breakdown due to the inability to answer the question: 'What comes next in terms of market positioning evolution or creation of a new category?'

The second executive committee was more future creation oriented. The amount of action regarding future creation was impressive and the whole organization was unquestionably committed to this task. Unfortunately, during the workshop its members received some bad news. The company had lost a bid regarding a traditional customer for conventional services. This bad news was regarded as an acid warning that insufficient care was being taken of its current portfolio of customers. Consequently, there is another aspect of a strategic breakdown, due to insufficient care being given to the existing customer base by the customer loyalty management process.

We can conclude that one of these two dimensions is usually neglected. This is a situation that cannot be sustained over a very long period without running the risk of ending up in a strategic cul-de-sac.

CHAPTER 18

THREE SUGGESTIONS FOR EMBARKING ON THIS NEW SET OF TASKS

*T*here are three criteria to address when establishing if the appropriate mindset is present for establishing a new starting point for the executive committee's work.

VISION

An easy way for the company to regularly revisit the business meaning of vision consists of regularly running the competitive advantage acid test (see page 36).

In the example of SPI's Belgian team, we observed that the vision is embodied by a leader who has built a 'dream team'. When vision is mentioned, an organization should be able to answer the traditional question: what are we in this market for? And the answer is to avoid referring to the current product–client combination in order to look at the business in a dynamic way.

Vision describes not only a mobilizing formulation reached by the team leader, but also the active support of the team. For instance, we were able to observe how the two subsidiaries, targeting the same customer group in different but nevertheless culturally and geographically very close countries, expressed their respective understanding of their mission:

- Belgium: information flow management.
- France: long description of the characteristics of the product-client combination.

In the first case the idea of vision was clearly mastered, in the latter we were still in an intermediate stage.

TEAM SPIRIT

The team must possess two characteristics, excellence and creativity.

Excellence is a functional responsibility of each member of the committee. Each member is accountable for their own area of expertise. Consequently, this means that they must not plunder the collective resources of the committee because of the existence of problems in their own area, unless these threaten the foundation of the company's competitive advantage. This implies that the executive committee member concerned must have the skills, the talent, the internal or external access to the resources to get an appropriate resolution to the problems within an appropriate time, while still respecting the corporate economic rules. If not, a solution must be found quickly.

Creativity regarding the future is obtained by joint actions, which can take place outside the current scope of the traditional business operations, for instance:

- *Multiplication of customer contacts*. Beware of falling into the classic trap of key account management where the executive committee member meets the same people as the people in charge who are daily managing the account. The goal is clearly to broaden the scope and not to be there to take orders or firefight.
- *Customer data analysis*, e.g. conduct an assignment with a peer regarding a specific issue to fine tune a cross-fertilization target.

- *Network development opportunities* with innovative partners.
- Increase everyone's *technological savvy*.

In this context the executive committee member is not acting as an expert but as a high-calibre generalist, occupying a position as a member of the government of a corporation and consequently acting to develop the future.

I always suggest going into the field in teams of two and not always with the same colleague. Two is a good size for a team and is manageable for the people you visit. Moreover, they don't wonder if there is a hidden agenda. Furthermore, a joint call allows the process of information sharing to be speeded up by having, in each case, a debrief regarding the observations made. To do this, both team members can independently write on the back of an envelope their impressions and then compare them.

This also prevents the executive committee members from falling into a trap that I have frequently observed in benchmarking. Someone achieves an interesting observation of radically different practices, which they were not expecting to discover. Delighted by their findings, they want to share them with their colleagues in order to improve the company's performance. In 90 per cent of cases the person inevitably gets an answer such as 'You must have misunderstood, that is not possible' or is heard with a sceptical ear, which slows down the speed with which the company reacts.

NO DEAD WOOD, NO FREE RIDERS, NO FIEFDOMS – BUT A DREAM TEAM

Prevarication is a good way to waste time and divert the executive committee's attention from the real issues.

In the decoration solutions distribution chain Heytens (see page 13) in 1999, the executive committee encountered a crisis due to the under-performance of the logistics department and its manager. If one looks at the rate of sales over the same period, there is no comment to make. Performance was not affected by this issue. We could even conclude that this judgement was too severe. However, the answer does not stay the same if we consider the creation of the future. For example, 20 shop openings were planned and only 9 had been achieved. At this stage, by not having taken the appropriate decisions quickly enough, the executive committee had contributed to some extent to the cannibalization of part of the company's future. This was not substantial, but was very clearly identifiable.

A way of summarizing the executive committee's current situation is to map its different members on the matrix in Figure 18.1 along two dimensions. In relation to the company's strategy, are the executive committee members:

1 Effectively working?
2 Effectively agreeing?

This is a very straightforward way of confronting the reality, but it should be done sooner rather than later. One cannot afford to prolong the pain, the price risks are too great.

IS THE RELEVANT INFORMATION AVAILABLE?

Too often at the executive committee level we are dealing with data or information that has become stereotyped. Those who are in charge of collecting this data are only sensitive to information that

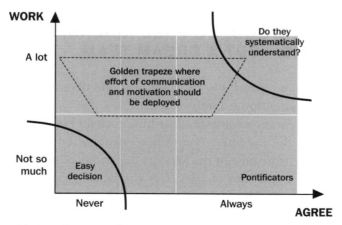

Figure 18.1 Who am I playing with?

matches the conventional patterns with which they have been trained or are used to dealing. Consequently, many organizations run the risk of conformity in thought, which prevents them from recognizing the subtleties of weak signals.

The reason is simple: when these signals materialize, the kind of talent that could draw benefits from them is not present. It is like fishing. When there is a bite, the sales people will be excited about the size of the fish, while for the executive committee member the bite will mean something even more interesting as well. He or she will interpret it as the result of his or her ability to recognize intelligently the opportunities of the situation. If we refer to the Latin definition of intelligence, it is the ability to find links between disassociated facts.

One, two and three

To reinforce the importance of the culture of the signal, I cannot resist drawing an analogy with the example of Aimé Jacquet, the coach of the French soccer team who led them to the title of world champions in 1998. Just before the final against Brazil, having watched hours of videotapes on the Brazilian team, he gave the following advice to striker Zinédine Zidane: 'In the case of a corner kick, position yourself 10 metres in front of the first goalpost.' He didn't add anything, nor did Zidane ask why. When the opportunity occurred, that is what Zidane did. The result was two goals and a decisive contribution to the ultimate result.

In fact Jacquet had recognized that the Brazilian team were a little too self-confident and used to leave their defence fairly loose in that area, counting on their talent and speed of reaction. The executive committee member is there to put his or her 'Zidane' at the appropriate place because he or she can then be confident about the result. Like Aimé Jacquet, executive committee members are not only delighted about scoring a goal, but even more so about the rationale of the process leading to that result. It worked in the past and it keeps on

> ### CONTINUED ... One, two and three
>
> working – what a delightful programme! But this raises a straightforward set of questions: do you have the videotape? Have you watched it again and again to uncover potential clues?
>
> If a Zidane is not available in your team you will have to start a few steps earlier by developing this kind of talent. Nevertheless, when you have such a person this example will still have the same relevance.

Experts in conformity are not interested in weak signals, they are fishing for today and if possible not for small fry, which are assessed by them and the rest of the organization as under-performance. There is another way to read this, due to too much attention being given to the nature of the information. By relying too much on *conformity of information*, we inevitably aim towards a *convergence of practices*, which is the step before customers' *perception of parity*.

The Austrian economist Joseph Schumpeter invented the word 'stochastic'. This describes a situation controlled by random events. Consequently, the challenge is not to master them but to adapt to the situation as smoothly as possible and not to lose the opportunities that these random events might announce. The proposition is simple: reduce the loop of reaction by adapting faster. This is so obvious that one can easily lose touch with this simple managerial practice.

The case of the Austrian ski team is my favourite example to remind my MBA students or my clients of the idea of adapting to unplanned events and how these kind of skills are developed.

> ### They go skiing
>
> In the 'white circus' (the skiing world cup, where competitors are taken from one ski location to another like a circus), if one asks which has been the dominant ski team over the last 50 years one answer comes spontaneously: the Austrian male and

CONTINUED ... They go skiiing

female ski teams. The reason is simple: a natural context plus a marvellous ski club and school system, training a very large number of gifted young boys and girls in their racing specialities, slalom, super giant slalom and downhill.

Since Jean-Claude Killy in Grenoble in 1968, nobody had won in all three disciplines. Based on the natural predis- positions of the talented young skiers, the Austrian special- ization model was producing its cohorts of talented champions such as Franz Klammer and Hermann Maier. Therefore the model should have continued to guarantee Austrian supremacy.

The emergence of a new breed of champions surprised the defenders of the specialization orthodoxy. Skiers from small countries were starting to win. It was not unusual for the Scandinavians, French or Italians (with apologies to those I have omitted) regularly to uncover and develop a challenger who could dominate his or her speciality for a while, such as Alberto Tomba or Luc Alphand. But this new case was different.

These athletes, for instance Kjetil André Aamodt from Norway, were able to win in disciplines that had all but become mutually exclusive. The Austrian trainers wanted to know and benchmark what was done and discover why they were not doing as well. They scrupulously assessed the classical areas of effort from which to build a future champion:

- Physical training.
- Training in the ski speciality.
- Mental training, how to support the pressure of winning.

The results were disappointing: the skills–development techniques were all but the same. They were even a little less systematic and intense than in the Austrian system. Conse- quently, the profile of a champion sounded rather like a gift

---

CONTINUED ... They go skiiing

from God than the result of a reengineered process where something different was deliberately being achieved.

In fact there was only one main difference. In the training plan one can read something called skiing. The purpose of this exercise was somewhat astonishing: the champions simply went skiing, every day, in any condition of wind or temperature and on any type of snow on any kind of slope.

Was this a waste of time? Certainly not. The purpose was simple: not to spoil the runner's adaptive faculties by training them in a context that had become too stereotypical compared to the diversity that daily reality can offer.

Why forget this, when the difference between winning and not, in a context of parity of performance, can be largely due to speed of reaction and adaptation to random events? The speed of adaptation, counted in nano-seconds, can at the end of the slope make a difference of a few hundredths or even tenths of a second, and this is the range where the difference that leads to victory is hidden.

This example clearly illustrates the principle that there is much to lose in terms of progress opportunities if:

- You do not possess a system that allows you systematically to confront the reality of the business context.
- You do not want to adapt accordingly to stay at the forefront of the competition.

A second example, dealing with the management style embodied by Dario Reggazzonni, the former head of Conrad Hotels for Asia Pacific based in Hong Kong, illustrates the required systematic commitment to this managerial approach and its consequences in terms of the process of adjustment. Confront the daily business reality is what Reggazzonni did three times a day, throughout his career.

The Conrad in Hong Kong

This second example is important for its systematic approach and its way of dealing with the freshly collected new observations. Between 8.30 and 9.30 am, after lunch when the patrons were leaving the various restaurants of the hotel and then in the evening when the guests were ready to go out for dinner, the top management team (Dario Reggazzonni, the marketing manager and a couple of other key people) wandered around in the lobby, paying attention to details, comments and gossip. Therefore they were not only listening to but also observing the relevance and effectiveness of the hotel's processes. In order not to be overwhelmed by the flow of observations and information, these information sessions were systematically followed by a management team meeting, in order to implement, without any delay, corrections and improvements on the spot.

These two examples are here to remind us of the subtle nature of the benefits to be extracted from this active confrontation with the business arena – not a virtual confrontation or a remote one, but an unquestionable dive into business reality. To summarize this principle and reinforce its strength as a universal way of behaving, I like to associate it with a famous painting by the Belgian surrealist painter René Magritte, which represents a very realistic brown curved pipe in the middle of the canvas with the title 'Ce n'est pas une pipe'. Magritte claimed that it wasn't a pipe, it was a *representation* of a pipe. It is this kind of nuance that I expect to see governing managers' discernment to avoid disappointing wake-up calls.

Do we have it or do we know where to fish for it?

Are we at the appropriate place to get the relevant information? The rule is to check the relevance of the place where the signals are supposed to be collected. I have gathered many examples in the field, but the most relevant in my opinion belongs to a medical equipment company manufacturing devices for surgery.

There are calls and calls: fooling oneself with good intentions

The observation was simple, the company considered that it had lost contact with its customers. This is a situation that many corporations finally have to confront. Within the executive committee, the sales and marketing manager reminded us that his company had had more than 1200 contacts per year with the physicians' community in a western European country.

A more senior executive, who used to occupy that position more than 10 years ago, raised a surprising question: 'How do you count contacts?'

After the initial confusion, the committee agreed that 300 public relations contacts, although useful, had to be subtracted. They represented the consolidated number of physicians participating in a symposium in Morocco.

Whatever the figures of effective contacts were, a second question followed: 'Where are these contacts taking place?'

The answer to this question was not as spontaneous as the previous one because the goal was not as clear. The purpose was simply to make the sales and marketing people aware that *beyond listening there is observing*. Just like 10 years previously when the former sales person had reminded his colleagues that he was allowed to stay with the physician in the surgery room.

The conclusion is clear: to a certain extent this company had lost its sense of the quality and relevance of the information being collected and then shared. The information quality tracing and tracking system was beeping warning signals! In fact, the supplier had lost the sense of tension that one can feel in these circumstances. What is the relative value of an active listening exercise with a surgeon after surgery in his or her office and of the observations achieved in the surgery room?

The answer is not either/or but *both* are necessary.

Effectively, a superior sector performer needs both. Just listening to the customer, even actively listening, makes a company run the risk of losing contact with its customer's *business reality*. By business reality I mean *the moment when the customer discovers the benefits of his or her collaboration with the supplier*. It is a critical moment where many good or bad things about the relevance and the effectiveness of one's own role can be learned.

The tough benefits of confronting reality – who are you working for?

The new managing director of SPI France decided shortly after taking charge to go with the couriers to confront the business reality, by observing how effectively the deliveries were handled and if there was anything to learn. At the first stop, he jumped out of the van with the courier who said hello in a way that unambiguously showed that he was familiar with the customer's people. He took the voucher envelope out of his bag and gave it to the clerk in front of him and added: 'Here are the Restaurant Tickets for the month of April.' This was in fact the name of the product issued by SPI's competitor Accor.

This happened three times in a row before the managing director decided to react: 'Who you are working for?'

'Sodexho.'

'Do you know the name of our meal voucher product?'

'Yes, sure, Chèque Restaurant.'

'And what did you say when you handed the envelope over to the previous company's clerk?'

'It is a pity, I can never remember!'

We all know that success lies in the fine details, which is why an organization should force itself to confront the reality of its information collection by answering the following two questions:

1   Can we formalize our *listening strategy* and assess it in a contradictory manner?
2   Can we formalize a more advanced step of internalizing the customer in the organization, the *observation strategy* at the point where the added value of the company's products and services is absorbed by the customer?

MASTERING THE OFFER: IS THE EXECUTIVE COMMITTEE GOOD AT PLAYING LEGO?

Mastering the offer is not only knowing what it is, but also being able to handle it with the ability of a child changing a Lego model from a truck into a ship. It means being able to deconstruct and reconstruct the offer with a question in the back of one's mind: is this achievable by the process?

One warning to be considered is that this context can be seen as familiar to many sales people, but one must take care not to run the risk of operating a two-speed company. The attitude of the sales force is to tend to please the customer by swallowing their wishes like a sponge absorbs water. Sales people consider that the process is here to deliver what the customer wants and that the organization will find a way to manage it.

In the foundry industry, I heard a very critical comment from the CEO of AFE (see page 43) at the year 2000 manufacturing managers' convention:

> If we want to keep getting superior performance in this industry, our close relationship with the customer is a waste if we are not able to co-engineer die casting parts that fit perfectly with what our process is the best in class at doing. If we define a product that fits better with the characteristics of our competitor's process, it means that we have not correctly done our job. Consequently, to effectively pretend to play this game, sales people must have a solid technical background and accurately master what the process is able to do.

It does not exist

'It does not exist' was the comment made by a sales person from a leading express shipment company in Israel to its commercial director after a meeting with an unusual prospect for its business.

We met the deputy chief engineer of a food company whose problem was its inability to assess the correct leadtime for fixing a process line. The main reason was due to the inaccuracy of the information provided by its express shipment company.

For instance, the electronic card shipped from Siemens in Germany was supposed to be delivered to Israel within three days. This was not occurring as promised. Examples of poor service were happening so frequently that the customer had run out of patience and this understandably led him to say goodbye to his current operator. Consequently, this person was very annoyed and rather sceptical regarding the ability of express shipment companies to fulfil their promises. Naturally, the sales person started his approach by presenting the characteristics of his offer. Reading out of the company brochure, he specified the terms of the service and how it was supported by a sophisticated system.

At the first opportunity the commercial director stopped him and started addressing the true customer concerns by running with the engineer a functional analysis of what should happen in the case of a food process line breakdown requiring electronic after-sales service parts from abroad. The discussion went as follows: 'When the electronic card reaches our Franz Joseph Strauss Airport hub, we scan the shipping document, then it is available on the desk account manager's computer within X hours. When we notice a shipment that concerns your company, we can therefore...'

To cut a long discussion short, we must mention how attitudes evolved. The deputy chief engineer lent back in his armchair during the first part of the meeting and the fact that he

CONTINUED ... It does not exist

had started to relax could be seen in his face. Then he sped over to his desk and started writing on the commercial director's handwritten flowchart. An hour later, we were shaking hands with the feeling of having achieved a mutually positive result:

- For the deputy chief engineer, his concerns would finally end up in the most appropriate hands.
- For the commercial director, DHL had a potentially very attractive new customer and an emerging ambassador.

I discussed the meeting with the commercial director and suggested to him that before sending a proposal, it would be wise to fax his current understanding of the situation in order to manage the customer's effort (in line with the suggestion on pages 101 and 239) and avoid investing too much if we were scouting the path for FedEx. While we were talking, I noticed that the sales person was walking back with us to the car looking at his shoes. When we arrived at the car, he suddenly turned to his commercial director and said: 'Nissim, what you sold, it does not exist!'

Nissim, a trifle astonished, started explaining to him how to find the various components of his proposal from the different products and services. Little by little the sales person started relaxing. In fact he was right, this proposal did not belong to the conventional list of products. The commercial director had played Lego with the core constituents of the company's offer.

We do not ask every member of the executive committee to play like this commercial director, who had merely fulfilled his functional mission. Nevertheless, having available a prioritized framework of what the corporation is able to offer to the market is a critical step in preparing oneself to confront the business reality.

To achieve this, you need:

■ A validated business model, the critical building blocks of the offer in order to be active in this sector.
■ A prioritized system for recognizing the various layers of performance available for each building block.
■ A clear idea of the potential development that will take place by area.

After going through these three steps, members of the executive committee are ready to confront the unexpected in the field with confidence. I have discovered that mastering the offer with a clear idea of how the company delivers its services or products is something that cannot be taken for granted. It is mandatory to check that a minimum of knowledge regarding the offer is mastered by all members. The point is to give the clearest possible vision. It is why we suggest discussing at the executive committee level a summary of the situation, which could have been formalized by the marketing representative.

Figure 18.2 shows a combination of:

■ The *business system*, the various steps through which the service's added value is put into action.
■ A *prioritized presentation of what is currently available* under each step of the business system. This prevents the vision of the company's offer being limited to a couple of newly minted, advanced services.

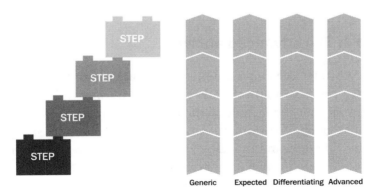

Figure 18.2 The executive committee's box of Lego

Step 1: The generic answer

This is the minimum demanded just to have access to the game. It mainly refers to characteristics of the company's operations: for instance, the density of the network, the number of sales people, the ease of access to the organization and so on. To keep a relevant image, George Fornay, CEO of Sony Computer Entertainment France, calls this stage 'being on the play list', adding 'this does not mean that you will play'.

Step 2: The expected answer

This is the minimum at which the customer will buy. For instance, for meal vouchers the details of the order must arrive in the printing shop 72 hours before delivery.

Step 3: The differentiating answer

To be different does not only mean to be better than the competition, but also to be able to offer answers in areas where the customer is not even expecting them. To do so, the organization must first gauge its ability to enter into intimacy with the customer where, through appropriate observations, it should be able to identify areas for benefit improvement or, more luckily, to conceive of the 'missing benefit'.

Step 4: The advanced answer

Here we enter the cultural dimension of the offer. This means all that we can do to attract and retain the customer. For instance, under this topic we include all the means and processes to keep the promises given to customers. Advanced customer-oriented organizations fine tune and capitalize on this aspect of their relationship with customers through appropriate communication.

The reason for this is simple: it emphasized some unique items that the company knows it will seldom have to use. 'You can bring us back what you want' announced Nordstrom, because it would rarely be obliged to honour this.

I was quoting this example in an executive seminar and a participant from a fast automotive maintenance chain added, 'It is the kind of thing I will never dare say because I cannot offer it.' That raised an obvious question in the audience of: 'Why?' The answer fell like a guillotine: 'Our performance is not strong enough to allow us to communicate in this way.'

This observation brings us back to a topic that I have addressed many times in this book, that process performance governs everything and deeply influences the culture that we need to thrive. In this respect, we can observe a mechanism for rigour testing to reinforce the consciousness of how the company wants to live out its relationship with the customer. The decision to do this and the associated message are hitting two birds with the same stone, the whole organization as well as the customer side.

Château bottled for the staff!

In Marseille in the south of France, there is a medium-sized company manufacturing sun blinds, 100 000 a year with a seasonal peak. This company's customers are small business people, who very often promise miracles to their own customers to get the order and then pass on the level of urgency to the supplier. This company has formulated a very simple promise that was stated by its owner: 'Any order is delivered within two weeks, which is competitively relevant. In the case of a delay of 24 hours the company offers a memorable gift, 48 hours 10 per cent discount on the invoice and the gift, 72 hours 20 per cent and the gift, which is more than realistic!'

However, there was also a subtle and colourful trick. The company's staff can always see the stock of memorable gifts, wooden boxes of Palette, a fine red wine from Aix-en-Provence. What was not given to clients because of under-performance was shared between the staff!

Summary

Embarking on this new approach is not a cosmetic decision nor a process that can be kicked into gear without considering if favourable conditions are well in place. The executive committee as a whole must show clear evidence of commanding a corporate vision with an unparalleled 'dream team' spirit. Executive committee members must rediscover the subtleness and impact of information by playing with it without any filters, equipped with a Lego brick-style corporate business model.

Finally, the executive committee members must be ready to accept that the results of field immersion can be painful because of what they may find out. This represents a clear test that they are plugging themselves into the heart of business reality. Nevertheless one warning: this painful field observation must not become the main goal of the approach. If that happens the painful observation will not be able to be balanced with more numerous positive ones because the company won't still be alive.

 Action point

Structure for executive committee members a Lego brick-style presentation prepared by sales and marketing. This permits the members to get rid of some inhibiting factors; the excuse of not knowing enough about the corporate offer is very often used as a reason to delay involvement. The point of this presentation is its bird's eye view style, not the details of the offer, which is more of a functional responsibility.

CHAPTER 19

READY TO OPERATE – EXECUTIVE COMMITTEE MEMBERS IN THE FIELD

A strategic breakdown with a customer is a situation where the customer suddenly stops its relationship with a supplier. This does not take place by accident. In many circumstances a breakdown of the relationship with a customer is announced by many warning signals from the customer itself.

The key question is: *have the supplier's contact people paid attention to the signals?*

Nothing to report

To tailor an executive programme seminar, we do not achieve anything without substantial investment in understanding the customer's business context and perception of performance. This preparation often brings us in front of our client's customers.

CONTINUED ... **Nothing to report**

The best illustration of this took place in France. The customer's headquarters requested that its subsidiary contact us to organize this preparation. Organizations are transparent, but country managers don't like this kind of demand coming from HQ. That is understandable! Consequently, when asking to meet reference customers one does not choose the worst, and the call is organized with high-calibre sales people. There is nothing wrong with that, it is only natural to try to give one's most favourable image.

The client is a service company, with around 10 000 customers in France and a sales turnover of €400 million. We met a newly acquired client whose turnover with the supplier was €4 million. I made this visit with one of the top three sales people out of a sales force of 100.

We met the general manager in charge of operations in Europe. Usually the sales person dealt with his subordinate, who was not present at the meeting. The visit was used as an opportunity to reinforce the critical mass of relationships at the account level. The client's general manager was an alumnus of our business school, which broke the ice more quickly. The context was consequently more than favourable.

I reminded our guest of the purpose of our visit and the goal of the seminar I was preparing. He reacted positively and explained that it should be easy to observe the supplier's performance because his company had, by chance, just prepared a presentation on the subject.

We went through the presentation, whose overall tenor was very good for the supplier. In summary, the consequences of the very positive perception were demonstrated by the volume, which had quadrupled over the previous 10 quarters.

Back in the car park, I asked the sales person what his conclusions were regarding this meeting. Trained at being positive, but also at never missing an opportunity for improvement, he finished his assessment with suggestions for possible

---

CONTINUED... Nothing to report

electronic data interchange (EDI). Then I started drawing on the window of the car the content of two slides that I found somewhat scary (see Figure 19.1).

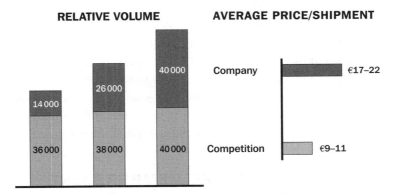

Figure 19.1 Relative performance volume and average price per shipment

I continued with two questions: 'Did you notice that? Why do you think they have prepared a presentation on your performance?'

After exchanging a few ideas, I got to the pricing policy, on which we had received a clear signal. Each time the competitor performed the service the company saved €6–11, so this means that it is under pressure to reconsider its allocation of business. My next question was: 'What do you plan to do?'

The answer was surprising: 'This account has already cost us so much to acquire that we will increase our rate in two months' time because it was agreed in the contract when we signed it.'

The message did not hit the right level of executives to organize an appropriate reaction. The total sales turnover dropped by 20 per cent for the same volume.

Why do I suggest that the executive committee be involved with the sales people? To anticipate the reaction in this kind of situation and create a reference set in terms of managerial attitudes. An executive committee member would have noticed the same threat that I did. But in his case, he would have sped up his company's reaction and also helped to instil a new set of reflexes among his sales people. In this case, I could only count on the reflex of the sales person combined with common sense and analytical skills. We are too limited to modify our routine.

Not paying attention to weak signals is a well-recognized way of reinforcing the customer's power of negotiation. They shoot first. The purpose of the 3Cs (see page 109) is to prevent this situation, by anticipating the economic management of the account. The purpose of seeking weak signals through joint calls is to get the information to achieve effective management of the account and moreover to provide help to the sales force by challenging their discernment.

EXECUTIVE COMMITTEE MEMBERS FINE TUNING THEIR FIELD INVOLVEMENT

At the executive committee level, the amount of time to be invested in joint calls must be agreed. This figure must be the same for everybody. Nobody in the executive committee can be exempted from such a task. I suggest checking that the figure is reached when taking the average figure over a period of three months. There is no rule for what is the most appropriate figure. For instance, in one instance I suggested going twice every month for half a day with the goal of collecting 30 to 50 samples of field perspectives for the next executive committee meeting. At each field session there was a target of three calls twice a month for an executive committee of eight members.

NO CONFUSION ABOUT THE GOAL

Among the *benefits* offered by this approach, we mentioned at the beginning of this part the message given to the customer that *our company cares*. However, the main purpose of the call is to give the customers the possibility of speaking about their own situation. We are not there to sell but to counter the comment that sales people speak too much in 85 per cent of cases and in 50 per cent the customer has not even been able to raise the questions they had in mind. Why is this? Sales people speak to reinforce their own confidence.

Zero

A couple of years ago I was working with an area manager of Somfy, a company based in the Alps who is the world leader in motorization and automation of almost anything in the home, such as roller shutters, sun blinds, curtains, solar protectors, garage doors, screens and so on. The company has a market share ranging between 50 and 100 per cent and substantial experience of managing a portfolio of brands in a business-to-business context. I met one of its medium-sized customers in the south of France for a positioning study of multiple brands in a business-to-business situation.

During the meeting, I was informed that the area manager was due to meet this customer quite soon. I considered this as a good opportunity to measure what amount of time was spent speaking about the customer's concerns rather than about the beauty of the product lines and services. I didn't mention the purpose of my next call and agreed with the customer to call on him again soon.

As promised, I called the customer and asked him about that area. His answer caught me by surprise: 'If that was your question I could have answered it the last time I saw you. It is a simple one, he spoke for the whole meeting, as usual.'

This example is very illustrative of situations where the company intends to develop a consultative selling style of relationship, but this does not work.

Because of his attitude the sales person handled the relationship as a kind of unrecognized 'transactional selling'.

> **The business is fine but the strategic health of the relationship is not as fine as the volume.**

This situation has no consequences as long as you can bet on the sustainability of your product and service leadership. However, when this is challenged, the cost in terms of effort to keep the customer becomes exorbitant, because the appropriate game was not proactively deployed at the account level. The sales person, in this case an area manager, had good intentions and was convinced that he was playing the correct game. He had the illusion that he was doing an appropriate job because he had been able to deliver all the company's selling arguments. This is not enough, and it is even sometimes inappropriate.

LISTENING AND OBSERVING: LAUDABLE GOAL, BUT HAS THE RIGHT CONTEXT BEEN CREATED?

The main purpose of the joint call is to give the customer or prospect the opportunity to speak in a context free of a sales perspective. In order to stick to this goal and give each customer the opportunity to speak, it is not very effective to come and announce that we are here to listen. I suggest meeting the customer with two kinds of document.

First, a *company presentation* to broaden the scope of the potential relationship. Given that a member of the 'government' of the company is present, it is a good idea for the customer to receive directly a reclarified message in terms of direction. Nevertheless, beware of the XBS/Crédit Lyonnais syndrome mentioned on page 159. In my experience five slides are sufficient and enough to support a fruitful introduction.[1]

Secondly, a *promotional presentation*, again with only four or five slides. This is a tool that allows us to add more substantial content to the purpose of the call. For a three- to six-month period, the company must be able to address, in a formalized way, a specific topic that shows one aspect of its progress in its relationship with the customer, and then pass to a new or updated version. The philosophy of this tool is the same as the one suggested for creating a dialogue-based context focused on core skills in business development (see page 99). I like this idea because it forces the organization to confront reality with lucidity and avoid falling asleep in the comfort of an institutionalized customer relationship. One generally has the impression in companies that the new services invented for customers were designed only yesterday. This second presentation, with a more specific customer account goal, is here to anchor the customer's interest.

In this context, I consider that it is more effective to leave a few slides with the customer rather than to hand out a glossy brochure, which does not encompass the same amount of perceived added value.

When conducting the interview:

This also will be the moment to discover the hard way that if speaking is a necessity, hearing is an art.

> **The art is to manage the silences in order to give to customers a real opportunity to talk about themselves.**

A CUSTOMER ACCOUNT CALL: BACK TO THE 3Cs263

Before meeting the customer, the executive committee member and the sales person must prepare for the call. To do this, I suggest referring again to the 3Cs to gain an overall idea of the account or prospect situation quickly.

Context

The account and its business perimeter addressed though four simple questions:

- What business is it in and how is it relatively performing?
- What is the nature of its expectations (needs–wishes–dreams) in our related area of business?
- What is our share of the customer and its evolution?
- Who is the reference competitor and how is it relatively performing?

Coverage

Three main topics must be covered:

- A quick discussion supported by an analysis of the *updated map* of the account will allow you to recognize the position of the person who should be at the meeting taking into account the overall drift of the relationship.
- *Assessing how the purpose of the meeting has been sold to the customer.* This represents an opportunity to check if the goal of the approach is as unambiguous for everybody as was expected when the process was conceived and then launched by the managing director in an information session to the whole organization.
- The number of contacts with the account must be carefully gauged, in order to judge if the *critical mass of relationships* has been reached. By doing so, one will avoid the trap of transactional selling on existing accounts, which leads to confusion. In fact we are trying to apply tools for the consultative selling context while the rest of the time we are in a transactional selling situation, where the availability of the product and the price are the key determinants of the deal. If such a situation occurs, I strongly suggested that you cancel the meeting. The approach is a serious process and if you are not perfectly prepared, it is ridiculous to mobilize the company's resources in this way. I agree that an objection can easily be heard and there is always something to learn from a customer, but this is a functional responsibility not an executive committee one.

Content

The content can be addressed through three simple questions:

- How do we keep track of the customer?
- What was the purpose of the last call?
- Does that demonstrate the existence of a structured marketing approach?

At the end of this discussion, both the executive committee member and the sales person must be sure that this joint call is taking place in the appropriate context. To synthesize this discussion, the executive committee member can show the sales person on the effort matrix that they are currently well positioned in the difference pentagon (see Figure 19.2). This signals that the approach should bring some tangible results.

I would like again to underline at this stage the critical importance for executive committee members of checking if the appropriate conditions have been met. This is a really key dimension of their role, which is directly linked with their ability to mobilize the necessary and sufficient resources.

According to the information that the 3Cs model provides, the executive committee member and the sales person can agree on the most appropriate way to give the customer the opportunity to speak about their concerns.

YOU NEED A BREAK, NOT A PAUSE

The debrief after the meeting is as important as the preparation for it. I am stating the obvious not just for the sake of common sense, but because during my various experiences I have been able to observe

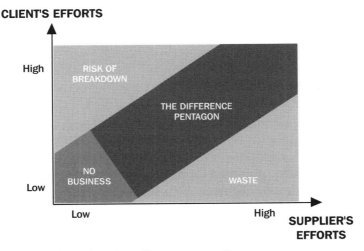

Figure 19.2 Assessing the effort context of an account

that an executive committee member and a sales person are not sensitive to the same elements. Consequently, if this step is skipped just after leaving the customer, you miss a valuable experience of both cross-fertilization and coaching. It shows sales people what executive committee members are sensitive to and little by little they can broaden their scope of attention.

After the interview, the executive committee member and the sales person should revisit the assumptions contained in the 3Cs. The discussion should follow a thread of questions, as below.

Context

The first step concerns the progress achieved in the understanding of customer intimacy:

- How should we formalize the added value of this joint call?

Then the critical point:

- Have we heard anything regarding the customer's concern? This is the kind of weak signal that we want. It can represent an opportunity to resegment a customer base, to invent a new category and then to naturally become its leader by getting the invention bonus.

Customer satisfaction

Reevaluating the relevance of the promises made to the customer must follow two steps:

- Revisiting the nature and formulation of customer expectations.
- Assessing the consultative selling achieved.

Consequently, we can judge the quality of our process-based marketing and the necessary conditions for reinforcing customer loyalty.

Coverage

A twofold question:

- How do we assess the critical mass of relationships?
- Is the deployment plan appropriate?

Can we observe signals of organic growth?

Three types of questions: maintenance, competition and preparing the future:

- How do we assess the effectiveness of our maintenance policy? This is the consequence of the above questions, which must be answered first in order to address the other growth opportunity areas consistently.
- How do we assess the attitude of the leading competitor on this account?
- Can the person met become one of our ambassadors to engineer a large-scale selling plan in his or her industry sector?

Content

The purpose is to assess how we can play with the various marketing tools:

- What do we plan to do in order to sustain the momentum we have launched with the joint call approach?
- What permanent relationship marketing plan should consequently be articulated?

In the context of a prospective customer, the debriefing should be slightly different and reflect three main concerns.

Context
Progressing on the factual side of the relationship:

- Characteristics of the account.
- Customer style, loyalty, practicality, versatility.
- Drawing up the map of the account.
- Can an industry-wide concern be identified?

Access

Considering the level of the competition's effectiveness:

- How do we formulate the prospect's expectations?
- How do we assess the effectiveness of the competitor according to our own system of performance assessment? The purpose of the call was to get the opportunity to make the customer recognize that we are different. The idea 'better than' is a second-league strategic tool.

Customer's efforts

Preparing the next step with insight:

- Can we get evidence of a real interest in our company? Have we left an opportunity for the customer to make an effort for our company?
- How should we organize our dialogue-based marketing approach?

This discussion between the sales person and the executive committee member must be documented in a way that reflects the main points of the debrief.

This document is critical. On the next joint call, the sales person can start by showing what was done the previous time. So the sales person should have copies of his or her experiences of joint calls with executive committee members. Each time, before going into the field with any sales person, the executive committee member must make him communicate what was done with his or her colleagues.

Information collected by the executive committee members during sales session should be distributed before the next executive committee meeting, which will have on its agenda the lessons from this field involvement.

Summary

When we are in front of the customer we cannot afford to miss the weak or even the all but inaudible signals that he or she delivers. These messages represent the acid test of the effectiveness of the whole approach. This does not occur spontaneously, it is a question of preparation. The preparation is critical to assess how well informed and with which appropriate conclusions the sales person is approaching the account or the prospect. A milestone in preparation is agreeing together on the most suitable means of inviting the customer for an open discussion regarding the future of his or her own company. Getting in front of the customer is one thing, but taking the time to give meaning to the clues collected is another issue that cannot be skipped.

Finally, one must also not forget that any information collection process must be followed by communication to reinforce the added value. Raising customer expectations and then leaving them lying around represents a free gift to the competition to catch up.

 ## Action point

Test in your own office with a sales person your ability to apply the 3Cs before a real call in order to get a fair assessment of the current relationship situation with this account. Then develop and compare with the other executive committee members the best demonstrated practices available to offer customers the opportunity to speak about themselves.

Note

1   Leonardo da Vinci said to François 1er during his stay in Amboisse, a city along the Loire river in France, that the art is to chop not to add.

....

CHAPTER 20

THE CROP – LESSONS OF FIELD INVOLVEMENT

T he purpose of assessing the relevance of this approach through the results of its pilot phase is not to demonstrate the effectiveness of the executive committee's commitment in the field in terms of business and sales development, but to observe what managerial lessons can be drawn.

Two crucial questions must be discussed:

■ How can the momentum in the approach be sustained?
■ What kind of ratios must be used to measure the managerial effectiveness of the process?

PROCESS–PEOPLE–PATRONS: THE RESPECTIVE BENEFITS

In the initial pilot phase of the example I used above (see page 213), the involvement of the executive committee was unambiguously observed. Each month between 30 to 50 customer contacts were counted according to the size of the subsidiary concerned. One of the goals was to bring back to the heart of the executive committee's discussion a new flavour in terms of business reality. A twofold benefit was targeted:

- Allow the executive committee members to confront business reality with rejuvenated lucidity.
- Boost accordingly the speed of reaction of the whole organization.

From this angle the expected goals were reached.

Moreover, this approach aims at three benefits, which I call the 3Cs for the 3Ps (see Table 20.1).

Table 20.1 The benefits of field involvement

Areas of attention	Benefit observed
Process	Control
People	Consideration
Patrons	Care

The purpose is not to unroll a catalogue of specific results, which I consider in their detailed formulation as the company's property, but to mention some illustrations of typical observed output.

Process effectiveness *control*

The head of information systems was astonished to discover the quality of the information support with which the sales people used to knock at the door of the customer. The observation was clear. There was a confusion between database information and appropriate field support. The vast majority of sales people were not operating with support that gave them a clear enough bird's eye view of the account situation.

In one case, he could count up to 17 pages of customer database printout. If this situation is multiplied by five calls a day, it is legitimate to wonder on what the sales person is spending his or her time. Still being practical, one can easily conclude that the sales person is operating in a sub-optimized context from an account information point of view. Consequently, the result of this field experience led the information systems manager immediately to implement an audit with the sales manager to provide the sales force with a systematic one-page account synthesis.

Consideration given to *people* in the field

In the Czech Republic, the idea of top management in the field was considered as a form of help to solve the tough commercial challenges. The initial reaction was a feeling of frustration, which was quickly settled when the sales people discovered that there is something more fruitful to draw from a relationship with senior management than help on a short-term commercial issue. Such issues must be addressed with the top functional manager. In contrast, this half day spent in the field was like a breath of fresh air to rediscover and even sometimes to discover the company from a radically different perspective. Sharing information and vision motivates.

Unusual *care* for *patrons*

Companies never disguised their surprise at meeting unusual senior managers from the supplier or partner organization. A comment often heard was: 'Our own top management would be well inspired to imitate you.'

Nevertheless, one of the critical purposes of this technique is to try to replicate the positive lessons of Nissim's case in the Middle East (page 225) or Muriel's case in Belgium (page 154): *catching the relevant weak signals.*

The crop of weak market signals in the example I am discussing was up to expectations, which in my opinion was not a surprise when one considered the quality of the team in each subsidiary's executive committee. They had the skills presented earlier to recognize the opportunities. However, there is a more critical issue than being tipped off about a potential new business.

TRANSFORMING WEAK SIGNALS INTO SUCCESSFUL MARKET ATTACK PLANS

Believing that weak signals will automatically be exploited is not a serious proposition and is even a little naïve. The business context is very seldom a transactional one, where the availability of the product or service itself engenders the business. The context must be created. The crop from the field involvement has provided a bunch of relevant and even insightful information, which when fine tuned will show where to deploy more accurately the company's efforts. Nevertheless, it is no more than that. So what are the conditions under which this potential business can be transformed into a tangible perspective and the opportunity grasped?

Achieving this is critical because it will bring a valuable side effect: sustaining the momentum of top management's commitment to organic growth, In my opinion this result, from a strategic and organizational point of view, is more important than additional business, which realistically it is wise to consider as merely a consequence of a well-oiled process.

Mobilizing the executive committee is something that is only possible with the personal involvement of the head of the executive committee. This is a rather hackneyed management recipe. I like an observation from Henry Mintzberg[1] regarding this option:

> Surely no technique ever received more top management support than strategic planning did in its heyday. Strategic planning itself has discouraged the commitment of top management and has tended to create the very climates its proponents have found so uncongenial to its practice.

Consequently one must pay attention that support for organic growth does not lead to a situation where the vast majority of the executive committee members end up bored with it or only superficially in favour. That pitfall in mind, I nevertheless suggest that getting the involvement of the executive committee leader is a necessary condition. For the sufficient condition, one must identify a means that will *prevent* the pressure of daily business from being a justification for no longer being so deeply involved in the process. If so, one after the other, the executive committee members will submit a legitimate reason for being excused.

To prevent the trap of routine, feedback on the executive committee's commitment must be clearly addressed in the agenda of, for instance, one out of three executive committee meetings to give clear signals to the members of the importance of collective involvement. This form of transparency is in line with what we have suggested under the message 'no dead wood' (see page 215). It concerns the collective responsibility that each individual member bears and contributes to the creation of the company's future.

The analysis should cover the volume and origin of the contribution:

- Total number of contacts.
- Number of contacts per executive committee member.
- The results per topic of investigation (process, people, patrons) per executive committee member.
- Total number of weak market signals.
- Number of weak market signals per executive committee member.

This is a key to how substantial the crop was. Therefore, it can represent for the executive committee member a first good reason to keep pursuing the experience. Nevertheless, there is a further very straightforward question.

Who should carry out the analysis?

In my experience, great benefit can be gained from conducting the analysis as a team, especially if it satisfies two characteristics:

- Decompartmentalized.
- Showing sustainability.

Regarding the latter, the marketing department is the most suitable body to play this role. Moreover, a permanent record must be kept and managed somewhere in the company. So half of the task is achieved and for the remaining part, I suggest as the most appropriate and fairest system for involving each executive committee member in the analysis on a rotating basis. This will bring an additional layer of commitment.

From an organizational point of view, we have satisfied the need to design and carefully implement an effective information-sharing mechanism. Then comes the expected acid test.

WAS IT WORTH IT?

The spontaneous suggestion would be to measure the additional business brought to the company through this means. I do not want to appear blasé, but this information will merely be interesting; important, but not empowering and generating a subtle pride in the achievement. At the executive committee level the result can be observed from many angles:

- *Step 1*. The executive committee has taken into account John le Carré's warning that 'an office is a dangerous place from which to see the world'. This is already good news if the number is substantial enough, i.e. 30–50 contacts each month.
- *Step 2*. However, these observations were only data. To transform them into information, some value must be added and they must be sorted along the three areas of investigation: process, people and patrons. This gives us three ratios and the possibility of observing a dominant characteristic and suggestions for aiming at a better-balanced situation. The goal of the approach is to uncover business development opportunities. So one should be able to observe in the patrons category a substantial number of these; if not, the direction of future efforts is clear.
- *Step 3*. A large number of weak market signals is a good thing, but weak market signals are not real business. Thus it is at this stage that the operational contribution of the executive committee reaches its end. The executive committee is therefore legitimately entitled to observe a tangible result to keep justifying its own efforts.

Now it is the turn of the whole organization to transform the weak market signals successfully into business. This process will qualify the relative attractiveness of converting a weak market signal into a selling theme. In Chapter 11 addressing the implementation of cross-fertilization, for instance, the various steps have already been addressed. So the problem is not to come back on the various characteristics of the different steps, but to warn the reader again of some subtle traps identified in this pilot phase and hidden in your own organization.

In a pilot phase, does a weak signal mean new business? The answer is yes, but the challenge is more ambitious. How can this conversion be incorporated in the list of corporate best demonstrated practices? If one wants this type of result one must measure it with the appropriate unit.

From market signal converted into a selling theme: how many days, weeks or months to launch a market attack plan?

Now the focus is on execution, not on the result of this execution. What kind of tempo must be found for this execution style?

During my MBA some 20 years ago, I read Peters and Waterman's *In Search of Excellence* and I was amazed by a very straightforward observation: 'Why does Exxon find more gas than its competition?... because they drill more.[2] Hamel and Prahalad[3] reinforced this point with a similar and complementary idea: avoid the 'gold-plated arrow'. In fact the speed of execution gives an organization the possibility of going into bat more often, as one says in cricket. However, in achieving this market attack plan the organization can reveal unexpected and critical problems.

Jean-Frédéric, I am furious

Assessing the result of the pilot projects of the executive committee field commitment, I was discussing with Ann-Mary, the marketing manager of SPI Belgium, a file of executive committee member field reports. Two cases drew my attention and in particular one relating an experience with franchisees in a food distribution chain. After initial success the

CONTINUED ... Jean-Frédéric, I am furious

potential cross-fertilization opportunity did not materialize to the expected degree.

Discussing this case with Ann-Mary, I came to the conclusion that between marketing and sales the coordination and support of various aspects of the action in this specific sales context were not well oiled. I tried to share this impression with the marketing manager, but she objected that there was currently so much potential business that it was difficult to address the challenge with the optimum care on every occasion. Two observations can be made:

- First of all, in this context it is absolutely objective, but what are the criteria to introduce in order to allocate priorities?
- Secondly, the excuse of so much potential business sounded like a waste or at least a sub-optimization of the leads, bearing in mind that no tree has ever reached the sky. However, what about the business in 2002 or 2003? What improved skills would then be applicable to show a distinctive and meaningful approach? Consequently, it is in this period of minor competitive tensions that the means to prepare for the toughest competitive time must be launched.

In this respect, the sales common sense of Sudha,[4] one of SAP's top sales performers, supports the point of analysing the context positively. While commenting on reluctant chief information officers and disappearing technology budgets, SAP's star saleswoman added, 'Why not take advantage of this slow period to endure the eight or ten months (and inevitable disruption) it takes to install new software?'

The same week as this discussion, I shared over the phone my impressions of insufficient effectiveness in the interaction between marketing and sales with Pierre, the area managing director. A few weeks later, I met the marketing manager

CONTINUED ... Jean-Frédéric, I am furious

again. Then I noticed that the discussion was not as friendly and fruitful as usual, as if enthusiasm had waned. I wanted to know what was happening, I insisted and finally I got this answer: 'Jean-Frédéric, I am very annoyed because you said to Pierre that things are not working so well between the sales manager and me.'

Tough times ahead! I did know that her boss had shared my impressions with her. That was not at all an issue, so I was ready to enter into a very appropriate explanation when Ann-Mary put her finger on the painful zone on her own: 'When you said to Pierre that things are not working very well with the sales manager, it is wrong and it has annoyed me because the communication between sales and marketing is excellent.'

Here was the key:

This was inhibiting a substantial share of the potential results in this new category of sales. Business development demands added value from both departments, not only through communica-

> **There was confusion between communication and demonstrated skills to achieve combined operations together.**

tion but also in terms of joint work achieved together in order to optimize the identified opportunity. Ann-Mary had opened the door and I kept investigating very simple topics such as:

- How much time did you spend with the sales manager to assess what had to be done and the reason for the initial success?
- How did you interpret it in terms of market opportunity?

Faced with a weak signal, my recommendation is straight-forward: hurry up slowly. Have a discussion regarding the meaning of the signal or the unexpected market success.

HURRY UP SLOWLY – SKIPPING THE STEP BUT NOT MISSING THE TRAP

In the food distribution franchisees case (see page 251), the sales manager, proud of the success of his team and in line with the cultural pattern of the corporation – fast – immediately implemented a phone campaign to get appointments for his sales force with potential customers among the distribution chain members.

This was not wrong, but unfortunately it was insufficient. Out of 50 calls, 41 remained unexploited, which meant that we were not able to qualify the interest of these prospects in the newly tailored offer. Five, including the initial success, were transformed into contracts and four were already with the competition. But what about 80 per cent of the potential targets? To some extent this sounds like a waste.

Instead of trying to achieve additional sales quickly, the sales manager should have corralled the company's strengths, talents and common sense to decide what is the most appropriate option to play:

■ Sell.
■ Be bought.

This case gave a good live demonstration that the selling option was not the optimal one. You might object that it is easy to judge afterwards. That is not what I am doing. I am only taking the view that the potential sales context, which governs the choice of the best or the least risky option, had not been carefully enough judged, if at all.

A clearly identified network or market segment, the 50 franchisees of a food distribution chain, had been recognized. So we were in the context of a large virtual account with a common denominator: the franchisee contract. Consequently, if one of the franchisee club members, facing a motivational problem or desiring social benefits for his or her staff, has a positive experience of designing and implementing a solution engineered by a specific supplier or a even a partner, it represents a missed opportunity not to test with the other members of the network if the solution wouldn't receive the same positive echo. So far, I have described an approach that sales managers can legitimately consider their own.

In fact, it is exactly at this point where the divergence of approaches takes place. Here I want a break to carefully assess if I can uncover a jewel. To take a break does not mean that I am not obsessed with speed, but it does means that the step has been fully and carefully covered in order to take the most appropriate decision that I shall believe in and consequently feel comfortable enough to make the best effort. The reason for the active break is simple because the obsession always remains the same: beating the break-even point (BEP) or, better, the break-even delay (BED) of these new accounts.

Individually each account represents a specific BED, but one that could be leveraged through a network sales operation. So the 'break' is the manifestation of a real change in approach. If one cannot observe this active break and its set of conclusions while auditing the approach, then one is still in the limbo stage of improving one's own best practices. There is no action but only talk and good cosmetics.

This break is in fact proof of strategic management at the account level, in the field. It means speed of reaction to take the appropriate decision in front of a business situation. By suggesting this kind of approach I am bringing back to the surface concepts addressed 150 years ago by General von Molkte, not the famous son who was at Verdun and the Somme during World War I but the father. He was the one who organized the Prussian army, creating what was at the time an unparalleled military organization that dominated Europe and over 10 years beat the Austrian and French armies successively. In his doctrine he noticed some very relevant attitudes and behaviours for the strategist. He wrote, 'The strategist possesses not only the ability to understand the meaning of events without being influenced by popular opinion, attitudinal changes or one's own prejudices but also the ability to make quick decisions and to take action without being intimidated by a potential danger.'

This definition is brilliant, but even more so when you know which rank von Molkte held when he outlined this strategic talent: lieutenant. Consequently, there is a big confusion to avoid between creating a strategy, Matsushita's 'big things and little things' (see page 46), and acting with a strategic mind at the appropriate level of operations. Borrowing this example from the military world, we get an analogy that forces us to question if corporations are strategic enough in their attitudes and behaviours at the operation level. And we can apply the questioning encompassed in the analogy to the above-mentioned sales manager. Finally, one must also notice how he insisted both on the importance of analysis and on simultaneously getting rid of paralysis by the analysis. An army cannot limp along, neither can a company.

Back to the reality of the case, it would have been wise to gauge if a network sale could have been articulated. The test was simple. This network of franchisees has some formal or informal means of expression, discussion or communication between the franchisees and certainly an opinion leader. So the challenge should have been to transform this happy accident, an unplanned sale, into a potential solution for all the members of the network.

We will all agree that the solution already implemented has specific value. As we said on page 75, the solution will be perceived as being a fixer or a necessary evil. However, recognizing it and assessing its impact on the customer process represents prerequisites for organizing effective leverage.

Then comes the challenge of sharing this assessment of the perceived impact with the validated opinion leader. From doing so I expect a threefold dividend:

- Formulating the appropriate selling theme.
- Confirming one's own opinion regarding the attractiveness of the target of the current solution offered.
- Assessment of the existence of an appropriate ambassador with whom to decide what kind of forum is needed to promote the solution.

In this specific case, I consider that the waste was very limited because the success of the conventional approach was so modest, 80 per cent of potential customers remaining untapped. Therefore there was no risk of redundancy in trying to implement a network sales approach for this potential large virtual account.

TAKING A BREAK WITHOUT DRAWING RELEVANT CONCLUSIONS IS ALSO MERELY COSMETIC

Analysing the same file of field reports, I found a similar case with certified professional accountancy (CPA) practices, which could be used as ambassadors to promote the service voucher solution among their customers in a specific industry sector. In this case, the target companies were small and medium-sized civil engineering companies.

A bug in the network sale

This also started with an initial success with one specific CPA practice, developing voucher solutions for civil engineering companies as a means of substitution for the *prime de panier*, a fringe benefit given by civil engineering companies to employees working on projects outside company premises and more than 5km from the company (the word *panier* means 'basket' in French and refers to the basket in which a worker used to bring a meal to work). The benefit is a set amount paid with salary and subject to social taxes. By substituting a meal voucher for the *prime de panier* the company can save on its employment costs and the employee has more choice over how to spend the voucher.

The natural reaction was to launch a sales development plan with this specific target, which resembles a typical case of network sales. The plan is obvious: leverage the sales effort. There are many CPA practices and they are certainly members of associations, which might provide the appropriate leverage in order to reach the whole group in one or a few shots.

SPI met one of the CPA associations in order to explore what kind of leverage opportunity they might represent. With the active support of one of its members, we had our first success. An agreement was reached and a forum opportunity identified. The forum chosen to promote the solution was a

---

CONTINUED ... A bug in the network sale

specific exhibition for CPA practices addressing a very large variety of needs, ranging from office equipment consumables to expertise panels regarding the new French regulation concerning a 35-hour working week. Moreover a specific activity was launched for new CPAs to make them aware of this opportunity.

The results were pretty mild and the subsidiary sales manager became rather suspicious about the effectiveness of this so-called network sale. The country manager, with more choice comments, expressed to me his own reservations about the approach. He tried to explain that the demanding business context was not appropriate for organic growth, which he considered to be more suited for a mediocre business context.

The network sale is not a panacea, but is an important step to check if the conditions are in place to make the desired results achievable. This situation is therefore an attempt to deal with large virtual accounts through a network sale. LVA is an account-acquisition technique, leveraging the cost of acquisition of these accounts through a network, which can receive the positive influence of an ambassador. So the correct question is at which level we can observe the consolidation effect of the network.

Consequently, did the attempt to operate at the level of an association of CPA practices represent the appropriate place? Unfortunately, I think not. First of all, the targeted network of small and medium-sized civil engineering companies is observable at the level of each individual CPA practice. This is because each CPA practice manages between a few and a substantial number of accounts of this nature. Then, in this context who is the ambassador? The CPA himself or herself? Not exactly, rather one of the clerks of the CPA practice, managing this kind of account on a daily basis, represents the ambassador level. The true ambassadorship is at the level of these clerks because they have contact with the decision makers, the entrepreneurs. They are able to achieve a win–win manoeuvre:

- Proposing savings as well as motivation solutions for the customer.
- Reinforcing the CPA's positioning as a fixer.

Then the issue becomes one of segmentation or optimization at the CPA practice: how to select the CPA practices where this specific sales pitch will have the most impact. This will certainly not be among the big five; a medium-sized practice with more than one premises where a clerk network can be implemented is certainly the place to run the pilot phase of this sales development project.

A sales pitch is one thing. Then comes the next question: what kind of context can we create around this event when the name of the company is Sodexho and means catering? Creativity is always welcome to show that one is able to combine outstanding sale professionalism with a memorable style. Consequently, these clerks will perceive the sales person as someone worth having a discussion with. In contrast – and this is very illustrative of the risk I want to prevent – with the misjudged target, the CPA association was wondering how it could charge intermediary fees to Sodexho.

In the previous two cases the mistakes were apparently of minor importance and sound like mere details. In fact they are not when one considers the consequences: the potential for new business was lost. Consequently, a network sale is a moon shot that relies on strict professionalism, where a deviation of a fraction of a minute can make the project disappear into the outer space of no business.

> With a mistaken analysis the tempo of the relationship always echoes costs, while if you hit the bull's-eye, the tempo of the relationship takes quickly value as its rhythm.

An organization involved in this kind of change needs a skilful coach in order to avoid falling back into the old habits of sub-optimization. The mission of this coach is to transform this pilot technique into reflexes, remembering Harvey McKay's recommendation about perfect training (see page 53). In these two cases the marketing manager and the sales manager could have sat together with a coach who would have made them well aware of the techniques that will control and boost implementation.

Then transforming talent into a best demonstrated managerial practice with the skill of choosing appropriately between implementing a conventional sales approach or engineering a sales network will become a quantitative matter, an issue of a critical mass of projects.

Once the sales technique is mastered the number of attempts is on our side, and so is the business. The next question concerns the strategic heath of the company. Has a competitive advantage been built? The answer is definitely yes. The combination of perfect training with the sense of multiplying the attempts put the organization beyond the competition's view range with a stealthy style. The competition will only be able to observe recurrent successes too late and the reasons for them will remain blurred, which allows time to keep pushing things even further. In summary, your organization hits your competitors where they ain't!

It is in this area that the correct assessment of the executive committee members' contribution should take place. The question is:

> What has the organization done with the weak signals that I collected in the field?

One indicator must count:

Getting this indictor and beating it is the rationale that con-firms to the executive committee member that his or her own active investment in this

> How many weeks does it take to be back in the field with a thoughtfully designed solution for a specific target?

field activity with sales people in front of the customer does create real value for the whole corporation. Consequently, it is worth continuing.

Summary

Spending time in front of the customer not discussing current operational issues is a first step for this limited but demanding and rejuvenated involvement of executive committee members. A corporation with the ambition to play a leading role in its industry sector cannot satisfy itself with such an approach because it quickly runs the risk of becoming cosmetic. To enter in the heart of changing things with the goal to stabilize the competitive balance to one's own advantage, the data collected must receive added value and become relevant information in order to show the best direction.

The company's filters will demonstrate their value due to the combination of their effectiveness and speed of process. By doing so, they can avoid weak market signals merely remaining good ideas. They offer the opportunity for them to become meaningful market attack plans for re-evaluated customer accounts.

This process is very simple, but that does not mean that it is easy. In fact, the simplicity appeals to the level of perseverance that an organization can demonstrate in implementing new attitudes, behaviours and methods before they become a full part of the company's culture or one of the company's best demonstrated practices. So sustaining the momentum is a serious issue that cannot be summarized in the relevance or the beauty of a new management concept. Each executive committee member must sincerely appropriate this approach and makes it theirs. The key is straightforward: it is an issue of return on investment that answers this question:

Mobilizing the energy of executive committee members in the field for this specific information-collection task is a very ambitious activity. At no point in this process can the executive committee members become diverted by a feeling that they can spend their time in a better way.

> **Through this field involvement what amount of value am I creating for my corporation on top of my current functional contribution?**

To prevent this, the company cannot merely rely on the benefits that the executive committee members will draw from this approach in improving the subtle accuracy of their own understanding of the mechanism to prolong and rejuvenate the company's success through their functional contribution. This in fact represents the icing on the cake, which constitutes a twofold information challenge.

First, a *formal report* must be regularly drawn up and presented to the executive committee covering the impact of the approach on the areas of *process* effectiveness *control, consideration* given to sales *people* and specific *care* demonstrated to *patrons.*

Secondly, the executive committee members must discover the added value of their respective contribution through *two items of quantitative information*:

■ The *number of new market attack plans* drawn up for specific refocused targets. The additional sales turnover is a sales and marketing question: the executive committee provides the opportunity in terms of raw material, but the turnover itself is the result of talent in functional effectiveness, which by definition must be considered as available in the company. If not, one comes back to the 'dead wood' syndrome (see page 215).

■ The *speed of execution of designing the market attack plans (expressed in weeks).* A weak market signal is a jewel that is irrelevant unless it is used within the appropriate window of opportunity. Consequently, how many weeks does the company process take to transform the weak signals into a market attack plan with an attractive selling theme? Assessing this systematically for each plan is a first goal, but then thinking of beating this figure becomes a challenge that keeps the momentum going, makes this process a concern of the whole organization and renders the company stealthier from a competitive point of view.

 Action point

Decide on the tempo of the executive committee members' field involvement – for instance half a day twice a month – in order to be unambiguous about the characteristics of the challenge once the committee has agreed.

Gain the support of an external or internal coach (a consultant or board member familiar with this kind of issue) in order to create the appropriate fit between the departments concerned. In the two cases mentioned in this chapter the focus was on the marketing–sales hinge, but this is an *ad hoc* case where the goal is to create a reference set for the combined operations required to transform weak signals into market attack plans with a permanent concern for speed of execution. By doing so, we nurture the right conditions to result in a motivating quantitative track record.

Notes

1. Henry Mintzberg (1994) 'The fall and rise of strategic planning', *Harvard Business Review*, January–February.
2. Tom Peters and Robert Waterman (1982) *In Search of Excellence*, Harper & Row, New York, p. 209.
3. Gary Hamel and CK Prahalad (1991) 'Corporate imagination and expeditionary marketing', *Harvard Business Review*, July–August.
4. Sudha (full name?) (2001) 'Blind optimism, thick skin and a cell phone', *Fortune*, August 27.

BUILDING BRIDGES THROUGH ORGANIC GROWTH

The organic growth process is now reaching a formal stage where the supplier can benefit from a comprehensive presentation of the

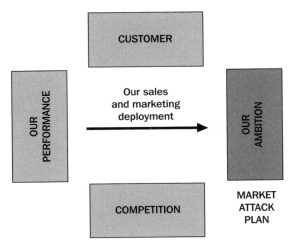

Figure 20.1 Structure of a customer account presentation, Step 3

growth opportunities associated with a specific account action plan. In this context, the sales deployment proposal is the result of a consistent process that has paid attention to avoiding the trap of insufficient consideration of both the customer and competitive context. In my experience the presence of such a formal, well-documented and articulated presentation represents a form of corporate goodwill that expresses the ability of a company to embrace tomorrow clearly from a secure today.

In summary, one clear goal in management is to build bridges between a corporation's various areas of interaction. That is why I am so keen to suggest playing with Lego bricks, especially in the executive committee meeting room.

AFTERWORD: KILLING YOUR AMBASSADOR

A WORD FROM THE AUTHOR

Very early in the process of writing this book, I wondered how to leave the reader with something other than just a summary of its contents and some good advice about solid resolutions to do things differently and more effectively. I was in search of a bridge between a book that represents a pause in the way we live and address our challenges, not exclusively business ones, and kicking us again into gear for the day-to-day business arena.

My central idea was to give the last word to somebody whom I know pretty well, with whom I share a common view and a similar committed style in addressing business challenges. It was not only difficult to choose a good team member or members but also to be sure to pass him or her the pen in the appropriate context. This is like in rugby: somebody must have done the preparatory job which, once the ball is passed, will open the way to scoring a try.

So the challenge was to create these appropriate conditions and this brings us back to Asia at the beginning of the year 2000. During a trip I met a colleague and friend of mine from Goizueta Business

School at Emory University in Atlanta: Nancy Roth Remington, the executive director of international programs. My business school has MBA exchange programmes with this school and, among many subjects, I shared with her the nature of my consulting projects and the academic research topics in which I was involved. At the mention of the express shipment industry and DHL, Nancy started telling me a great story about her experience with this sector. All the ingredients of a live case about organic growth seemed to be gathered. At that time, there wasn't any idea of using this case in the conclusion of my book, which was still in a limbo stage. Nancy spontaneously promised that she would write a draft of this story and after some e-mail correspondence across the ocean, sharing observations and comments, she ended up with a good case about the collapse of a customer relationship that we agreed to call 'Killing your ambassador'.

The title summarized a true story regarding the waste of a growth opportunity by a service supplier. Over the course of the story, the early-stage ambassador has such a painful experience of the customer relationship that she moves from active enthusiasm for her service supplier to a strict resegmentation of her needs between the potential players, all having become necessary evils. More damaging still, the customer takes charge of the business relationship, relegating the service supplier involved, DHL, to 'just-in-case' status and consequently freezing its potential for organic growth.

This case was used confidentially in our respective programmes and I mentioned a couple of times to some of my contacts in DHL that I had something interesting to share with them coming from Atlanta, but I had not yet found an opportunity to do this. It was not the kind of document you could send by mail with a brief message that I would be happy to get their observations and comments, thank you. Then the book was in its final stages and I was discussing with Nancy the merits of putting 'Killing your ambassador' at the end of the book as an appendix when I thought that something different and to some extent more daring could be done with it.

This case clearly regards a failure by DHL to manage a growth opportunity with a US account, which could have represented substantial potential for organic growth. So I decided to organize the final wrapping up of my concept of organic growth around this story to remind readers that business life is not a walk in the park, however brilliant or attractive the management concept can be. It represents an opportunity to show an unconventional way of stressing the strong determination required of managers if they want to achieve change.

To keep the rugby analogy, the preparatory job was well done in this case but it is still unquestionably bad news. Consequently, it is not the kind of ball one would be happy to receive with the mission of taking it beyond the line. I needed to find a manager who would agree to comment on this failure. To give even more impact to the comment, only a senior manager of DHL would be appropriate. I decided to propose this challenge to someone who would be able to read the case with the same business perspective as mine and who would nevertheless be able to welcome such a 'hot ball' for its value in terms of managerial lessons for his own organization. Consequently he could envision how to convert it into a superb try.

This was the challenge that I proposed to Peter Davies, chief operating officer of DHL International Americas, because a top-class manager knows how to welcome both good and bad news and in my opinion Peter was a leading light to join me in this challenge. The reader may wonder why I didn't offer the opportunity to DHL's CEO. The reason is simple: DHL stakeholding had changed and at that time I didn't know the new German CEO. However, when Peter Davies agreed to comment on the case, he did so with the full agreement of his CEO. Consequently, this afterword expresses the transparent opinion of the whole organization through the words of one of its senior managers.

Peter Davies' observations bring us back in the heart of daily business reality, with a case that he agreed to comment on because as a top executive he knows that in service, failure is painful but should never be a drama and above all business is about comebacks. In a world where the certainty of failure exists side by side with the imperative to deliver top-quality service, we know that companies will be judged by their ability to recover from broken promises. So this story and comments are the fitting conclusion for a how-to book on organic growth. They remind us to confront tough situations head-on and without excuses, for only by continually rejuvenating process excellence can we also maintain strong customer relationships. When the debris of failed customer relationships clouds collective memory, the potential for organic growth is dead. That is what Nancy and Peter help me to deliver as my final message.

Nevertheless one question remains: how can this 'hot ball' be converted into a try? Am I a dreamer to propose such a challenge? No, because Peter's epilogue after the case pulls us back to the business reality that is waiting for us if we have the courage not to stop our efforts midstream. This case demanded a lot of work from Peter and Nancy and I would like to take the opportunity to thank them warmly again. Once he had written his comments for the conclusion, Peter could have been overtaken by the feeling that this was only of marginal use and asked whether it was really worth anything other than transparency.

In fact there was a hidden jewel behind this effort: an unusual management system was being developed. As COO, Peter manages a team of country managers from the Arctic circle to Patagonia. He was ready to express openly how a senior manager, representing his own leading company, knows how to receive bad news and outline what lessons to draw and how to react accordingly. By doing so he is writing a memo to his own organization, but there is something more to do if one wants to stay at the leading edge of one's industry sector. Here is the jewel: by submitting himself to this exercise Peter created the conditions to launch a powerful acid test to assess how aligned the rest of his team was with his beliefs.

The educational trick is simple: Peter, as COO, has commented on the failure and written a 2000-word comment. So what would we read in a 2000-word comment by the different country managers? Something in line with 5, 50 or 75 per cent or even exceeding what the boss wrote on this subject? The jewel is a free gift for internal benchmarking, dealing with the company's true collective and individual aptitude to address the most critical subjects and consequently avoiding the trap of confusing understanding and assimilating, which means in our business context living with it in a way that is competitively effective for the company.

In this afterword we can see again the importance of formalization to create an active reference that supports internal contradictions and permanent assessment of one's own perceived performance.

KILLING YOUR AMBASSADOR: THE CUSTOMER'S EXPERIENCE
by Nancy Roth Remington, Executive Director of International Programs, Goizueta Business School, Emory University, Atlanta

Perseverance pays off

Dave Durham was a pest. He was unfailingly nice but he phoned repeatedly. He wanted our office to consider DHL for our international air shipments, but in 1994 this was not a pressing issue. We had relatively few shipments and, besides, we didn't need DHL.

UPS had moved its worldwide headquarters to Atlanta several years before, joining CNN and The Coca-Cola Company as Atlanta's best-known international trademarks. The strong relationship between the company and my employer – a major US business school – was underscored in several ways: frequent corporate speakers in classes (including the chairman); significant corporate donations; and a fine corporate discount for package delivery. Daily pickups and a drop box conveniently placed in the school further encouraged us to choose UPS. The ties had become so strong that a senior faculty member once wrote an internal memo admonishing staff and faculty to 'remember our friends' after he saw a Federal Express truck parked outside our building. What would a senior UPS executive think if he came to the school as a visiting lecturer and saw a competitor's truck picking up a package?

Modest needs, strong loyalty
However, Dave had done his homework: the business school's International Programs Office had a modest but growing need for air shipments. Our portfolio of international programmes was the largest in a nationally ranked university whose annual budget was over $1 billion and whose president had embraced 'international-

ism' as a key goal. Furthermore, the university was one of the largest employers in Atlanta's second largest county, and the school's endowment stood at $5 billion.

When Dave first contacted us early in the 1994–5 academic year, our volume of international shipping was small by DHL standards: about 100–150 envelopes and small packages per year. The university, however, included units much larger than the business school, which represents only about 10 per cent of faculty and students. Since each school maintains its own records for dealing with suppliers, it was nearly impossible for anyone to determine the total volume of air shipments within the university. Nonetheless, Dave was frank in explaining that he had targeted our office as the 'doorway' to the university. The business school's volume of international air deliveries had tripled between 1993 and 1995 and he had clearly determined that the university couldn't be far behind.

Can friendship keep pace with demand?

Until 1995, using UPS was easy. We almost never called our account executive, and nothing seemed to go wrong. Nevertheless, our needs were changing. My office spearheaded the business school's commitment to growing both the size of our international student population and the variety and scope of international programming – all within the context of a personalized, student-friendly community. The reason: to differentiate ourselves in a crowded MBA marketplace.

Just when we needed advice on how to handle shipments into uncharted territory, trouble struck. First, I spent days on the phone trying to rescue a package from a Mexico City warehouse where *siesta* time threatened to derail an important recruiting event hosted by the president of Coca-Cola Mexico and two of my deans. Several months later an incoming German student reported that his visa had been delivered to a nearby hamburger shop and he was only able to retrieve the grease-spattered UPS letter pack after tracing the shop's owner to a mountain vacation cabin.

The next chaotic situation involved a box of gifts that our Executive MBA class planned to give to Austrian managers. Although we had repeatedly asked our UPS representative how to label the package to ensure on-time delivery, Austrian customs refused to release the box. Repeated pleas from the US and from our Austrian colleagues with ties to the government came to nothing. Three weeks after the event was over, the box was returned to Atlanta.

The summer gave us a reprieve from problems until a freak snowstorm in Barcelona brought all deliveries to a halt. Germany, Austria, Spain – surely UPS should know how to deal with delivery to countries in western Europe? What would happen in Asia, the former Soviet Union and east central Europe, where significant numbers of acceptance packages carrying visas would soon be sent?

Persistent, attentive, then a fine solution

Two months after the Spanish snowstorm I stared at over 200 lb of printed materials that needed to be in Seoul in two weeks. I had stalled on sending the boxes because I had no idea of how to get a guarantee of delivery. With the materials bound for a programme sponsored by the US Ambassador to South Korea, who was the former president of my university and the person who had urged our participation, landing empty handed was not an option. I had just about decided to bring everything with me as overweight baggage when Dave left another message.

Dave had pursued us for over a year. I had never allowed him to visit and he had been a little pushy, but maybe that meant he would answer our calls if we needed him. Possibly his persistence was a sign that DHL cared about its customers and would not let our packages end up in a Frankfurt hamburger shop or stuck in Austrian customs. I returned Dave's call.

I regaled him with my delivery tales of horror, my way of letting him know that I needed help but would not tolerate sloppiness; the price in personal and institutional credibility was too high. Dave listened patiently, and when I was finished he asked a number of specific questions: type of volume of international air mailings, seasonality of mailings, potential for mailings from other business school offices. In less than 15 minutes he had proposed a solution involving a service I had never heard of and which was less expensive than I could have dreamed. The packages were picked up the following day and materialized in my Seoul hotel room exactly as promised.

DHL raises its flag in UPS land

After the Seoul success, my assistant confirmed prices for individual letters and small packages, which constituted the bulk of our normal needs. The rates were competitive with those offered by UPS and FedEx. Good rates, flawless service to an uncommon location, and a knowledgeable and attentive account representative: I was sold. I immediately shifted all of the international shipping in my office to DHL and informed the school's director of finance and administration of what I was doing. UPS was new to international shipping and we couldn't count on international delivery, I explained. DHL could get the job done. I would continue to ship all domestic packages through UPS but would send international deliveries by DHL.

An ambassador is born

I immediately sought to convince our Admissions Office (which handled a higher volume of international air deliveries) to switch to DHL as well. Next, my assistant arranged for Dave to meet an administrator in a key central university office. We were happy to help Dave find his way around the university. He had come through for us, and a good discovery was worth sharing.

Flawless delivery, as promised

For the next year, deliveries fulfilled all expectations. We shipped small packages and visas to Tashkent, Bucharest, Beijing, Frankfurt and many places in between – all without a hitch. I happily signed the invoices; by using DHL, international shipping had ceased to be a problem. In fact, DHL was giving us a competitive advantage in our quest to offer better service to international students and colleagues whose opinions mattered. To reinforce the wisdom of switching from the home-town company to DHL – and to respond to potential questions from our Finance and Administration Office – I periodically asked international applicants (especially those in 'tricky' locations like Romania, Nigeria, or Kazakhstan) which air delivery company was the most reliable in their home countries. Invariably, the answer was DHL.

The only request that Dave could not fulfil was placing a drop box outside our building next to the ones supplied by UPS and FedEx. He said that our initial volume didn't justify the drop box and the daily pick-ups; this meant that a secretary in each department would need to call in advance for pick-ups. He said he would try to have a drop box installed as soon as our volume increased.

An internal champion shares the good news

I couldn't force faculty and staff loyal to UPS to change their air delivery habits, but I lost no opportunity to suggest using DHL whenever the issue of reliable international delivery arose. Why not share a good idea and reap the credit for helping others to solve their problems? In the meantime UPS trucks continued to pick up regularly from their drop box, but I heard no further comments about my switch from the school's administration – or received any sales calls from our UPS rep.

Dave visited my assistant and other university offices annually and supplied us with up-to-date materials. He never called me after we had made the switch, but then we experienced no problems, so I was happy not to get involved. The drop box was not mentioned; perhaps next year.

Who's minding the store?

In fact it was only the delivery of packages that was flawless. DHL's billing department was certainly not as responsive, personable or effective as Dave. After convincing the Admissions Office to use DHL we found that for nearly a year my assistant's name appeared on all business school bills, regardless of where the request originated. Repeated calls to DHL's billing department by secretaries in Admissions and by my assistant had no effect. For a year we endured extra work, delays in bill payment, calls from the billing department and frustration all around. My assistant and I regarded DHL's blockheaded billing clerks as an aberration; once the problem was solved, it quickly receded from our minds.

Sticker shock!

A little over a year after the successful Seoul shipment of 1996, I was signing a DHL invoice when I noticed that the charges for letter pack delivery had risen considerably, by about 15–18 per cent! My assistant recalled getting a new DHL rate book, but Dave had not called to warn us about a major price increase that was three to four times the rate of inflation. My assistant phoned him to ask if there wasn't some mistake in billing. Dave reported that the increase was correct and resulted from two factors: regular annual increases and lower than anticipated volume at the business school.

When Dave and I first spoke I had explained when and how our delivery needs spiked at different, and predictable, times of the year. But when I called to discuss the large price increase Dave said that the company could not take our seasonality fully into account, since it looked at deliveries on a quarter-by-quarter basis. Our volume in some quarters was fine, but not in others. Further confounding DHL's accounting system, our high seasons sometimes spanned two DHL quarters. Dave said he was sorry, he hoped our volume would rise and our per-package price could fall. So did we, to lower overall costs and to get a drop box.

The big price increase caused a problem in my budget, which had been calculated on the old rates with a normal price increase. Even though I had to scramble to allocate additional funds to shipping midway through our fiscal year I didn't feel too annoyed: on-time delivery and a lack of complaints from our colleagues and future students were worth juggling budget dollars for.

A fateful phone call

My assistant director enjoyed working with Dave and we all felt well served. Then, in autumn 1998, Dave left a series of voicemail messages. As we played phone tag for several days, Dave's repeated voice messages, like his initial persistence, made me wonder if a new and better rate, or some other nice offer, was in the offing. The reason was different: Dave wanted to tell me personally that he'd received a promotion. He was pleased with the recognition but was sorry he would be moved before his replacement had arrived in Atlanta. He gave me the name of our new account representative and assured me that we would be in the hands of a good man. He planned to update the new rep on the history of our account and he knew we'd continue to receive good service. I wished Dave well, felt a pang of regret and informed my assistant of the change.

Old friends are not soon forgotten

Shortly afterwards I made a startling discovery. While reading the application of a newly accepted student from China I saw a UPS delivery receipt nestled in the front of the file. What had happened? The year before I'd spent hours discussing with the Admissions Office why we needed to switch to DHL: DHL offered reliability and speed of delivery to tricky locations at nearly the same price as UPS. What had caused the change? Everyone was mystified. A few weeks later I encountered a large stack of UPS letter packs containing acceptance materials all bound for international locations. Who had changed the Admissions Office policy of using trusted DHL to deliver all international materials?

The admissions director quickly uncovered the reason. Her overworked assistant who was in charge of mailings found it difficult to use DHL. Without a drop box, the assistant needed to call ahead for pickups. Many days, the labelling and stuffing of acceptance packets was a just-in-time operation. The convenient UPS drop box gave her one-stop, no-hassle access to domestic and international air delivery. Why did she need to call DHL, she wanted to know. The admissions director also wondered if using DHL was really so important. The office's big workload would soon get heavier. Would DHL really give the Admissions Office an advantage, she asked, that was worth pressuring an overwhelmed staff member to take on more work?

Who's making the decisions?

My assistant director shared my enthusiasm for DHL and she had arranged for Dave to meet one or two members of the Admissions Office staff. During the two years Dave managed our account he had visited annually, always seeing the same people in Admissions.

But during this period he had not realized that his key contact was not the person responsible for the actual mailing of acceptance materials. Over this same period the volume of international air shipments shifted to the Admissions Office, as we consolidated operations to save money and increase effectiveness. By summer 1998, about 75 per cent of all international air shipments were originating from Admissions, as opposed to 50–60 per cent only two years before. Dave may also have missed this change.

I hadn't checked on the mailing habits of the Admissions Office for two years; I had thought there was no need. Although the Admissions staff had agreed to switch to DHL – and indeed had for a period of time – clearly their behaviour had changed. Incentives for the mail handlers to use DHL were not so obvious: the hoped-for drop box had never materialized, old billing problems might still darken their memories, the price had increased significantly over that of UPS, and using DHL required extra time and thought. Besides, the credibility of non-professional staff was not on the line if a visa arrived in Beijing in fifteen days instead of five. By mid-January 1999 I found only UPS receipts in the folders of accepted students, and I still hadn't decided whether to ask the admissions director to push her employee to return to DHL, the more difficult and more expensive option.

Trust is a high-stakes game

In January 1999 one of the school's most senior professors, a man whose demand for quality was well known, was preparing to lead the school's acclaimed Beijing seminar for a second time. The planning team, of which I was a part, discussed the professor's desire to bring distinctive gifts for the senior US, European and Chinese executives who would interact with our group, as well as for distinguished colleagues in our Chinese partner school. Unlike the previous year, when he'd divided all the gifts among the 40-odd students participating in the programme, he wanted to ship the gifts to China. What were our options? DHL could handle the transport, I confidently affirmed.

The line-up of speakers included impressive US multinational companies: Ford, The Coca-Cola Company and Motorola. All had ties with our school and through them we intended to extend the school's international reputation. In the first year of the programme the gift supplier had experienced problems – it was 'the factory's fault' – with the result that the order was delivered to the professor's home the night before he flew to China. He wanted no repeat experience of lugging extra boxes across the Pacific. Insuring the production and delivery of this year's more expensive and heavier gifts was my responsibility. Normally this would have been a job for my assistant, but because the project involved China I wanted to handle the job. 'I trust your judgement,' he said when we agreed on what was needed. Given the previous year's problems, the responsibility felt like a heavy weight. At least I knew I could count on DHL.

I asked my assistant to call our new DHL account rep and ask loads of questions about what we should do; the memory of the stranded box of gifts in Austria quickly came to mind. At my insistence she called twice, outlined our needs and came back with explicit directions on what to do. I realized that the new rep would probably think we were over-anxious clients. No matter, this was a very important job as far as I was concerned. The boxes were picked up as promised and I turned my attention to my own lengthy business trip to Asia that was only two weeks away.

Late-night wake-up call

'Hello Nancy, this in Xin. Sorry to call late on a Sunday night, but in Beijing it's Monday morning and the boxes aren't here. The programme has started, the DHL employees are totally unhelpful, and Professor Thomas is getting pretty upset.'

Oh my God! In a moment disaster flashed through my mind: my reputation going down the drain, nearly 100 disappointed US and Chinese students, excuses being offered to the heads of Motorola, Coca-Cola and other top companies – 'We're sorry, it's a delivery problem...' Everyone would look like a fool, especially our school. This was my fault, I had insisted that DHL could deliver the gifts.

I plied Xin with questions and tried to keep a calm voice. Xin was the ideal troubleshooter. Born and brought up in Beijing, he'd attended the prestigious school serving as the host for our seminar, he'd spent four years in a top Chinese state-owned enterprise making successful deals and besting his counterparts – and he was one of our students. If Xin had a hard time getting the DHL employees to cooperate, we were in big trouble.

Client scrambles, shipment stays put

For the next hour I kept both home phone lines open, one for Beijing, the other for the DHL all-night hotline, where I hoped to determine what had really happened to our packages.

The DHL customer service rep quickly determined that the packages had arrived five days before in Beijing. 'Then why aren't they in my professor's hotel room?' I pleaded. 'Where are they?' As I gave the package trace numbers to Xin my son came in and wanted to know if I'd be off the phone at any time soon; it was nearly 11 pm and he wanted to say goodnight. 'Sorry,' I whispered, 'I know it's late but I have an emergency in Beijing.' He rolled his eyes. Usually emergencies were confined to the office. Why had this one overtaken me at home late on a Sunday night?

Xin returned to the open line with Beijing. The DHL office confirmed that the packages had not been released from customs. 'Why?' I asked.

'The office won't tell me,' Xin replied. 'It doesn't know. The only way to learn something is for me to go in person to the customs office at the airport. I'll call you back when it's morning in Atlanta.'

The DHL all-night operator had been holding the line during my discussion with Xin.

'My assistant in Beijing says the packages are in customs. What does your system tell you?'

'I don't know, the computer only shows when the packages arrived in Beijing.'

'But it's five days later, why are they being held?'

'Sorry, our computer software doesn't have a field for that kind of information.'

'Then please call Beijing. It's morning there, ask what the problem is.'

The all-night operator put me on hold and a little later came back on the line. 'I'm sorry,' he said. 'The number in our book doesn't seem to be correct. I can't get anyone on the phone in Beijing, it just keeps ringing.'

'But how is this possible? No one in the office at 10.30 am in Beijing, no one telling us that the materials were sitting undelivered in Beijing?'

'Sorry, we don't do that.'

'What do you mean? If someone ships large boxes by air express to China, you can assume the materials are needed on an urgent basis. How can DHL not deliver on time and then *not* tell us why the shipment is being held up?'

There was no answer to the last question, just another 'sorry'. The all-night operator told me he would go off duty early the following morning and would be sure to send a summary of our conversation to the Atlanta office. I should call the same hotline number at 9 am, the Atlanta office would answer and it would have a full record of what had happened.

I hung up the phone and went to look at my son, who was asleep. My frustration quickly turned to anger. DHL had created a mess that not only threatened to make my school and me personally look incompetent, it had also ruined the end of the weekend for my family. Clearly, our packages had not been a priority for DHL. That was about to change.

The customer asserts control

Monday morning came quickly, and with it another call from Xin in Beijing. He had gone to the DHL office and also to the airport customs holding area, accompanied by a low-level DHL employee. There, the DHL employee had stayed silent and Xin had done all of the talking.

'Why weren't the packages released?' I asked.

'The customs official gave me many reasons,' he replied. First, the items should not have been sent to an individual at a hotel, they should have been sent to the school where the seminar was being held. Next, the value of each box exceeded the limit set for a single individual to receive. And finally, the lading documents should have been typed. So much for the advice of our Atlanta DHL rep!

Time was not on our side

We had 38 hours to get our boxes out of customs. At exactly 9 am I called the DHL hotline and was immediately put through to the Atlanta office. The customer service manager was pleasant, he had the information from my previous night's call, so I recounted the new information from Xin, including the fact that the Beijing DHL personnel had been less than helpful. The Atlanta customer service manager said that he would immediately send a fax to the China office to 'give it a push'. I asked that he also involve DHL headquarters, since our problem was extremely time sensitive. Beijing employees might not know Atlanta but they would surely pay attention to a message from headquarters or possibly a well-known US city like New York.

Before getting off the phone, the manager gave me his direct number and I repeated my request that another DHL office send a message that would help to build pressure on the Chinese employees. I asked that he call me with the names of DHL managers who would write to Beijing so I could pass this information on to Xin for his Tuesday morning visit to the Beijing DHL office.

Angst and the waiting game

By 5 pm I had heard nothing from the customer service manager so I called him. Yes, he'd sent an e-mail and a fax to China. 'What about involving other DHL offices in the US?' I asked. No answer. 'But this was a critical part of the strategy for getting the Chinese to pay attention to us,' I pleaded. 'If headquarters or another big US office gets involved, we'll have a much better chance that our packages will get out. Please call me before you go off duty so I can tell our man in China who else has written.'

The DHL manager listened politely, gave no sign of what he might do, and we ended the conversation.

At 7 pm I had heard nothing so I called the Atlanta customer service manager's direct line. Ringing, no answer, no answering machine. I called the all-night operator. The operator was professional, took the tracking numbers, noted that the packages were in Beijing – and could add no new information. There was no record of my conversations during the day with the Atlanta office –

'Our system can't add that,' she explained – so I started to make dinner and stewed.

Xin called at 8 pm on Monday night (8 am in Beijing on Tuesday morning, 29 hours to go). The Beijing DHL employees were suddenly acting very differently to before and one of the senior people was preparing to accompany Xin to the airport customs office instead of sending back the low-level clerk. Throughout the day I waited nervously. Everything was in the hands of my student Xin, the now better-motivated Chinese DHL employees – and Chinese customs.

Twelve hours later I called Xin at his Beijing hotel, but instead was connected with the senior professor. He sounded remarkably calm. Nothing new had happened. 'We're certainly not paying for this, even if we get the packages,' the professor affirmed. I wholeheartedly agreed. But the issue of the moment wasn't payment, it was getting our packages. We had exactly five hours to retrieve the boxes from Beijing customs.

New angle, new ally

Xin took over the phone. There was a new possibility, he explained. The manager of the Beijing hotel had proposed a plan to re-address the boxes and assign them to the hotel. The manager would write a letter to customs explaining that the professor to whom the packages were addressed was indeed a guest at the hotel and was leading a large group of US graduate students. The boxes contained gifts, not items to be resold at a profit. The manager was convinced that this tactic would work, reported Xin.

I authorized Xin to give gifts to helpful customs officials and the hotel manager and asked him to call me as soon as something happened. An hour or so later I called the all-night customer service line. I gave the tracking numbers and was told that the packages had arrived seven days before in Beijing: the same old information.

We got them!

Just before 11 pm Atlanta time, two hours ahead of our deadline, I received a joyful call. The packages had been released. I was exhilarated – and furious with DHL. Why had the packages been released? No one was really sure. Why hadn't they been released earlier? No answer to that either. Another explanation for the hold-up emerged: on releasing the packages Beijing customs explained that the mailing labels should have been typed. Why was our DHL rep in Atlanta so clueless about what needed to be done to deliver packages to the capital of the largest country in the world?

The only bright spot had been dealing with the courteous and efficient DHL all-night customer service representatives. In fact, just after Xin had called to say that he'd received the packages, a DHL operator called to report the same good news. It was midnight. 'Forgive me for calling so late,' she started, 'but I knew you really wanted to have this information, and you said you'd be up pretty late waiting to hear.' I did appreciate the follow-through – the only real follow-through we'd experienced since learning three days before that the packages had not arrived.

Atlanta post mortem: I won't pay!

Back in Atlanta my first visit was to the senior professor in charge of the Beijing seminar. The programme had been a great success. DHL, on the other hand... 'We aren't paying them a penny,' he declared. I immediately agreed and then apologized for the mishap; it was my suggestion to use DHL that had set the entire sorry operation in motion. 'That's OK,' he replied. 'We're just not paying.'

As soon as I left the office I got worked up again: this problem had been completely avoidable. DHL's own staff in China did not move until I spun into action and called US managers to help us. Even worse, judging from the information I'd gleaned in Beijing, the company knew that its Beijing office was a big problem, full of pride at being the first China office and unwilling to accept or act on advice. To compound the human problems, the company's own package-tracking system couldn't update the status or location of our packages. And the customs agents, insisting on typed labels – our account rep had been useless in advising us on what to do. We certainly were not going to pay.

Payment refused, the real discussion begins

When the bill came, I wrote 'Refuse payment' in a thick black marker across the top and sent it back. I also held up payment of all other DHL bills until the issues surrounding the China packages were resolved. Sure enough, the account rep called shortly after I had mailed my response to his bill. This was his first call to me since his arrival in Atlanta six months earlier.

I explained the entire saga: breakdowns in the DHL system, the lack of interest among Chinese DHL employees, changing stories of Chinese customs agents, nights spent with DHL operators and days with the Atlanta-based customer service rep, and the fact that nothing had happened until I had become personally involved pushing as many people as I could to get our packages released.

It's the customer who's at fault

The rep's first reaction was startling: 'Why didn't you call me?'

'It was a Sunday night,' I patiently explained. 'I don't expect you to give me your home number. The all-night DHL rep told me to check in with the Atlanta office at 9 am and that's what I did.' But I didn't say what I was thinking: 'It was your lack of knowledge that got us into this mess.'

'Why hadn't I called him on Monday?' he persisted. I repeated my story of following what the DHL reps had told me to do. The rep listened patiently to the long China saga and then wanted to make one point very clear: if only I had contacted him first thing on Monday, he could have spared me time and frustration and solved the problem quickly.

I pointed out that DHL's system never alerted him that an irate Atlanta customer had spent two nights with operators and much of one day with the Atlanta customer service manager. We had relied on his information and this had not been accurate. Finally, in a fit of frustration I asked him: 'Why would we have believed that you could help us when you and your system had created the problem to start with?'

The account rep's concern was clear: he wanted us to agree that he could have helped soften our problem. My interest was entirely different: I wanted acknowledgement that DHL would take responsibility for the problem, cancel our payment and apologize. Then I felt we could move on.

After 15 minutes of conversation the rep said he was sure he could get us some kind of discount, but he wasn't sure he could rescind the entire bill.

'Fine, then I'll take my business elsewhere,' I said.

'You're kidding! You don't mean you'll stop using us just because of this?'

'Yes, I will. If I can't trust that you're going to be honourable and stand behind your business, then I can't work with you.'

'I'd support cancelling the charge,' the rep said. 'But I don't know if the higher-ups would. Really, if you'd have called me I could have helped.'

'We've been through that,' I said in a bit of a rude tone. 'Nothing happened until my student called me and I got involved. My student and I both pushed DHL into action while DHL's own computer system couldn't even tell us what had happened to our packages and never even alerted you, the account rep.'

'I agree that half of the fault was the DHL system but the other half was China.'

'China' – I was thoroughly exasperated now – 'China in this case starts with the DHL China office which became involved only because my MBA student was able to get information and personally went to the Chinese customs office twice. If your superiors want to think about this, I'll wait to hear from you.'

The conversation ended. I was limp with frustration and anger. Shortly afterwards I learned that the bill would be cancelled. There was no sense of relief or elation, no sense of victory. When the China problem had arisen, my only thought was of cancelling the specific charge. Now the account rep's reaction was leading me to wonder if we should continue using DHL at all.

Epilogue

I had stalled in making a decision on how and if to tell the Admissions Office to use DHL again for its tricky international shipping. During this time, the admissions assistant had continued to use UPS and the convenient drop box. By avoiding the subject of which shipper the Admissions Office should use I had, in fact, moved towards a decision: a three-pronged approach to fulfilling the business school's shipping needs: UPS for USA ground and air packages, FedEx for general international shipments and DHL for the tricky locations.

The new strategy would mean more work for us, since we wouldn't have the convenience of one-stop servicing from a single company, but the prospect of speaking with the DHL account rep was so unpleasant that I preferred to expend more energy than to deal with him; my assistant readily agreed.

Two months after the bill had been voided and the rep's visit was receding from memory, I boarded a flight to New York City. While buckling myself into the seat I recognized a familiar profile, a former international student who had graduated five years earlier. 'What takes you to New York?' I asked.

'I work for IBM, big consulting job.'

'Been with them a long time?' I followed up.

'No, just a year and a half. I was with UPS before.'

The temptation was too great, the China delivery débâcle too close to resist probing a little. 'Tell me,' I asked, after we had spent a little time catching up. 'If you had to ship a package to, say, Bucharest, what company would you use?'

He lowered his voice: 'DHL, for sure.'

THE COMPANY RESPONDS
by Peter Davies, Chief Operating Officer, International Americas, DHL Worldwide Express

In early June 2001 I was sharing breakfast in Brussels with Jean-Frédéric Mognetti, whom I have known for many years. Indeed, he ran some strategic management learning projects for me in Europe. He was giving me some feedback about this book *Organic Growth*, when he proposed that I add a final practical touch to its conclusion. His objective was to bring the reader back into daily business reality with its subtle pitfalls and traps, after having demonstrated the benefits of a rejuvenated way to approach internal growth. His idea sounded attractive.

The concept addressed in the book was familiar to me, considering that I was among Jean-Frédéric's early supporters in this project. Consequently I was happy when he asked me to review the conclusion of the case study called 'Killing your ambassador', given my experience in the express shipment industry.

Pride and feeling of effectiveness

My satisfaction was confirmed when I read the first few pages of this Atlanta-based story. Without any doubt, I think that the reader will easily share with me DHL International's pride in this specific account conquest.

So a first observation can be made both in terms of 'good news for growth' and a warning for customer portfolio management: sales people's tenacity pays. Impregnable customer positions do not exist. This rule is applicable to DHL's own portfolio of customers too.

Caught on the wrong foot...

It did not require a profound understanding to realize the appropriate emotions and therefore I could not let pass the quintessence of this reported experience with us. Consequently, I am happy to comment about this case study. Odd that I should say 'happy' given that we let one of our customers down so terribly. But for a corporation, this does also represent the fact that senior management, in any company, cannot be satisfied with their own marketing reports. On average, in DHL our customer satisfaction indexes are good – even very good – but one does not succeed in the long term through average figures. Excellence is rooted in detail.

No manager likes unhappy customers, but my role as chief operating officer is not only to accept the situation but also to move ahead, recognizing this case as a highly valuable set of warnings. Beyond the loss of growth opportunities with this specific account, it represents, if one takes the time to fairly gauge it, key milestones of a checklist for securing tomorrow's growth.

Realistically

Before addressing this sharp reminder of complacency, meaning whether we created the appropriate conditions for an effective growth context, I would like to consider a prerequisite regarding any service organization that mobilizes a sophisticated combination of technology and human involvement.

Failure is an inherent dimension of service managed on a daily basis. While we permanently design rigorous standards of process control and try to prevent customer disintegration, realistically and statistically failure will happen, which does not represent at all a justification of its occurrence. To illustrate this risk that any service organization runs structurally, I suggest that you bear in mind – as I repeat so often to my teams – a message of Tom Peters in his seminar 'Beyond close to customer': 'If you do not want to have any problem with your customers, there is only one way... do not open...' So, if we are in this game, proactive vigilance becomes the motive.

For sustainable growth, avoid confusion!

The context of this account conquest merits a few comments. I consider that our sales person, Dave, accomplished a great performance by creating the conditions to 'be bought' by this customer who saw in our services the best matching answer to her specific needs. The dialogue-based marketing between DHL and this account – or, more accurately because we are in a business-to-business context, between Dave and the business school international program director – went very well. It is what one must systematically aim for to build a sustainable growth context. But beware stopping in the middle of the stream!

There was confusion between achieving a deal and becoming dominant at the account level. UPS's reaction is not covered in any depth, but one can notice that the company received some valuable internal support from other business school departments that considered its service to fit pretty well with their own specific needs. Sales in a business-to-business context require solid segmentation and positioning reflexes. This makes clear demands on what you are credited for and where. Before expecting growth based on your initial distinctive advantage, it is mandatory to check its relevance elsewhere in the company. Our outstanding service for the most remote places in the world seems not to be on a par with the pre-print shipping documents or the drop box highly appreciated by other departments. If the customer has put these items at the top of the list, we are fooling ourselves if we disregard them and expect to grow at the same time.

To succeed in the long term being unique is a necessary condition, but unfortunately not sufficient. Consequently, it is mandatory not to tolerate any weakness in one's own competitive formula if one wants to play a leading role at the forefront of one's industry sector. In this case, our ability to recognize the weak signals was lost in the relationship with the customer.

Sunk cost is the next step after a Pyrrhic victory

This case has to be viewed, paradoxically, as an opportunity to improve and concentrate on the essence of not only customer service but also, having won the customer, really making sure that one is able to keep it. A simple message, which was clearly missed on this occasion. Consequently, we do not demonstrate in this specific case our ability to secure the first level of organic growth: growing by not losing and maintaining in our portfolio our newly acquired customer accounts.

The impact of this specific failure, as with any failure, on a profit and loss account is twofold:

- First, from research I carried out in DHL on the impact of the sales force, it costs us six times as much to gain a new account than to keep one.

- This automatically leads on to the second point: longevity of customer relations leads to continuous retained business.

It is easy for us to forget this simple yet obvious fact. It is often assumed that once a new account conquest has been achieved the difficult job is over. Clearly, it is the contrary and we failed to understand, as managers, the extent and relevance of sales and marketing staff not being fully aware of the breakdown point of customer acquisition nor indeed of the cost of maintaining a portfolio of customers.

We all want market growth, but we cannot let our sales and marketing people operate without a clear idea of two critical factors:

- The cost of acquisition of a new account.
- The cost of maintaining our portfolio of customers.

Value is embodied in the effectiveness of the process

As a senior manager in DHL, I am extremely sorry that we treated this customer in this way. I can assure them and you, the reader, that we spend much time and money providing the highest level of service of any international express carrier, we are the number one brand (according to internal market research), yet for all that we failed this account – why?

Through insufficient attention, the context for failure existed even on the sales process side. The sales process clearly lacked a satisfactory customer recognition programme and response mechanism, yet I know that these do exist in DHL. What lies behind that is a distinct lack of sales awareness and training. The attention to detail demanded (quite rightly by customers) had in this instance led us to believe that once the customer has been gained, due to the promise and initial delivery of superior services compared to those of our competitors, we could reduce our sense of care without any detriment to our relationship. Subconscious action on our part led to conscious action being taken by the customer. Why don't we read our business plan more often? Clearly our customers do!

Once the core process had failed, the process of informing the customer through our track and trace failed also, which led to a massive deterioration of providing information on a timely basis through a lack of proactive follow-up.

The culture of the process of excellence, by being systematically consistent with what is promised to the customer, represents a sharp reminder to us to recognize that the effort to develop an effective permanent relationship marketing programme is intimately linked to this first layer of excellence. Permanent relationship marketing can just temporarily offset the consequences of poor process performance. Not recognizing this sequence leads to putting the cart before the horse, which usually means waste and therefore no growth, further exacerbated by the cost of recovery.

One cannot be wrong twice

It is natural for a customer to be unhappy with a failed service, but it is made substantially worse if our process does not proactively inform them on a regular basis of the status of a shipment. We all experience this phenomenon while waiting for a delayed flight, for example. It is extremely frustrating to be told that a further announcement will be made in one hour only to find yourself, usually surrounded by an unhappy family, four hours later still with no information. Interestingly the staff themselves, given the lack of process — or if that was not the case, they were not trained sufficiently well — instinctively resort to common sense and often solve the problem. However, while that is laudable it is a distinct failure of the management who placed staff in that position in the first place.

We are always learning and the clear lesson from this business story concerns our internal processes and problem-solving capacity at the customer interface. If we related this to air travel and our pilot lacked any sense of flight planning, the consequences would be dire! That interface must be recognized not only by those staff who interact directly with our customers, but more importantly in the level of attention to detail, attitudes and committed behaviour that senior management can show to our staff and customers alike.

Conclusion

DHL is an international brand leader in its sector. The end of the case gave me a short break when I read the IBM executive's opinion. We hold a significant worldwide market share so we have to execute and show to our staff and customers that DHL can diminish the consequences of our own process failure not only by getting it right first time but by being able to restore our promise with an appropriate style.

In this regard, we undertake on a daily basis statistical data showing our performance, not just in delivery terms but in all aspects of the many thousands of processes we have to fulfil to satisfy customer requirements. These are intended to provide management performance figures necessary to perform our everyday mainline business and we are accountable for them. Clearly, in this case, we let ourselves down and more importantly our customer and workforce. There can be no excuse for poor service; we have to be continually vigilant against complacency.

As important, there is a solid lesson for DHL in the sales process. Having won an important account from the competition, to lose it through the very discipline we excel at – service – is tantamount to irresponsibility. The costly consequences are clear in the mind of the customer. As Al Ries formulated it in his book *Marketing Warfare*, from now on the customer has a new supplier ladder in his mind and DHL is repositioned, I hope, on the challenger bar with a limited growth potential area. In summary, with this customer we created a new business category and we experienced the hard way that the innovator remains the leader in its new category as long as it does not make any mistakes, which represent the opportunity offered to our colleagues to catch up.

Of course, realistically I am not happy to be writing this summary, but perversely it is good news that if we recognize these failings and act on them, our tenure as the leading worldwide express carrier can continue with greater focus on managing the business for the good of our customers, workforce and shareholders.

INDEX